not by MIGHT nor by ower

A Pentecostal Theology
of Social Concern
in Latin America

not by MIGHT
nor by Power

A Pentecostal Theology
of Social Concern
in Latin America

DOUGLAS PETERSEN

PREFACE BY JOSE MIGUEZ BONINO

regnum

Oxford
Akropong, Buenos Aires,
Irvine CA, New Delhi

First published 1996 by Regnum Books Internation in association with
Paternoster Publishing, P.O. Box 300, Carlisle, Cumbria CA3 0QS UK

Regnum Books International

P.O. Box 70, Oxford, OX2 6HB, UK

17951 Cowan, Irvine, California, USA

P.O. Box 76, Akropong-Akuapem, Ghana

Jose Marmol 1734, 1602 Florida, Buenos Aires, Argentina

Post Bag No. 21, Vasant Kinj, New Delhi 110057, India

02 01 00 99 98 97 96   7 6 5 4 3 2 1

British Library Cataloguing in Publication Data

A catalogue record for this book is available from the British Library.

ISBN 1-870345-20-7

Typeset by WestKey Ltd., Falmouth
Printed and bound in Great Britain
by Clays Ltd., Bungay, Suffolk

Contents

9/82l

CHAPTER THREE

THE PRACTICAL OUTWORKING OF DOCTRINAL CONFESSION IN LATIN AMERICAN PENTECOSTALISM

CHAPTER FOUR

SOCIAL EXPRESSIONS OF CENTRAL AMERICAN PENTECOSTALISM

CHAPTER FIVE

LATIN AMERICA CHILDCARE: A CASE STUDY IN PENTECOSTAL PRAXIS

CHAPTER SIX

TOWARD A SOCIAL DOCTRINE FOR LATIN AMERICAN PENTECOSTALS

Preface by José Miguez Bonino

Perhaps one should let a book simply speak for itself. However, two considerations led me to yield to the temptation to accept the author's invitation to write what he called 'an extended preface'. The first one is personal: Since I first met Doug Petersen and then had a long conversation with him—in Costa Rica, in 1991, in a restaurant from which the after shocks of the recent earthquake chased us out a couple of times—we have engaged in an on-going conversation in personal encounters, through long letters, and faxes or on the phone, while he was working on his dissertation. It has been for me a very enriching experience. From the beginning it was clear to me that Doug is a convinced and militant Pentecostal, who ardently believes in what he is doing and at the same time wants to uncover the deeper meaning of this commitment and think through its theological implications in order to improve and enlarge its efficacy.

The second consideration has to do with the contents and the nature of this book. There is no need to prove the significance of Pentecostalism as undoubtedly the outstanding expression of the enormous dynamism in the Latin American religious field. Sociologists and anthropologists of diverse schools and places—Latin Americans, to be sure, but also Europeans and North Americans—compete to offer interpretations of the meaning and growth of Pentecostalism. Their work has given us some valuable insights into the social, economic and cultural factors that have been involved in the origins and expansion of the Pentecostal movement in Latin America (and, in different forms, in other areas of the world). Their work, however, has suffered from two limitations. Almost none of the interpreters comes from within the movement: they are at best 'observer participants' (the category that Lalive d'Epinay was the first to explicitly assume for himself) with the possible advantage of a greater objectivity but lacking access to a personal experience which they do not share and which is at the very heart of what they study. On the other hand, most of the studies have attempted to 'explain' Pentecostalism as a social and cultural phenomenon,

ignoring its specifically religious nature. And even those (like
Cartaxo Rolim) who would insist on looking at it primarily as a
religious phenomenon end up by reducing the religious dimension
itself to an epiphenomenon of social or economic conditions (class
analysis, the culture of poverty).

Theologians, on the other hand, with a few notable exceptions,
when they consider Pentecostalism at all, seem to satisfy themselves
with the characterizations borrowed from the social sciences. We
are only now beginning to see attempts to look at Pentecostalism
'from the inside', either by Pentecostals themselves or by theologians who try to bring theological reflection into their understanding of Pentecostalism.[1] It is in this context that I read Doug
Petersen's book. His work, however, has some peculiar features. A
most important one, in my view, is the fact that it is basically centred
in a specific situation and project: Central America and the 'Latin
American ChildCare' programme of the Assemblies of God. From
that experience and perspective he addresses some important issues
for the whole Pentecostal movement in Latin America: (1) the
nature of the Pentecostal experience, (2) the process of indigenization, and (3) theological thinking and the 'rationale' for (existing
and future) 'Pentecostal social concern'. It is in relation to these
themes that I would like to make some comments and to suggest
that the book opens up important theological questions that need
to be addressed, not only within Pentecostalism, but in wider
evangelical and indeed Christian thought.

Toward the end of the book the author indicates that throughout, he has argued that 'the Pentecostal experience of Spirit baptism
is basically one of empowerment'. The 'subjective' side of that
experience is the new sense of certainty which the author describes
as 'boldness' (the biblical *parousia*), 'confidence', 'assertiveness',
'determination', even 'optimism'. Others had already noticed these
traits in the behaviour of Pentecostal individuals; Petersen wants us
to relate it to the theological understanding of the work of the Holy
Spirit. He also tries to look at it as a response to a central Latin
American need: 'The theme of power, belief in one's access to

---

[1]There is a rich and growing number of publications. Journals like *Pneuma* and the
bibliographies in this book and other recent works provide abundant information to follow
this theological production. I want to refer specifically to the work of Steven J. Land,
Pentecostal Spirituality: A Passion for the Kingdom (Sheffield: Sheffield Academic Press, 1993)

power, allegations of supernatural intervention and the fear of others' power are all part of the emotional and cultural life of Latin Americans', he says. Pentecostalism, he concludes, is effective 'because it addresses the real historical situation with an effective power'.

'The power of the Spirit' is by no means a new theme. But the questions as to what are the realms of the action of this power, how it relates to the different forms of power that operate in human life, what kind of Christian action witnesses to the power of the Spirit and can be recognized as a historical manifestation of it seem to me to be central concerns for theology. In fact, as Pentecostalism becomes a significant social factor by the sheer weight of its numbers and dynamism, 'power' overflows the space of subjectivity, the gathered community and the charismatic manifestations, to gain a public, even political dimension. Recent experiences of evangelical Christians—and in many cases specifically Pentecostals—show that this is no mere speculation but very concrete reality. When Petersen, Steven Land, Murray Dempster, Roger Stronstad and other Pentecostal theologians invite their people to relate the 'Lukan' experience of the power of the Spirit as expressed in the Book of Acts to the kingdom theology of Luke's Gospel, they are sketching a wide theological programme which has to do with hermeneutics, trinitarian reflection and social and political ethics as much as with evangelization, prayer and praise. But this is a challenge to all the Christian churches, who have frequently failed to think of the power of the Spirit beyond its action in certifying the authority of the Scriptures or operating in the community of the church.

Our author faces the question of indigenization in a very pro-vocative and unaccustomed empirical way. The central thesis is that the speed and reach of growth is such that external control becomes actually impossible. The point is significant because the Assemblies of God, certainly the largest and most widely extended Pentecostal church in Latin America, is also the most organic and well organized and frequently seen as strongly attached to the international net-work. In concrete terms, there are normally three channels through which foreign influence is exercised: missionary personnel, finances and education. The relation between the number of missionaries from abroad and the total leadership of the Assemblies churches in Latin America is such, argues the author, that direct supervision would be practically impossible; in fact, growth takes place fundamentally through local initiative. Through a number of examples Petersen shows the autonomy of national bodies in terms of main decisions. On the second issue, he shows that the disparity between funds coming from abroad—normally in capital investment or in special projects—and the total investment in the work of the Assemblies coming from local contributions is such that the partial or total withdrawal of funds from abroad could probably limit the scope of some of the service projects but would not significantly affect the life of the churches. Much of the very interesting statistical information given throughout the work substantiates these claims. Probably the third channel—the printed material for the formation of leadership at different levels which is provided internationally—would deserve a specific study. At the same time, it must be noted that Pentecostalism still functions to a large extent through 'oral' transmission and that the reception and authority of the leadership is legitimized charismatically and not academically. Doctrinal and ideological control would be very difficult.[2]

It seems to me that the book makes a solid case on this issue. The reader will reach his/her conclusions. In terms of the purpose of this book, the author can rightly rest here his case. But I think that, beyond this factual approach, the question of indigenization deserves a theological consideration. I have no doubt that Pentecostalism represents the most clearly, if not the only truly indigenous form of evangelical presence in Latin America. Some observers (among them some Pentecostal theologians) have called attention to the dialectical relation of continuity/discontinuity between traditional culture and religiosity and Pentecostal piety and expression. On the other hand, others have pointed out that traditional Pentecostal doctrine and symbolic language is reinterpreted by the people in terms of the cultural and social conditions of their own situation. To put it in very simple terms, Latin American (or African, for instance) Pentecostals understand and live such doctrines as the authority of the Bible, eschatological expectation, the relation between faith and the world or the charismatic manifestations, in terms of their condition of exclusion or social acceptance,

---

[2]An interesting study by Cheryl Bridges-Johns on Pentecostal education explores some aspects of this question: *Pentecostal Formation: A Pedagogy among the oppressed*. (Sheffield: Sheffield Academic Press, 1993).

the characteristics of their language and culture and even some of their traditional understandings of religious symbols. A visit to Pentecostal churches in Argentina, Brazil and Peru will easily illustrate the truth in this observation. However, it is not enough to recognize it. A theology which intends to serve the real life of the church had to ask at least two questions: Is the reception of these traditions a real process of transformation in which the old is reinterpreted in the light of Christ and under the direction of the Spirit? (The question of legitimate inculturation and unacceptable syncretism cannot be avoided.) On the other hand, when traditional doctrine and symbol is re-signified and re-defined in practice, is the new signification compatible with the traditional doctrine or does it really mean a critical transformation and even correction of it? This latter question seems important, given the fact that Pentecostalism (and not only Pentecostalism) has inherited a doctrinal baggage shaped by the conditions and conflicts of the 19th and 20th century North American religious situations which may not be adequate to express and articulate the present Pentecostal experience of the gospel and the Spirit. I believe that the stress put by the author on the genuinely Latin American nature of this Pentecostalism unavoidably leads to such questions.

Finally, there is the question of the theological rationale for 'Pentecostal social concern'. That such concern exists hardly needs to be proved. That it is more than a spontaneous attitude of benevolence but moves into the area of an intentional and self-conscious social action seems to me evident from the material gathered in this book—besides many other evidences which could be easily added. Dr. Petersen, however, wants something more: (a) a recognition of the structural issues involved in such social action and (b) a theological articulation which relates the experience of the Spirit to active presence and service in society. The question is raised very clearly in chapter 3, documented concretely in chapters 4 and 5 and developed theologically in chapter 6. The urgency present in the whole book in this respect seems to me to be totally justified. The observations made earlier in this preface in relation to the question of power demand such theological articulation. The 'Kingdom of God' motif which emerges in the author's response and similarly in other Pentecostal authors appears as a fruitful way to engage this task. Personally I would like to think that a Pentecostal reflection on the Kingdom of God and the eschatological dimension of the

Pentecostal experience to social responsibility can be best developed
in a Trinitarian perspective in which the experiential unity of body
and spirit, personalization and community and apocalyptic expectation of the Pentecostal spirituality and the emerging sense of the
unity of Pentecost and Jubilee (Acts 2 and Luke 4)—the power of
the Spirit and the peace and justice of the kingdom—are set in the
context of the creative, redeeming and fulfilling purpose and action
of the triune God.

This is only one way of reading this book. It is offered here as a
sign of gratitude for the opportunity which Doug gave me of
accompanying him on the road to the completion of the work and
as an expression of hope that he and other Pentecostal people and
theologians will accompany us on the long road to understand
better the call of the Spirit and respond to it in trust, hope and joy.

José Míguez Bonino
Professor Emeritus
Instituto Superior Evangélico de Estudios Teológicos
Buenos Aires, Argentina
November, 1995

Acknowledgements

I initiated the research on this book almost 20 years ago when I began my work with Latin American ChildCare. From the beginning of my missionary career I have been involved with this programme of spiritual formation and social action, that provides quality education as well as feeding and medical assistance to 75,000 poor children in 18 different countries. It has always been the desire of LACC to bring a sense of justice to children who are victims of poverty. We consciously designed programmes to bring change in the conditions that perpetuated a life of poverty by establishing creative educational institutions within the existing social systems, thus providing an alternative future for children in slum areas. Throughout these years of development we also felt the need to develop a firm theological position to undergird our own social involvement. Moreover, with the rapid expansion of our programme from just a dream to an established institution that included more than 2,000 teachers, directors and other national leaders there was a constant need to provide orientation. Theological reflection and practice were linked closely together.

The Oxford Centre for Mission Study presented me with an unusual opportunity to develop, in a formal and scholarly fashion, the theological reflection and practice of my lifelong work. This book, with editorial revisions, is the substance of the thesis I presented for the Degree of Doctor of Philosophy.

I would like to acknowledge and thank the following people for their contribution and support for the preparation of this book: Dr. José Míguez Bonino, Emeritus Professor of Systematic Theology and Ethics, Instituto Superior Evangélico de Estudios Teológicos, Buenos Aires, Argentina; Dr. David E. Cook, Fellow of Green College, Oxford University and Dr. J. Andrew Kirk, Head of Department of Mission, Selly Oaks Colleges, Birmingham and the Directors of the Oxford Centre for Mission Studies. Their thoughtful guidance and broad range of experience was exceeded only by their patience and extraordinary investment of time in the development of this research. I would also like to thank three exceptional friends, Murray Dempster, Everett Wilson and Mary Mahon, who have read through a draft of the book. I am grateful for their comments and suggestions, but most of all for their friendship.

I am indebted to the Division of Foreign Missions of the Assemblies of God, USA, for the immense amount of time and resources with which they provided me. I mention with great appreciation, in particular, John Bueno, Field Director for Latin America, who has been my fellow colleague, encourager, friend and mentor.

I am also grateful for the funding for my research which was provided by the Research Enablement Program, a grant programme for mission scholarship supported by the Pew Charitable Trusts, Philadelphia, PA, and administered by the Overseas Ministries Study Center, New Haven, CT.

Most importantly I express my appreciation to the members of my family, my children, Kimberley, Christie and Doug Jr., and especially my wife, Myrna. Their love, trust, patience and support have been without limit. It is to them that this book is dedicated.

Doug Petersen
March 15, 1996

Chapter 1
The Emergence and Development of Classical Pentecostalism

THE FOCUS OF LATIN AMERICAN PENTECOSTALISM

The origins and the rapid growth of the Pentecostal movement in Latin America have only recently become the focus of serious scholarly investigation. As Pentecostalism has become increasingly viewed as the prevailing form of Protestantism in the region, and with recognition that Pentecostal and Protestant Christianity may be assuming a significant social role, scholars have begun to research the emergence and institutional development of these two movements. Social science studies have generally related Pentecostalism to the dislocation of the masses brought about by economic deprivation, the breakdown of traditional society and the consequent loss of traditional values.[1] These conditions, accelerated by rapid demographic and economic change after World War II, provoked crises that contributed to the emergence of populist political movements and, generally, the groping of the displaced masses for their own solutions to an anomic existence. However correct scholars may have been in relating the rise of Pentecostalism to the crises of the masses, the view that the movement is a reaction to deteriorating conditions—'a haven for the masses'—obscures its constructive features. At the root of Pentecostalism is its power to generate an attitude of assertiveness among its leaders and its rank and file members. The often socially marginalized persons attracted to the movement find in the Pentecostal experience the power to resist compliance with the status quo and to struggle for a better life.[2]

---

[1] The now classic study by Christian Lalive d'Epinay, *El refugio de las masas: estudio sociológico del protestantismo chileño* (Santiago: Editorial del Pac'fico, 1968), and later published in English as *Haven of the Masses: A Study of the Pentecostal Movement in Chile* (London: Lutterworth, 1969), tends to adopt the deprivation views of preceding scholars, especially the revitalization theory of Anthony F. C. Wallace, 'Revitalization Movements', *American Anthropology* 58 (April 1956): 264—281.

[2] See the discussion of the impact of Spirit baptism as experienced by the socially marginalized later in this chapter. Also see chapter 2 for a description of 'popular, autonomous Pentecostal churches'.

Assessments of Pentecostalism have tended to perpetuate defective assumptions and inadequate explanations about the character and development of the movement. Despite penetrating analyses by social scientists like Emilio Willems and Cornelia Butler Flora, among others, both Marxist and Catholic writers have often attributed the growth of the movement to foreign resources and leadership, and, further, assumed that Pentecostals are indifferent to and even obstructionistic in their attitudes towards the fundamental issues of social injustice, repression, discrimination, corruption and poverty, which are often characteristic of Latin American life.[3] Although these writers have acknowledged the apparent compatibility of Pentecostalism with Latin American popular culture, many have consistently ignored the group's essentially autochthonous character.[4] Nor was it recognized that in Latin America, where secularization is much less marked than in most of the Western world, social advances are correspondingly less likely to occur without religious legitimation. In Latin America, popular social movements are more likely to have religious underpinnings than in other Western societies. Not until recently has it been conceded that Pentecostal groups, with large numbers of committed workers, effective national leadership and considerable combined resources, have acquired, in part because of their essentially religious focus, a potential for playing a significant role in Latin American social change and development.

The character of Latin American Pentecostalism as a social movement rather than as an institutional or cultural invasion is indicated by the movement's grassroots origins. In the process of becoming a recognized religious alternative in several of the republics, Pentecostal groups have in the aggregate organized the most extensive network of popularly directed associations outside the Roman Catholic Church. Pentecostals throughout Central America,

---

[3]Much indirect criticism has appeared in the writings of Liberationist and Roman Catholic interpreters of Latin American social change. Direct criticism has come from writers who relate evangelical growth to imperialism, like Hugo Assman, La Iglesia *Electrónica y su impacto en América Latina* (San José, Costa Rica: Departamento Ecuménico de Investigaciones [DEI], 1987). Judith Chambliss Hoffnagel similarly proposes a reactionary view of the movement in Brazil in her 'Pentecostalism: A Revolutionary or Conservative Movement', in *Perspectives on Pentecostalism: Case Studies from the Caribbean and Latin America*, ed. Stephen D. Glazier (Lanham, MD: University Press of America, 1980), 111—121.

[4]See, e.g., Luise Margolies, 'The Paradoxical Growth of Pentecostalism', in *Perspectives on Pentecostalism: Case Studies from the Caribbean and Latin America*, 1—5.

and elsewhere in Latin America, have already begun to demonstrate their potential for mobilizing large numbers of people, ostensibly in their efforts to extend the evangelical faith, but in the process they are also creating institutional structures capable of performing various educational and community developments, social service and political functions.[5] In their own way these national Pentecostal networks of largely autonomous local congregations are not merely at the margins of the Latin American clamour for a more rewarding, secure future. It should be noted that in these societies, where discrimination, neglect and indifference are too often characteristic, Pentecostalism has typically gathered strength precisely among the most disadvantaged or dissatisfied sectors such as the peasantry, the urban poor, women, Indians and ethnic minorities, young adults and the independent middle groups. Thus, quite unlike some of the stereotypical portrayals of Pentecostalism as generating a passive, otherworldly and *status quo* attitude among its adherents, it has actually challenged its followers to engage in their own kind of here and now social struggle. Its programme of grass roots personal regeneration, significant in both its degree and volume of effectiveness, has far-reaching implications for mobilizing people in the service of social transformation.[6]

Although the Central American Pentecostal movement is essentially indigenous, there has been a significant relationship of Latin American Pentecostals to their namesake North American denominations regarding certain common values and tendencies. A review of the origins and nature of the Pentecostal movement in the United States in its initial phases will help identify the reasons why the movement-or more specifically, features of it-found a receptive environment in the region and how Latin Americans contextualized

---

[5]This study will largely focus upon the Pentecostal movement in Central America. The five countries of Central America are the republics of Guatemala, El Salvador, Honduras, Nicaragua and Costa Rica. These five republics share a similar history and economical base-largely agricultural. Panama, often considered a part of Central America, did not receive independence from Colombia until 1903 and its economy has been based on international trade. Belize, also part of the Central American isthmus, was a British colony and received independence only in 1981.

[6]See chapter three for the role that conversion plays in the social mobilization of believers. A positive interpretation of the social role of Pentecostalism as preparation to participate in a new society, rather than simply a flight from the old, is presented in Emilio Willems, *Followers of the New Faith: Culture Change and the Rise of Protestantism in Brazil and Chile* (Nashville, TN: Vanderbilt University Press, 1967).

these values and tendencies from North American Pentecostalism to determine their own social and spiritual activities.

It must be recognized that an interpretive consensus on the nature of North American Pentecostalism still does not exist. Because of the limited scholarly treatment to date and, the movement's inherent pragmatism and, as well, its deep regional, ethnic and theological divisions, a cohesive articulation of Pentecostalism is uneven at best. Nevertheless, increasingly penetrating studies, many by non-Pentecostals, have demonstrated the assertive, millenarian character of the early Pentecostals and, with the evolution of the movement since its introduction early in the century, the appropriateness of many of these emphases in addressing the concerns of contemporary Latin Americans.[7]

It should also be kept in mind that although the rapid spread of Pentecostalism in the region occurred after World War II, the movement was well established much earlier, having begun in Brazil and Chile by 1909 and in Central America during the following decade. Several Latin American Pentecostal groups thus predate the formation of some of the largest North American Pentecostal churches, including all those of the 'finished work' tradition.[8] In the case of the Mexican Pentecostals, some groups developed more or less simultaneously with their North American

---

[7]Although the symposium published in Glazier, op. cit., was a turning point in the interpretation of Pentecostalism in Latin America, the works of David Stoll, *Is Latin America Turning Protestant? The Politics of Evangelical Growth* (Berkeley, CA: University of California Press, 1990) and David Martin, *Tongues of Fire: The Explosion of Protestantism in Latin America* (Cambridge, MA: Basil Blackwell, Inc., 1990) tended to focus the findings of much previous research, including the landmark investigations published by Lalive, *Haven of the Masses*, (1969), Willems, *Followers of the New Faith*, (1967), and Francisco Cartaxo Rolim, *Religiao e Classes Populares* (Petropolis, Brazil: Editorial Vozes, 1980). Some popular treatments in the meantime had perpetuated the notion that Latin American Pentecostals were dependent on foreign influence and resources.

[8]The 'finished work' Pentecostals rejected the then prevailing view that baptism with the Holy Spirit occurred only after a perfecting experience and taught, rather, a progressive sanctification. This doctrine opened the door to many Protestants in the Baptist and Reformed traditions by making Spirit baptism an experience received by faith apart from the believer's spiritual progress. The organizations in these traditions, including the International Church of the Foursquare Gospel, the Assemblies of God, the Open Bible Standard, and the Pentecostal Church of God, now have in the aggregate a larger proportion of Latin American Pentecostals than have the Pentecostal churches in the Holiness tradition. See R. M. Riss, 'Finished Work Controversy', *Dictionary of Pentecostal and Charismatic Movements*, eds. Stanley M. Burgess and Gary B. McGee (Grand Rapids: MI: Zondervan Publishing House, 1988), 306—309 (hereafter cited as *DPCM*).

counterparts, even to the extent of developing as a single movement that straddled the United States-Mexican border.

The extension of Pentecostalism to Latin America was not a result of North American churches sending professional missionaries to reproduce their institutions overseas, but rather the development of national churches within their own culture utilizing patterns of religious assertiveness and motivation which were then available for selective adoption by Latin Americans. The role of North American churches and their missionaries can best be described as catalytic, providing models which Latin American Pentecostals adapted to their own situations and which, in any event, only they, because of their familiarity with popular Latin American cultures, were capable of implementing on any significant scale. Ultimately and critically what North American Pentecostal missionaries conveyed to Latin America was not their institutions, which in any case were not transferred intact, but the encouragement to become assertive and take control of their own destinies.

Prima facie evidence of this process of the early 'latinization' of Pentecostalism is easily adduced. The relatively few professional missionaries in Latin America supported by Pentecostal missionary agencies (as compared with missionaries supported by nonpentecostal missionary agencies) through the decades provides a revealing picture of Latin American Pentecostal autonomy.[9] The resultant growth of the region's Pentecostal groups extends far beyond the size of the mother-denominations in the United States (which in any case insisted that their missionaries subscribe to the missiological doctrines of the indigenous church). Large aggregations of Pentecostals in Latin America have received little North American direction or economic assistance. And clearly the most notable demonstration of grass-roots initiative is found in the large proportion of Latin American Pentecostal groups that have

---

[9]See table 1 in chapter 2 for a ratio of Assemblies of God members and adherents to the number of missionaries from 1951–1992. The numbers of missionaries maintained by most sending agencies in Latin America are given in David B. Barrett, *World Christian Encyclopedia* (New York, NY: Oxford University Press, 1982). Catholic scholar Prudencia Damboriena, though arguing that Protestantism is 'an invasion' into Latin America after World War II, nevertheless, when he gives statistics, shows that the number of strictly Pentecostal missionaries is relatively small in *El Protestantismo en América Latina*, 2 vols. (Freiburg, Madrid: Oficina Internacional de Investigaciones Sociales de FERES, 1963), 2:96.

emerged spontaneously (sometimes but not consistently referred
to in the anthropological sense as 'indigenous' churches), independent of any direct foreign assistance.[10] As Pentecostals in Latin
America emerged from within their own social conditions, they
demonstrated their concern for the social issues which their
premillennial theology and alleged otherworldliness seemed to
belie. Stereotyped and categorized, the Pentecostals have been
usually considered Fundamentalists, despite their rejection by
American Fundamentalism until at least the 1940s.[11] The litmus
test of Pentecostalism, however, has never been confessional but
experiential. Participants in the movement can be better understood by looking not at what they say but rather by analyzing
their experiential expressions. The functional consequences of
Pentecostal teaching, moreover, clearly place them in the position
of a social movement intent on realizing temporal objectives.

Even the most fractious Pentecostal groups have grown precisely
because they addressed the felt personal, social and spiritual needs
of their communities. Donald McGavran, citing the reasons for
Pentecostal growth, has pointed to the adherents' 'personal
Pentecost'—an individual experience of being baptized in the Holy
Spirit as an empowerment for service—as basic to the movement's
success.[12] Rather than being categorized theologically, socially or
psychologically, adherents of the movement are best defined as
individuals who have a strong conviction about participating in the
subjective Christian experiences that are universally acceptable to,
but often de-emphasized within, other Christian communions.
Whatever else may be said about Pentecostals, they are character-

---

[10]In chapter 2 an argument is formulated and statistically supported that Latin American
Pentecostalism, including classical Pentecostal groups, such as the Assemblies of God, is
an authentic indigenous religious expression of Latin American believers. David B. Barrett,
evangelical researcher, classifies Pentecostals by affiliation, ethnicity, theology, etc.,
making obvious the point that the movement has grown spontaneously and cuts across
most denominational categories. See David B. Barrett, 'Statistics, Global,' DPCM,
810–830.

[11]In 1928 a resolution was formulated by the World's Christian Fundamentalist Association. This resolution, cited by H. Vinson Synan, 'Fundamentalism,' DPCM, 326,
disavowed Pentecostals. Billy Graham and the Neo-Evangelicals recognized Pentecostals
in the 1940s over the objections of the Fundamentalist right wing. For the role of Billy
Graham and the Neo-Evangelicals, see Cecil M. Robeck, Jr., 'National Association of
Evangelicals,' DPCM, 634–636.

[12]Donald McGavran, 'What Makes Pentecostal Churches Grow,' International Bulletin of
Church Growth 13 (January 1977). 97–99.

istically more audacious about experiencing and demonstrating certain aspects of their faith than are the members of most other branches of the Christian tradition. They can hardly be described as retiring, 'spiritual', and otherworldly. Not only may they be best viewed as a social movement but they have implicitly adopted a social agenda that began with a radical concept of the church as an alternative community.

While inclusion in the community of believers may imply, as it does for other Christians, admission to the means of grace, for Pentecostals it also represents access to personal empowerment. The fragmentation of Pentecostals into widely diverse groups, while affirming the importance of the local community, asserts the right of the individual to choose a given association which provides maximum spiritual support. The objective however, is not just the growth of the group but the spiritual development of the members. While inclusion in a Pentecostal community emphasizes the availability of spiritual enduement to all, the individual is made part of a comprehensive, redemptive programme for humankind to which his or her empowering should contribute. Despite the failure of many individual members and, perhaps, of entire congregations to keep this central focus, the movement as a whole still promotes a vital spirituality. If Pentecostals have often claimed that their essential mission was to restore the energy of the primitive Christian faith, their emphases have had in fact, a revolutionary effect on virtually all sectors of contemporary Christianity. The supposed religious 'lunatic fringe', has unleashed human potential that has taken the movement from marginality into mainstream within three generations.

Both conventional, and sometimes sensationalist, portrayals of the Pentecostal movement have tended to obscure the centrality of a deeply held personal faith.[13] Such spiritual experience and commitment have brought adherents their own rewards in satisfaction, and have resulted in stable, trusting communities of believers, have inspired altruistic, sacrificial service and have often sustained the

---

[13]Examples of sympathetic treatment of the movement by well-known church and mission leaders are found in John A. Mackay, *The Other Spanish Christ: a study in the spiritual history of Spain and South America* (New York, NY: The Macmillan Company, 1933) and more recently Mackay's article 'Latin America and Revolution-II: "The new mood in the Churches," ' *Christian Century*, (24 November 1965), 1439. Also see Eugene Nida, 'The Indigenous Churches in Latin America', *Practical Anthropology* 8 (May–June 1961): 97–105.

rank and file through times of ostracism and deferred realization of their collective vision. Spontaneity and popular styles in worship, or even glossolalia, by themselves hardly explain the movement's rapid growth. Observers of the movement in all parts of the world find that a large proportion of families inducted into the movement claim to have had some experience of physical healing or other seemingly miraculous intervention that has assured them of divine concern and the power to overcome demoralizing circumstances. Examples abound of the influence Pentecostal women have had on their husbands who, as a consequence of a conversion experience, have changed their attitudes and practices and have brought peace to their households.[14] Ultimately, this integrating faith of personal spiritual experience, miracles of the supernatural, and the commitment and vision of hundreds of thousands of Pentecostal ministers, lay leaders and persuaded members, whose efforts have played a major part in the emergence of Latin American churches, are the phenomena in need of investigation and analysis in understanding Pentecostalism's popular appeal.

While the rapid growth and impressive numbers attributed to these churches suggest a dynamic, spiritual faith, many questions about the nature of Pentecostalism remain. Critics have pointed to its apparent instability, its tendency to exclusivity, its lack of theological depth, its opportunism and the failure of some of its prominent leaders. Not the least of the issues raised has been the movement's alleged neglect of social concerns and apparent compromise with dictatorships and reactionary sectors of the Latin American republics. Much research on the character of the movement itself is still required in order to evaluate these and other criticisms.

Despite a general recognition that the early movement emerged from among humble social elements and has flourished in Latin America primarily among such groups, Latin American Pentecostals have been frequently criticized for their apparent neglect of social concerns. Their antipathy to doctrines advanced within liberation theology and their supposed neutrality towards or identification with military dictatorships have merely given support to what critics have considered to be an already apparent disposition to approach social change only by amelioration if at all. However, recent theories of social movements as well as empirical studies, bring such a stereo-

---

[14]See the biographical story of Cokie and So-ia in chapter 4, pages 109–110

typed interpretation into question.[15] Both because of the nature of its organization and because of its radical religious character, Pentecostalism possesses an inherent agenda of social action, an agenda waiting to be identified, made explicit and activated.

In view of the fact that Pentecostalism has been described as a movement 'of the people', rather than a movement 'for the people', and explained as 'not having social programmes' but as 'being a social programme', it is clear that Pentecostals are in some ways involved in the process of social transformation. Beyond the regular community support that churches provide for their members, as well as their concern for social mobility, recognition, and power especially to very needy people, Pentecostals, when given the opportunity, have also developed institutional structures dedicated to specific needs. The areas of children, youth, and family problems, especially, have been at the heart of their social concerns. This inherent agenda for social concern within Pentecostalism can be found in the movement from its early formative years at the Azusa Street Mission.[16]

THE AZUSA STREET EXPERIENCE

The appearance of the Pentecostal movement precisely at the beginning of the century with a tangible evidence of divine presence—the gift of tongues—gives the movement a tidy, if misleading, inaugural beginning, often ignoring the frequent appearance of ecstasies and tongues throughout church history,[17] and the well-developed Wesleyan-Holiness tradition that gave birth to Pentecostalism. The movement has had an uninterrupted existence since students at Charles F. Parham's Bethel Bible Institute in Topeka, Kansas, were baptized in the Holy Spirit on the evening of January 1, 1901.[18]

---

[15]Susan Eckstein, ed., *Power and Popular Protest: Latin American Social Movements* (Berkely, CA: University of California Press, 1989; Orlando Fals Borda, ed., *The Challenge of Social Change* (Beverly Hills, CA: Sage Publications Inc., 1985); Arturo Escobar and Sonia E. Alvarez, eds. *The Making of Social Movements in Latin America: Identity, Strategy, and Democracy* (Boulder, CO: Westview Press, 1992).
[16]For a description and critical analysis of Pentecostal social concern see chapters 4 and 5.
[17]B. C. Aker, 'Initial Evidence, A Biblical Perspective,' *DPCM*, 455–459.
[18]By far the best scholarly work on Parham has been done by James R. Goff, Jr., *Fields White Unto Harvest: Charles F. Parham and The Missionary Origins of Pentecostalism* (Fayetteville, AK: The University of Arkansas Press, 1988). It is Goff's contention that Parham must be regarded as the founder of the Pentecostal movement. According to Goff, Parham was the person who was responsible for identifying the linkage between tongues as the initial evidence with the reception of the baptism of the

Parham's account of this historic event has been recorded in almost every study of the occasion:

In December of (1900) we had our examination upon the subject of repentance, conversion, consecration, sanctification, healing, and soon coming of the Lord. We had reached in our studies a problem. What about the 2nd Chapter of Acts?... having heard so many religious bodies claiming different proofs as the evidence of their having the Pentecostal Baptism, I set the students at work studying out diligently (sic) what was the Bible evidence of the Baptism of the Holy Ghost ....

Leaving the school for three days at this task, I went to Kansas City for three days services (and returned) to the school on the morning preceding (sic) Watch night services in the year 1900. At about 10 o'clock in the morning I rang the bell calling all the students into the Chapel to get their report on the matter in hand. To my astonishment they all had the same story, that while there were different things (which) occurred when the Pentecostal blessing fell, that the indisputable proof on each occasion was, that they spake with other tongues. About 75 people beside the school(,) which consisted of 40 students, had gathered for the watch night service. A mighty spiritual power filled the entire school. At 10:30 A.M. Sister Agnes N. Ozman, (now La Berge) asked that hands might be laid upon her to receive the Holy Spirit as she hoped to go to foreign fields. At first I refused, not having the experience myself. Then being pressed further to do it in the name of Jesus, I laid my hands upon her head and prayed. I had scarcely repeated three dozen sentences when a glory fell upon her(,) a halo seemed to surround her head and face(,) and she began speaking in the Chinese language, and was unable to speak English for three days.[19]

Although scholars acknowledge Parham's credentials as the founder of the Apostolic Faith movement,[20] the first twentieth

---

(footnote 18 continued)

Holy Spirit. For a primary account of the life of Charles Parham see the biography written by his wife, Sarah E. Parham, *The Life of Charles S. Parham* (Joplin, MO: Tri-State Printing Co., 1930; repr., Birmingham, AL: Commercial Printing Co., 1977).

[19] Parham, *Life*, 51—53.

[20] It was not until Pentecostal historian Klaude Kendrick published *The Promise Fulfilled: A History of the Modern Pentecostal Movement* (Springfield, MO: Gospel Publishing House, 1961) that Parham was given any scholarly treatment. Parham was accused and even arrested for committing an immoral act, quite likely sodomy, in 1906. The charges were later dropped but Parham's reputation was permanently damaged. Given the severity of the charges it is no wonder that Pentecostal historians, up until Kendrick, chose to ignore

century Pentecostal organization, his contribution to early Pentecostalism consists mainly of his having made tongues, which he
understood to be xenoglossy (the inspired use of an unlearned
known foreign language), the sign that the powerful apostolic
ministry of the Book of Acts had been restored.[21]

Parham and others believed that the supernatural gift of modern
languages would make possible the evangelization of the entire
world in the brief time remaining before the anticipated Second
Coming. Thus, from its beginnings, the Pentecostal movement has
had a global projection which, indeed, was soon realized as news
of the experience rapidly spread among like-minded people in

(footnote 20 continued)
him. The moral charges are covered in Goff, *Fields White Unto Harvest*, 128—146. Goff's
thesis is that Parham has been excised from Pentecostal history for this alleged moral
indiscretion. He is surely right. However, the central place he wished to accord Parham is
overstated. As we shall see, Parham's influence upon William Seymour, pioneering pastor
of the Apostolic Faith Mission in Los Angeles, California, lasted for a total of only five weeks.
Further, Parham's direct contribution to the benchmark Azusa Street revival was minimal.

[21] Agnes Ozman's account of the same incident varies substantially from that of Parham.
It is her claim that she was not aware of the doctrine of the baptism of the Holy Spirit
with speaking in tongues as the initial evidence until after her experience.

> Before receiving the Comforter I did not know that I would speak in tongues when I
> received the Holy Ghost for I did not know it was in the Bible. But after I received
> the Holy Spirit speaking in tongues it was revealed to me that I had the promise of the
> Father as it is written and as Jesus said …. I did not know then that any one else would
> speak in tongues. For I did not know how the Holy Ghost would be manifest to others.

According to Ozman she concluded several months after her experience that tongues
was the initial evidence and contradicted Parham's story that the students had arrived at
this conclusion prior to January 1. Given the fact that there only exist three eyewitness
accounts (the other being Parham's sister-in-law) it is difficult to ascertain with any degree
of accuracy whether it was Parham or the students themselves, in particular Agnes Ozman,
who concluded that speaking in tongues was the initial evidence of the baptism of the
Holy Spirit. However, the link between tongues as the initial evidence as the sign of
having received the infilling of the baptism of the Holy Spirit was of great theological
significance for later Pentecostals. Agnes N. O. LaBerge, *What God Hath Wrought*
(Chicago, IL: Herald Publishing Co., 1921), 3.

It appears as though Parham's theology was somewhat fluid and certainly unorthodox. He
was intrigued with the teachings of British Israelism and incorporated much of this doctrine
into his own teachings. He understood the baptism of the Holy Spirit as a sealing of a special
elect 'the bride of Christ' that would save this group from going through the great
tribulation. Parham discarded water baptism as a needless rite, later to practise single
immersion and taught that the wicked would suffer eternal annihilation. For an account of
Parham's shifting views see his journal *Apostolic Faith* (Baxter Springs, Kansas) and Charles
Parham, *The Everlasting Gospel* (n. p., 1919–1920). In light of Parham's shifting and unorthodox
theological positions it is difficult to accept Goff's assertion that Parham's doctrinal
conclusions would 'alter the landscape of American religious history'. Goff, *Fields*, 61.

various parts of the world. As Parham's 'missions theory of tongues' was not demonstrated in practice, however, increasingly the gift was considered to be glossalalia (incomprehensible, speech-like sounds) and was usually taken as evidence of Spirit baptism, the normative experience of the movement, even if not required by all Pentecostal groups. From the beginning, however, Pentecostals gave recognition to other revelatory gifts of the Spirit in addition to glossalalia, including prophecy and interpretation of tongues, as well as to healings and miracles. A personal spiritual experience accompanied by the gifts of empowerment provided the essential theological pattern for early Pentecostalism.

In the summer of 1905, the movement entered a new phase as it moved outside of Parham's control. A paternalistic racist,[22] Parham nevertheless permitted William Joseph Seymour, a black Holiness evangelist, to attend the class he began in Houston, Texas.[23] For five weeks Seymour sat under the instruction of Parham until he left to accept an invitation to serve as an associate pastor in a Los Angeles black Holiness church where, without

---

[22]For a review of Parham's alleged racist tendencies see Goff, *Fields White Unto Harvest*, 107–112; 131–132.

[23]Seymour was not allowed to enter the classroom to receive the teachings but rather had to remain out in the hall and listen through the open door. Douglas Nelson has written the most comprehensive account of the treatment of Seymour. See *For Such a Time as This: The Story of Bishop William J. Seymour and the Azusa Street Revival* (Unpublished Ph D. dissertation: University of Birmingham, 1981). Nelson argues that Seymour should be considered to be the founder of the Pentecostal movement. Traditionally Pentecostal historians have felt that the Pentecostal movement had no founders. It is their contention that the theological formulations of Pentecostalism cannot be isolated in the theological ideas of a single person but rather that their ideas stem from various sources. According to these scholars, people like Parham and Seymour should be considered to be no more than pioneers. The standard accounts of the early Pentecostal movement include Klaude Kendrick, *The Promise Fulfilled: A History of the Modern Pentecostal Movement*, 1961; Vinson Synan, *The Holiness-Pentecostal Movement in the United States* (Grand Rapids, MI: Wm. B. Eerdmans Publishing Co., 1971); Vinson Synan, ed., *Aspects of the Pentecostal-Charismatic Origins* (Plainfield, NJ: Logos International, 1975); Walter J. Hollenweger, *The Pentecostals* (Minneapolis, MN: Augsberg Publishing House, 1972); William Menzies, *Anointed to Serve: The Story of the Assemblies of God* (Springfield, MO: Gospel Publishing House, 1971); James R. Goff, Jr., *Fields White Unto Harvest*, 1988; and Edith L. Blumhoffer, *The Assemblies of God: A Chapter in the Story of American Pentecostalism*, 2 vols. (Springfield, MO: Gospel Publishing House, 1989) among others. Robert Mapes Anderson, a non-Pentecostal scholar, in *Vision of the Disinherited: The Making of American Pentecostalism* (New York, NY: Oxford University Press, 1979) argues that the Pentecostal movement should be understood as a sociological phenomenon that erupts as a religious protest from within a social context characterized by poverty, working class segments and marginalization.

having experienced the baptism himself, he introduced Parham's Apostolic Faith message.

William Seymour preached his first sermon at the little Holiness mission in Los Angeles on the text Acts 2:4. He boldly announced that speaking in tongues was the initial evidence that indicated that one had received the baptism of the Holy Spirit. Distraught over the controversial content of the message, Julia Hutchins, the pastor of the small Holiness church, under additional pressure from the Holiness leadership in the area, locked the front door of the mission before the next service and refused to let Seymour continue.[24] Then Richard Sperrys who lived on Bonnie Brae Avenue invited the ousted Seymour to stay in their home. Seymour began holding services in the house and soon the crowds extended out to the front porch. Several received the baptism of the Holy Spirit with the evidence of speaking in tongues including Seymour himself. Within a few short weeks the crowds from the noisy meetings were spilling into the street. It was time to find a larger building.

On April 14th 1906 Seymour held his first service at an old abandoned warehouse in a downtown area at 312 Azusa Street. By September, after a substantial but not dramatic summer increase in attendance, the meetings gained widespread publicity. During the following period of about three years the mission attracted world-wide attention and this interest added to the infant movement's international reputation. While it was certainly not a spontaneous spiritual eruption, having gained most of its teachings, practices— and much of its best leadership—from the Holiness groups, it was nevertheless a highly fluid, decentralized movement that quickly adapted to new situations.[25]

The Azusa Street mission, located near the Los Angeles Times building, benefited from the publicity generated from occasional journalistic coverage, as well as from the social fluidity and religious tolerance occasioned by the city's multi-ethnic, immigrant population. Frank Bartleman, a Holiness preacher and journalist, who had been with the local group since its beginning, gave wide circulation to accounts of the revival's progress. When the San Francisco earthquake occurred on April 18th 1906,

---

[24]*Apostolic Faith* (Los Angeles), I (Sept. 1906).
[25]Donald Dayton, *Theological Roots Of Pentecostalism* (Grand Rapids, MI: Zondervan Publishing House, 1987); Vinson Synan, *The Holiness-Pentecostal Movement*; etc.

Bartleman hurriedly had tens of thousands of 'earthquake' tracts printed to capitalize on the forebodings of catastrophe that spread throughout the area in the wake of the tremors. His dramatic account left no doubt that the band of believers understood the earthquake to be God's judgement.

> The San Francisco earthquake was surely the voice of God to the people on the Pacific Coast. It was used mightily in conviction, for the gracious after revival. In the early 'Azusa' days both Heaven and hell seemed to come to town. Men were at the breaking point. Conviction was mightily on the people. They would fly to pieces even on the street, almost without provocation. A very 'dead line' seemed to be drawn around 'Azusa Mission', by the Spirit. When men came within two or three blocks of the place they were seized with conviction.[26]

Current events thus gave the infant movement apocalyptic relevance. Most American Christians at the time were intent on figuratively or literally bringing about the realization of God's Kingdom on earth, but the first generation of Pentecostals expressed their understanding of the gospel of the Kingdom in their complete rejection of existing systems.

For almost three years the mission at Azusa Street held services three times a day seven days a week. Bartleman described Asuza Street as a 'veritable Jerusalem' as thousands of people from all over the world made the journey to Azusa Street to undergo their own personal Pentecostal experience.

Bartleman reported that in spite of persecution from the press as well as from local churches the crowds kept coming. He particularly underscored in his writings that a primary reason for God's approval was the elimination of racial barriers. In spite of the fact that the Azusa Street revival began through the efforts

---

[26]Frank Bartleman, *How Pentecost Came to Los Angeles: As It was in the Beginning* (Los Angeles: n. p., 1925), 29. Bartleman, more than any other person, chronicled the events of Azusa Street in his published writings and diary. He is credited for having produced 550 articles, 100 tracts and six books. See Cecil. M. Robeck, 'Frank Bartleman,' *DPCM*, 50–51.

[27]Bartleman, *How Pentecost Came to Los Angeles*, 29. Nelson's thesis in *For Such a Time* is that Seymour completely breaks down the racial distinctions between blacks and whites and thus established a community that most typifies the restoration of the New Testament Pentecostal experience in Acts. 2. For Nelson the elimination of racial barriers at Azusa

of a black man, Bartleman attested, 'there were far more white people than colored coming. The "color line" was washed away in the blood.'[27]

The Spirit of God was the real leader according to Bartleman who wrote,

> Brother Seymour was recognized as the nominal leader in charge. But we have no pope or hierarchy. We were 'brethren.' . . . . All was spontaneous, ordered of the Spirit. We wanted to hear from God, through whomever he might speak. We had no 'respect of persons.' The rich and educated were the same as the poor and the ignorant, and found a much harder death to die. We only recognized God. All were equal . . . . Those were Holy Ghost meetings, led of the Lord. It had to start in poor surroundings, to keep out the selfish, human element. All came down in humility together, at His feet. They all looked alike, and had all things in common in that sense at least. The rafters were low, the tall must come down. By the time they got to 'Azusa' they were humbled, ready for the blessing. The fodder was thus placed for the lambs, not for giraffes. All could reach it.[28]

Seymour began his own journal, *Apostolic Faith* Los Angeles, California, and soon had a subscription list of 40,000 people.[29] Azusa Street became the focus for the Pentecostal movement that would spread around the globe. Its teaching of the restoration of New Testament principles of spiritual empowerment, coupled with the experience of the baptism of the Holy Spirit as initially evidenced by speaking in other tongues, became the doctrinal cornerstone for much of Pentecostal theology. The greatest demonstration of its acceptance would be the emergence of the Assemblies of God.

However, the revival at Azusa Street did not take place in a

(footnote 27 continued)
Street is more critical than any theological concerns such as glossolalia. The fact that Azusa Street maintained a semblance of racial equality for such a short period undermines his claim. Even Seymour, in less than a three year period, had all blacks in official leadership positions. See Anderson, *Vision of the Disinherited*, 188–189.

[28] Bartleman, *How Pentecost Came To Los Angeles*, 32–33.

[29] Wayne E. Warner, 'Publications,' *DPCM*, 744 reports that Seymour by the end of 1907, boasted a 40,000 press run. Both Parham and Seymour called their magazines by the name of *Apostolic Faith*. Parham's was published out of Baxter Springs, Kansas; Seymour's was published out of Los Angeles, California until 1908 when Florence Crawford became the publisher and moved the magazine to Portland, Oregon. See the various 'Apostolic Faith' entries, and the 'Publications' entry in *DPCM*.

vacuum. To understand the Pentecostal movement that emerged
so forcefully from such a humble context it is necessary to understand the existing religious movements present at the turn of the
century that provided the theological roots for this Pentecostal
movement.

WESLEYAN ROOTS

Pentecostals find some of their earliest roots in the radical Holiness
movements that emerged in the later part of the nineteenth
century.[30] John Wesley's doctrine of sanctification[31] that referred
to Christian perfection as a second work of grace resulting in the
uprooting of sin provided the cornerstone for Holiness advocates.
They taught that by concentrating on the blood of Jesus Christ
and by experiencing the power of the Holy Spirit the believer
could enjoy freedom from depravity of spirit and be absolutely
cleansed from all sin. By the end of the nineteenth century,

---

[30]For the best surveys of the Holiness-Pentecostal movement in the nineteenth century
see Vinson Synan, *The Holiness-Pentecostal Movement in the United States*, and D.W. Dayton,
The Theological Roots of the Pentecostalism. Interestingly, there were significant similarities
between the goals of the religious conservatives and the 'social gospel liberals'. Walter
Rauschenbusch, the great advocate of the social gospel, was theologically conservative
rather than a liberal and deeply concerned with personal religious experience. Like the
conservatives Rauschenbusch pleaded for spiritual renewal. The conservatives understood
that this spiritual vitality would work its way out in the personal life of the believer, while
the social-gospeller maintained that spiritual renewal must be experienced in the corporate
life of the church. Walter Rauschenbusch, 'The New Evangelism', in *American Protestant
Thought: The Liberal Era*, ed. William R. Hutchinson (New York, NY: Harper and Row,
1968), 111–116. For an excellent biography of Rausenbusch see Paul M. Minus, *Walter
Rauschenbusch: American Reformer* (New York, NY: Macmillan Publishing Company,
1988).
[31]Though it is hard to describe Wesley's exact understanding of Christian perfection,
because of his changing views, it is doubtful that Wesley ever intended that the believer
would enjoy complete freedom from sin. His development of the doctrine of sanctification
is almost exclusively Christocentric. For his classic work see John Wesley, *Plain Account
of Christian Perfection* (New York, NY: Track Department, n.d.). Donald Dayton, 'From
"Christian Perfection" to the "Baptism of the Holy Ghost"', in *Aspects of Pentecostal-Charismatic Origins*, ed. Vinson Synan (Plainfield, NJ: Logos International, 1975), 39–54 argues
that Wesley never understood the work of sanctification to be the result of the receiving
of the baptism of the Holy Spirit but rather as a manifestation of practising Christ-likeness.
According to Dayton, the first sustained effort to associate the baptism of the Holy Spirit
with sanctification was carried out by the Oberlin school, especially by its two leaders
Charles Finney and Asa Mahan. Particularly see Asa Mahan, *Baptism of the Holy Ghost*
(New York, NY: W. C. Palmer, Jr., 1970). The Keswick movement evolved as a result
of Mahan's meetings in Oxford (1874) and Brighton (1875). Dayton provides the most
comprehensive analysis of this connection in his *Theological Roots of Pentecostalism*.

however, this idea of sanctification was becoming less influential in the identity of the average American Methodist.

The revivals of the Great Awakening in which Methodism entered America and of the Second Awakening in 1857-1858 had waned and by 1890 the membership of the Methodist Church was comprised of a middle class society that arguably had more interest in secular and materialistic pursuits than in the old-fashioned message of personal piety and holiness.[32] The lower classes, the less educated groups, rural adherents, immigrants and the poor within Methodist churches felt isolated and marginalized without voice or representation. These fringe clusters felt that the malaise of the church could be blamed almost solely on the loss of emphasis upon Wesley's plea for sanctification and holiness. Radical and unsophisticated groups argued that an instantaneous second work of grace that could permanently purge the believer of one's sinful nature was available through the power of the Holy Spirit. This extreme position of entire sanctification was viewed with disdain by Methodist leaders who were embarrassed by the claims and actions of their less educated members. The negative reaction of the church leadership served only to confirm what this underdog segment of Methodism already knew. Orthodox Methodism mirrored secular society and was concerned more with respectability and prestige than with personal holiness. Given this context the Holiness advocates chose to 'come out' from the Methodist Church and launch their own radical Holiness movements based upon the doctrine of entire sanctification as a second work of grace.[33]

For Holiness adherents the Holy Spirit was the agent who provided the power for such Christian perfection.[34] Sanctification

---

[32]'Decline' between the Civil War and World War I is a highly contested point. Charles Yrigoyen, for example, characterizes this period as one of expansion and growth for Methodism. Charles Y. Yrigoyen, Jr., 'United Methodism,' in *Encyclopedia of the American Religious Experience* eds. Charles H. Lippy and Peter W. Williams (New York, NY: Charles Scribner's Sons, 1988), 1:525–537. For standard sources on Methodism see Emory S. Burke, ed., *The History of American Methodism*, 3 vols. (New York, NY: Abingdon Press, 1961); Richard Cameron, *Methodism and Society in Historical Perspective* (New York, NY: Abingdon Press, 1961); Stuart Andrews, *Methodism and Society* (London: Longmans, 1970).

[33]For a comprehensive review of the 'come-out' movement in Methodism see Charles Edwin Jones, *Perfectionist Persuasion: A Social Profile of the National Holiness Movement* (Metuchen, NJ: Scarecrow Press Inc., 1974).

[34]The prevailing view among Holiness units was that sanctification was both instant and progressive until a state of entire sanctification was attained. See J. W. Horne, 'Sermon', in *Peniel; or Face to Face with God*, eds. A. McLean and J. W. Eaton (New York, NY: W.C.

resulted from a crisis experience with the Holy Spirit. In spite of bitter opposition and ridicule from within the orthodox church the Holiness followers did not shy away from their attack upon what they viewed as the church's unholy and unacceptable accommodation to the sinful characteristics of the world. They viewed what they considered to be the hopelessly back-slidden state of the church as evidence that a second religious experience or 'second blessing' was essential for holy living.

Revival campaigns led by itinerant evangelists became the logical methodology for propagating this climactic religious experience. These revivals were characterized by emotionalism, visions and dreams that were understood to be God's expression of approval. Hell-fire and damnation preaching, ridicule of organized religion and a call for repentance were part of the new revivalism. A crisis-experience with the Holy Spirit provided the only channel by which the believer could escape from one's sinful nature and be 'set free'.

The doctrinal statement from the First General Holiness Assembly in 1885, reflecting this extreme brand of holiness, stated that, 'by the baptism of the Holy Spirit, the justified believer is delivered from inbred sin, and consequently is saved from all unholy tempers, cleansed from all moral defilement, made perfect in love . . .'[35]

This concept that Christian perfectionism is available to the believer by way of a crisis experience or a 'second blessing' formed the standard position of the majority of Holiness followers. The idea that the Holy Spirit could control one's life and provide an experience-certified relationship with God came to be the unifying principle in later Pentecostal thought.[36]

Although the Pentecostal movement cannot be understood apart from its Wesleyan-Holiness roots, another strand of the Holiness movement that denied the Wesleyan position of entire sanctification would probably have even more of an impact upon Pentecostalism.

(footnote 34 continued)
Palmer, Jr., 1869), 26. Blumhofer, *Assemblies of God*, 1989; Synan, *The Holiness-Pentecostal Movement in the United States*, 1971; Dayton, *Theological Roots of Pentecostalism*, 1987 as well as three entries from *DPCM* address this issue. See Charles W. Conn, 'Christian Perfection (A Pentecostal Perspective),' 169–180; Charles Edwin Jones, 'Holiness Movement,' 406–409; David Bundy, 'Keswick Higher Life Movement,' 518–519.
[35]S. B. Shaw, ed., *Echoes of the General Holiness Assembly* (Chicago, IL: S. B. Shaw, 1901), 29–30.
[36]Paul Polmerville, *The Third Force in Missions* (Peabody, MA: Hendrickson Publishers, 1985), 79–104.

THE KESWICK INFLUENCE

The Keswick movement emerged from a series of annual 'higher-life' conferences held in the resort town of Keswick in the United Kingdom. This movement was committed to the propagation of the gospel through annual conferences, church revivals, missionary endeavour and biblical teaching on a deeper and higher walk of victorious Christian living. The Keswick leaders rejected the view propagated by the followers of the Wesleyan-Holiness movement that the baptism of the Holy Spirit was a 'second work of grace' leading to the eradication of sin in the life of a believer. They argued instead that sanctification was a gradual process and such a process began at conversion. The Keswick teaching was that sanctification was complete 'in Christ', but progressive in the life of the believer. Critical for later Pentecostal thought, the Keswick teaching emphasized that although the baptism of the Holy Spirit was indeed a crisis experience, it was divinely given not for that eradication of sin which would entirely sanctify the believer, but rather 'an enduement of power' for service.

The religious roots for the Keswicks began in the early part of the nineteenth century particularly with the teachings of the Anglican layman, J. Nelson Darby. Darby was part of a renewal movement in the Church of England that eventually organized itself into its own splinter group called The Plymouth Brethren. Darby and The Brethren introduced the dispensational system that was based on the assumption that God deals with humankind setting out different rules and regulations in successive time periods or dispensations.[37] Darby contended that the Bible could be rightly interpreted only when a distinction was made between biblical

---

[37]Darby's dispensational teaching has had significant influence upon fundamentalist-evangelical traditions. Generally seven time periods are identified in dispensational thought; viz., dispensations of innocence, conscience, civil government, promise, law, grace and the kingdom. Though there are divergencies in the interpretations of the above, consistent to most who accept dispensationalism is that there must be a distinct separation between the understanding of the literal interpretation of the biblical text as it relates to the church and the literal meaning of the biblical texts that relate to the nation of Israel. Dispensationalism was the standard teaching at educational institutions such as Moody Bible Institute and Dallas Theological Seminary, as well as almost all early Pentecostal Bible institutes. Two of the major North American advocates are L. S. Chafer, *Systematic Theology*, 5 vols. (Dallas, TX: Dallas Theological Seminary, 1944) and C. C. Ryrie, *Dispensationalism Today* (Chicago, IL: Moody Press, 1965). For the impact of dispensationalism on Pentecostalism see G. T. Sheppard, 'Pentecostals and the Hermeneutics of Dispensationalism: The Anatomy

imperatives intended for an earlier dispensation and divine imperatives intended for the present dispensation. According to Darby's schema, the Christian era initiated the current dispensation of grace. This dispensation of grace would soon be ended with the Second Coming of Christ which would usher in the dispensation of the millennium.[38]

Darby preached his dispensationalist system in many centres of America with considerable success. The Holiness-revivalists D. L. Moody, R. A. Torrey, A. J. Gordon, A. B. Simpson as well as popular teachers such as A. T. Piersan and C. I. Scofield[39] accepted the basic outline of dispensational thought and incorporated this blueprint of the ages into the core of their own theological thinking. At the heart and soul of this view was the 'soon return' of Jesus Christ. Bible prophecy as a predictor of the 'signs and the times' of the Second Coming gave rise to the conviction that the whole world needed an opportunity to hear the gospel before the imminent and cataclysmic end. Within this context of urgency to preach the gospel to the entire world in 'the last days' the Keswick Holiness preachers taught that the baptism of the Holy Spirit would supernaturally endue the believer with extraordinary power for such a task. While different functions were attributed to Holy Spirit baptism, the major emphasis was on an enduement with power to evangelize.

The Keswick understanding of the baptism of the Holy Spirit as enduement for service was more palatable to a far greater number of believers than were the Wesleyan-Holiness teachings of baptism for entire sanctification. The more mediating position of the

---

(footnote 37 continued)
of an Uneasy Relationship', PNEUMA: *The Journal of the Society for Pentecostal Studies* 6 (Fall 1984): 5–31. Sheppard quite correctly argues that Pentecostals were not dispensationalists originally. It is Professor Sheppard's contention that an acceptance of a dispensational theological position threatens Pentecostal identity 'hermeneutically, sociologically and politically' and that such a stance is inconsistent 'even for the most basic Pentecostal understanding of Acts 2 (5)'. For the strong impact of dispensationalism on the Latin American evangelical movement see Wilton Nelson, *Protestantism in Latin America* (Grand Rapids, MI: Wm. B. Eerdmans Publishing Co., 1984).

[38]In Darby's teaching, the notion that the Second Coming of Christ would occur previous to the thousand year millennium, was used by many to remove any motive for social action. According to this perspective man was incapable of building a better world and, further, the Lord was going to right all the wrongs of society during the millennium. Such a pessimistic view offered little motivation to improve social injustices.

[39]Scofield popularized dispensational teachings for millions of people with the publishing of the Scofield Reference Bible in 1909.

Keswick teaching presented a balance between holy living and the infilling of the Holy Spirit for enduement with power to evangelize and perform miracles. This balance provided an attractive panorama of a 'higher life' that appealed to those eager to commit their lives in Christian service.

Robert Anderson correctly states that the theological assumptions of the Keswick movement were critical in the later development of Pentecostal thought.[40] Though Pentecostals can trace their origins to the Wesleyan-Holiness movement it is clear that the subsequent early influence of the Keswick teachings regarding dispensationalism, premillenialism and more importantly their understanding of progressive sanctification, as well as their experience of the baptism of the Holy Spirit for empowerment, became predominant theological elements in later Pentecostal thought. With the development of the Wesleyan-Holiness demand for believers to 'come out' from contemporary Methodism and with the rise of the Keswick 'higher life' teaching, the stage was set for the turn-of-the-century experiential outpouring of the Holy Spirit which started the modern Pentecostal movement.

PENTECOSTAL UNIQUENESS AND DENOMINATIONAL FRAGMENTATION

Though the impact of the Holiness movement upon the formation of Pentecostal thought cannot be denied, there were some important differences between the movement and Pentecostalism. Many of the people attending at Azusa Street were, according to Bartleman, 'seasoned veterans [of the Holiness movement]. One of the reasons for the depth of the work at Azusa,' he claimed, 'was the fact the workers were not novices. They were largely called and prepared for years, in the Holiness ranks and the mission field.'[41] Nils Bloch-Hoell similarly comments on the large proportion of recognized and lay ministers who attended at the Azusa Street Mission, as well as the numerous conferences that attracted clergymen from long distances in pursuit of enlarged spiritual comprehension.[42] Since the Holiness movement theologically and

---

[40]Anderson, *Vision of the Disinherited*, 43.
[41]Bartleman, *How Pentecost Came to Los Angeles*, 52.
[42]Nils Bloch-Hoell, *The Pentecostal Movement; Its Origin, Development, and Distinctive Character* (Oslo: Universitetsflorlaget, 1964), 39–40.

experimentally fed on concern for an ever-increasing demonstration of power, for a heightened sense of urgency in light of the imminent Second Coming and for confirming evidence of spiritual superiority, it is not surprising that it was unable to constrain the tendency to overflow self-imposed limits. The effective use of communication techniques, entertaining music, the inclusion of topical material into sermons and the element of surprise and congregational participation incorporated in the Pentecostal theology of spiritual empowerment made a broad appeal that caused the previously accepted patterns of the Holiness movement to appear increasingly sober, elitist and restrictive.[43]

Moreover, the Azusa Street mission always essentially a black church, despite the number of whites initially in attendance, had a more universal character than was typical of the racially segregated Holiness churches and the Midwestern Pentecostal centres started by Parham. 'The thinly veiled Anglo-Saxon racist strain in Parham's scheme made its acceptance by minority racial and ethnic groups difficult and unlikely', comments Anderson.[44] If the Azusa Street mission quickly reverted to its origins as a black church, it briefly lowered the barriers of race and nationality. 'God makes no difference in nationality', an often cited quotation from the mission's publication stated, 'Ethiopians, Chinese, Indians, Mexicans and other nationalities worship together.'[45] A reported twenty different nationalities were represented. 'It is', said an eyewitness of the work 'noticeably free from all nationalistic feeling. No instrument that God can use is rejected on account of color or dress or lack of education.' Based upon his research into the Azusa Street Mission, Robert Mapes Anderson observed that 'the ethnic minority groups of Los Angeles found themselves welcome at Azusa, and some would discover there the sense of dignity and community denied them in the larger urban culture'.[46]

The geographical and sociological backdrop of the early movement was the South, the border states and the Southwest, as well

---

[43]The rift that soon developed between Holiness leaders and the emergent Pentecostal groups indicates the unwillingness of the former to accept the legitimacy of the Pentecostals' claims, despite their many similarities. See C. E. Jones, 'Holiness Movement', *DPCM*, 406–409.

[44]Anderson, *Vision of the Disinherited*, 40.

[45]Cited in Anderson, *Vision of the Disinherited*, 69.

[46]Ibid., 69.

as metropolitan centres like Los Angeles, Houston, Chicago and New York, all areas which were made up in large part of immigrants from rural America and Europe. After the Populist movement of the 1890s failed to bring substantial help to the nation's small farmers, their social status, rural values and powers of political leverage were in disarray. While only a comparitively small number of such farmers or immigrants took their place in the emerging Pentecostal movement, those who did were, in many cases, persons of notable ability and ambition, articulate, and capable of providing leadership.[47] At the same time, these people were also cut off from their religious past as migration or modernizing influences deprived them of their traditional forms of emotional support. Under these pressures interconfessionalism became widespread, as evidenced by the growth of non-denominational movements and the appearance of new groups, many of them emphasizing Christian perfection, that had, in effect, seceded from the established church traditions.[48]

The young Pentecostal movement also quickly showed its adaptability by its capacity to transfer their experiences into a number of other settings. Thus, the origins of the movement in numerous cities can be traced directly to the Azusa Street Mission and beyond to the conversion of several existing Holiness associations. G. B. Cashwell became a missionary to the various Holiness churches in the South, including the previously organized Church of God (Cleveland), destined to become one of the leading Pentecostal denominations.[49] Similarly, Charles H. Mason, of the Church of God in Christ, visited Los Angeles and subsequently led his group into the Pentecostal ranks.[50] In addition, the now formally organized centre commissioned various home and foreign missionaries, some of them qualified by the apparent gift of tongues for ministry to a particular language group. Widespread circulation of literature, coming from the pens of the Pentecostal editors in impressive numbers, quickly carried the message overseas. As a result members of Holiness groups around the world were rapidly linked together in their fascination with the new teachings.[51]

---

[47]Ibid.
[48]Bloch-Hoell, *The Pentecostal Movement*, 13.
[49]Synan, *The Holiness-Pentecostal Movement*, 114.
[50]Hollenweger, *The Pentecostals*, 482.
[51]See listing of publications in Goff, *Fields White Unto Harvest*, 241, as well as W. E. Warner, 'Publications', *DPCM*, 742–751.

While the Azusa Street Mission was establishing practical precedents, the movement continued to evolve elsewhere, especially on the East Coast, where similar conditions and contact with revivalists advanced the movement, and in Chicago, which John Alexander Dowie and others had already made a centre of religious ferment.[52] There William H. Durham, a Baptist minister, carried the message that he had received under the influence of Seymour in Los Angeles and applied it with equal effectiveness.[53] If Azusa Street had given the movement world-wide publicity, Durham's contribution was no less important in practically extending the faith through his contact with leaders from other nationalities. A. A. Argue, a founder of the Canadian Pentecostal movement, visited the mission, as did Luigi Francescon, an originator of the movement in the south of Brazil and in Argentina, as well as in Italy. Daniel Berg and Gundar Vingren, who introduced Pentecostalism into the northern states of Brazil, were influenced by Durham, as were other Scandinavians whose influence reached Willis Hoover, founder of the movement in Chile in 1909.[54] In each of these instances, people from various regions of the globe travelled to Azusa Street, Los Angeles or Stone Church, Chicago to hear Durham. Durham did not leave United States soil to perpetuate his Pentecostal teaching. Instead, potentially influential leaders came to experience Pentecost, and then returned to their country of origin to contexualize the Pentecostal message within their own cultural matrix, political-economical reality and personal concerns.

Durham in his brief Pentecostal ministry, moreover, further removed the Pentecostal movement from its Wesleyan-Holiness origins by effectively advocating a Baptist view of sanctification. Rather than achieving perfection as a single act of grace, the process continued throughout the believer's life as one continued to walk by faith. This view, while creating one of the movement's many internal controversies, over time gained wider support in the form of the 'finished work' position.[55] It provided a form of Pentecostal interpretation with which believers from the Baptist and Reformed

---

[52] E. L. Blumhofer, 'John Alexander Dowie', *DPCM*, 248–249.

[53] H. V. Synan, 'William Joseph Seymour', *DPCM*, 778–781.

[54] Standard accounts of Hoover's work in Chile are those found in John B. A. Kessler, *A Study of the Older Protestant Missions and Churches in Peru and Chile* (Goes, Netherlands: Oosterbaan and Le Cointre, 1967) and Willis C. Hoover, *Historia del Avivamiento Pentecostal en Chile* (Valparaiso, 1948).

[55] See R. M. Riss, 'William H. Durham', *DPCM*, 255–256.

persuasions could more readily identify, eventually making the Pentecostal message more acceptable to the American evangelical religious main stream.[56]

In spite of significant differences which emerged as the movement began to take institutional form, it was clear that the majority of Pentecostals had remained largely committed to the Holiness teaching of immediate, entire sanctification. Thus the Church of God (Cleveland, TN) became Pentecostal in 1907. The Church of God in Christ, a Holiness church in existence since the 1890s and the Pentecostal Holiness Church, made up of several Holiness groups, came into existence in 1906 by adding a third peak experience to those that they had already come to accept.[57] The Church of God, which came to exert strong influence in Latin America, entered Mexico and Central America in the 1930s, in some cases identifying with existing Pentecostal work begun as early as 1906.[58]

Other early Pentecostal groups, also influenced by the Holiness movement but made up in part by elements with a Reformed background that were generally committed to the Keswick teaching of baptism for empowering in service, formed a second distinct Pentecostal tradition with the founding of the Assemblies of God in 1914.[59] From this group emerged later denominations, including the International Church of the Foursquare Gospel (1923), the Open Bible Standard (1935), and the Pentecostal Church of God (1919).

A third major grouping resulted from a split within the ranks of the existing Pentecostals took the form of dissent in identifying itself as Unitarian in an otherwise Trinitarian tradition. Ministers who

---

[56]See note 11. When Pentecostal groups were invited to become charter members of the National Association of Evangelicals in 1942, it was the moderating approach of Harold Ockenga, associated with the Reformed Tradition, and Carl F. H. Henry, associated with the American Baptist tradition, which won the day over critics who wanted Pentecostals excluded. The first Pentecostal to be elected President of the NAE was Thomas E. Zimmerman, General Superintendent of the Assemblies of God, the first Pentecostal denomination in 1914 to adopt the reformed and baptistic Keswick position on sanctification and on Spirit baptism as an empowerment for witness. According to 1987 figures, the NAE has 5 million members in denominations associated with the organization. Of these 5 million members, 3.1 are Pentecostal, and the Assemblies of God contributes 66 per cent of all Pentecostals. Cecil M. Robeck, Jr.,'National Association of Evangelicals (NAE),' *DPCM*, 634–636.
[57]See the explanation given in Hollenweger, *The Pentecostals*, 24–26.
[58]Manuel J. Gaxiola-Gaxiola, 'Latin American Pentecostalism: A Mosaic within a Mosaic', *Pnuema: The Journal of the Society for Pentecostal Studies* 13 (Fall 1991): 115.
[59]E. L. Blumhofer, 'Assemblies of God', *DPCM*, 23–28.

had adopted the 'Oneness' doctrine, seceded from the Assemblies of God in 1916 and formed their own organization, the General Assembly of Apostolic Assemblies, merging with an existing group to form the Pentecostal Assemblies of the World in 1918. The United Pentecostal Church (created by the merger of several groups in 1945) belongs to this lineage, as well as some Apostolic groups.[60]

This fragmentation of the Pentecostal movement into three major branches and an expanding number of denominations, only one short decade removed from the initial Azusa Street revival, had implications for the missionary endeavours among Pentecostals.

EARLY MISSIONARY DIMENSIONS OF THE PENTECOSTAL MOVEMENT

While the lack of institutional stability within early Pentecostalism simply did not permit participants in the movement to carry out extensive programmes of overseas work, a relatively few hardy visionaries determined to fulfil their calling with heroic tenacity. If it had been initially assumed that new missionaries would not need to learn the language, they soon returned or settled down to some more conventional style of missionary ministry on finding that their gift was not linguistic.[61] Moreover, the lack of financial structures to maintain them in overseas ministry resulted in many returning home after a relatively brief term of service or, in a few cases, becoming an integral part of the overseas ministry and largely losing association at home during their prolonged absences. The institutional importance of the North American Pentecostal churches for the Latin American revival is, accordingly, tenuous, except for the personal impact a few missionaries had on the nationals whom they influenced, leaving the contribution to these Latin American groups largely one of exemplary practices, precedent and inspiration.[62] Moreover, beyond the regulations of the Holiness tradition, Pentecostal beliefs gave adherents, in the words

---

[60]D. A. Reed, 'Oneness Pentecostalism', *DPCM*, 644–651.

[61]Goff, *Fields White Unto Harvest*, 75.

[62]Whereas in 1906, the year of the Azusa Street revival, an estimated 6,000 to 8,000 Pentecostals were found throughout the United States, by 1909, the year Pentecostalism was introduced into Chile and Brazil, the Pentecostal movement in the United States may have grown to as many as 60,000 adherents. By all accounts their resources were extremely modest, and given the Pentecostals' general aversion to formal organization, they lacked the administrative apparatus to promote an institutional missionary programme of any size

of Robert Mapes Anderson, 'authorization for visions, trances, dreams and transports, dancing and various physical gyrations, loud singing and shouting, prolonged prayer, and fasting', a range of creative behaviour far beyond the conventional limits in symbolic protest of the status quo.[63]

The Azusa Street revival did, however, add fuel to the already substantial propaganda of the revival movement making its appearance throughout the world, encouraged by the still growing Holiness movement and a conservative reaction to the rationalist tendencies in the established churches. Much attention was given to the Welsh revival identified with Evan Roberts in 1904 and the, perhaps, derivative experiences at Pandita Ramabai's Mukti home near Bombay, where Pentecostal phenomena were reported.[64] T. B. Barratt, a Methodist pastor, returned to the Scandinavian countries with the Pentecostal message after experiencing his own baptism in New York.[65] Conceived originally as a means of raising funds for one of many projects, Barratt's trip to the United States was depressingly fruitless. Hearing of the Los Angeles revival, Barratt had an outstanding experience while a guest at a Christian and Missionary Alliance residence in New York in early October, 1906, and spoke in tongues a week later in a similar meeting. Barratt returned to Norway with enthusiasm for the experience and emerged as the apostle of Pentecostalism in Europe, where the movement was also soon promoted by other strong leaders, including the Baptist Lewi Pethrus in Sweden, Pastor Jonathan Paul from

---

(footnote 62 continued)
and stability, let alone, given their eschatology, a programme of intentional organized social reform. In fact the initial Pentecostal work in Brazil, Chile and Central America all occurred without the direct benefit of professional missionaries from one of the organizations that later came into being.

While the efforts of institutional missionaries were important to the later developments in Central American republics and elsewhere in Latin America, they were not uniformly successful. The earliest Pentecostal periodicals did engage in advising their readerships of the activities of various missionaries and assumed the function of clearinghouse to receive and disburse funds sent on the missionaries' behalf. By 1910, the number of missionaries sent overseas by all Pentecostal groups to all fields, according to Gary B. McGee, was over 185 of which perhaps no more than a score had embarked for Latin America. Many of these missionary adventures, however, ended in death or failure. See 'Missions, Overseas by 1910 (North American),' *DPCM*, 612.

[63]Anderson, *Vision of the Disinherited*, 93.
[64]T. Ellis, 'Pentecostal Revival Touches India,' *Heritage* (Winter 1982–1983).
[65]Thomas Ball Barratt, *The Truth about the Pentecostal Revival* (Larik, Norway: Alfons Hansen and Soner, 1927).

a Reformed background in Germany, the Anglican Alexander Boddy in England, the Waldensian Luigi Francescon in Italy and, in the 1920s, the Baptist Ivan (John) Vornaev in the Soviet Union.[66]

Elsewhere, many overseas missionaries heard of the revival and experienced the baptism of the Holy Spirit, as in the case of William Wallace Simpson, of the Christian and Missionary Alliance, who became a Pentecostal in China in 1912, and Alice Eveline Luce, daughter of an Anglican vicar, who received the baptism in India in 1910 and became a Pentecostal missionary in Mexico and to Hispanics in the Southwestern United States shortly thereafter.[67] Thus, some outstanding early Pentecostal missionaries were not initially sent, but affiliated after resignation from their respective missions.

Pentecostal influence in Mexico and in Puerto Rico, stemmed directly from the Azusa Street mission, where Hispanics had been part of the movement from the beginning. The *Iglesia Apostólica de la Fe en Cristo Jesús*, a Oneness group, traces its origins to a meeting conducted by a visitor from the United States in the home of her family in the state of Chihuahua in 1914.[68] The Assemblies of God traces its Hispanic beginnings along with those of the work in Mexico to the missions established by Henry Ball in Pasadena, Texas in 1915, although Spanish-speaking congregations along the border were part of the organization from its beginning in 1914.[69] Puerto Rican Juan Lugo,[70] baptized in the Holy Spirit in California in 1919, introduced the message to his home community the next year, while Mexican Methodist, Francisco Olazabal, baptized in the Spirit in 1919, promoted Hispanic work in the United States and Puerto Rico with extraordinary results thereafter till his death in 1937.[71] The ministry of Mexican-born Maria Atkinson, begun in 1924 after her healing from cancer, made an important contribution

---

[66]Peter D. Hocken and Desmond W. Cartwright, 'European Pentecostalism,' *DPCM*, 268–278.

[67]Gary B. McGee, 'Alice Eveline Luce', *DPCM*, 543–544.

[68]Manuel Jesús Gaxiola-Gaxiola, *The Serpent and the Dove: A History of the Apostolic Church of the faith in Jesus Christ in Mexico, 1914–1974* (Unpublished M. A. thesis: Fuller Theological Seminary, Pasadena, California, 1977), 4–9. The thesis has subsequently been published in Spanish *La Serpiente y la Paloma, Análisis del Crecimiento de la Iglesia Apostólica de la Fe en Cristo Jesus de Mexico* (Pasadena, CA: William Carey Press, 1975).

[69]Gary B. McGee, 'Henry Cleophas Ball', *DPCM*, 40.

[70]Everett A. Wilson, 'Juan L. Lugo,' *DPCM*, 544.

[71]Everett A. Wilson, 'Francisco Olazábal', *DPCM*, 643–644.

to COG work among Hispanics in the Southwest and northern Mexico until her death in 1963.[72] Only in 1935 did the Assemblies churches in the Republic of Mexico separate to form their own Assemblies of God organization.

Thus, in the Hispanic Pentecostal beginnings in Mexico little distinction was made in the initial years between the loosely organized Pentecostal groups of both languages and on both sides of the border and this looseness in national organization was equally true for Hispanic Pentecostal beginnings in Puerto Rico. One probable explanation for this slow evolution toward autonomous organization is the large population of Mexicans and Puerto Ricans in the United States; the Mexican population is concentrated in Texas, California and the Southwest, and the Puerto Rican population on the mainland is concentrated on the Atlantic Coast. Race and ethnicity among Pentecostals of Mexican and Puerto Rican descent apparently played a significant role in producing cooperative organizational alliances between Mexican Pentecostals in the United States and Puerto Rico. In extending the Pentecostal message to Mexico and Puerto Rico, common race and ethnicity seemed to play a more significant role than cultural factors related to particular geographical regions.[73]

In contrast to the direct ties of Pentecostalism in Mexico and Puerto Rico to the United States, the next chapter will demonstrate that in Latin America, especially in Central America, Pentecostalism developed in the contextualized sensitivity to the cultural, linguistic, theological and geographical needs of the adherents in the region. Furthermore, Everett Wilson has reconstructed case studies on the birth and development of Pentecostalism in Latin America which clearly show that the movement in Central America developed autonomously, even more so than Pentecostalism in Brazil and in Chile.[74]

Although the institutional development of European Pentecostalism, Hispanic Pentecostalism in Mexico and Puerto Rico, and Latin American Pentecostalism took place in markedly different

---

[72]Ibid.

[73]Everett A. Wilson, 'Hispanic Pentecostalism,' *DPCM*, 390–400.

[74]Everett A. Wilson, 'Passion and Power: A Profile of Emergent Latin American Pentecostalism,' in *Called and Empowered: Global Mission in Pentecostal Perspective*, eds. Murray W. Dempster, Byron D. Klaus and Douglas Petersen (Peabody, MA: Hendrickson Publishers, 1991), 67–97.

ways, and with varying degrees of connection to the rise of North American Pentecostalism associated with the Azusa Street revival, the dynamics found in the Pentecostal experience itself seemed to carry an inherent social concern. Rooted in the nature of Pentecostal experience was an embryonic impulse toward social concern which would make the movement particularly successful in Latin America, but which still needed explicit theological articulation and interpretation.

PENTECOSTAL SOCIAL DYNAMICS AND SOCIAL ACTION

What, specifically, were the features of this early twentieth-century Pentecostal faith that made it appropriate for Latin Americans, and what, specifically, were its social concerns? It might further be asked, as a movement with alleged millenarian characteristics, what were the implications of its supposed alienation from the mainstream of American life? The course of the movement's evolution demonstrates that Pentecostals were far less inclined to deny the realities of temporal existence than aspects of their teachings and practices might suggest. On the one hand, members were selective in repudiating the world, being typically inclined, for example, to renounce benefits like wealth and power, that were in any event not readily available, given their lower economic class status, than the more modest rewards of peer acceptance by 'brothers' and 'sisters' in local congregations and improved occupational status as ministers and church leaders, achievements that were within their reach. On the other hand, their radical rejection of the religious establishment, for example, was hardly a matter of despising religion, but of aspiring to compete with the dominant denominations in which, for the most part, they were not qualified educationally to lead. Ultimately, as David Martin shows, Pentecostals were able to carve out a faith which helped them accommodate the realities of their existence while rejecting many of the values and perspectives the larger world imposed.[75]

The explanation that people joined the Pentecostal movement because they were essentially the victims of deprivation and social dislocation, the portrait drawn of the movement that still persists,

---

[75]David Martin, *Tongues of Fire*, 282.

has been demonstrated as inadequate.[76] Luther P. Gerlach, a serious sociological investigator of the movement in the 1970s, concluded that, given the range of social and personality types found among adherents, nothing as simple as deprivation-organization models could explain the growth of Pentecostalism or its appeal for its participants. 'In reality', he asserted, 'the only thing which does distinguish Pentecostals from the general American population is their specific religious practices and beliefs. This cannot be used to prove them generally defective.'[77] The ongoing pragmatism of the evolving movement demonstrated that Pentecostals shared a world view in common with most Americans; however, the Pentecostals' rejection of the world was symbolic rather than literal, demonstrating that they were not as impractical as some of their own declarations or their detractors might suggest.[78]

Even what outsiders considered to be the most bizarre features of the movement, tongues, emotional expression in their meetings, faith healing and their belief in the imminent end of the world with the return of Christ, as they understood these beliefs and practices, affirmed their sense of personal worth and gave them control over their lives by sustaining the individual forced to cope with the insecurities of change.[79] Norwegian historian of Pentecostalism, Nils Bloch-Hoell, sees the Pentecostal movement, with xenolalia and healing, 'as primitive attempts to solve the problems of assurance or certainty which were present at that time'.[80] The quest for inner resources, far from suggesting pathological behaviour, may have indicated the essential sanity of individuals who were forced to live with increasing dissonance. The themes expressed in Pentecostal

---

[76]The work of David Martin, *Tongues of Fire*, largely discredits this position already called in question by Stephen Glazier, *Perspectives and Pentecostalism*, among others in Latin American Pentecostalism. Duke University Professor Grant Wacker insists that from the initial stages of the Pentecostal movement a deeply rooted character trait in its followers was a stubborn, audacious and assertive streak that he describes as 'willfulness.' Wacker documents several case studies to demonstrate this 'Pentecostal pragmatism'. Grant Wacker, 'Character and the Modernization of North American Pentecostalism,' a paper presented at the 21st Annual Meeting of the Society for Pentecostal Studies (Lakeland, Florida: November 7—9 1991), 8.

[77]Luther P. Gerlach, 'Pentecostalism: Revolution or Counter-Revolution?' in *Religious Movements in Contemporary America*, eds. Iwing I. Zaretsky & Mark P. Leone (Princeton, NJ: Princeton University Press, 1974), 678—679.

[78]Wacker, *Character and Modernization*, 13—21.

[79]Ibid., 9—13.

[80]Bloch-Hoell, *The Pentecostal Movement*, 12.

meetings—radical conversion, sanctification or holiness in daily life, divine healing from all sickness, and the premillennial rapture of the 'Bride of Christ'—according to James Goff, 'contained a release within the individual's religious psyche which portrayed a future release from the problems faced in the here and now. More importantly, they provided comfort in this life in dealing with disappointments and fears.'[81] As Charles Jones points out, the construct of Pentecostal faith and the expression of Pentecostal worship created a symbolic world for the faithful to inhabit and from which they could negotiate a life of meaning despite the uncertainty of their circumstances.[82]

The beliefs of Pentecostals may thus be seen as alternative ways of acquiring existing rewards of society, emotional well-being, recognition, security, purpose, rather than as providing alternative rewards themselves. 'For many reasons the attempts at solution to which these groups felt attracted were not only subjective and experimental, but emotional and finally ecstatic', concluded Bloch-Hoell. Yet, he continues, 'The solution purported to afford a sensible, verifiable proof of God's existence and at the same time, to serve as a means of revival in an eschatological harvest.'[83] The experiential basis of having a 'verifiable proof' for God's existence and of participating in 'an eschatological harvest' with its implication of an ever-widening market illustrate well the dialectic in which early Pentecostals lived. On the one hand, Pentecostals lived in a world of practicality marked by experiential proof and limits; on the other hand, Pentecostals lived in a world where individuals were not held captive to prevailing social and intellectual notions of rationality because God was establishing a new eschatological order.[84]

It has seemed to some observers that rather than rejecting contemporary currents of change in American life, the movement was more a precursor of change by its anticipation of numerous social and cultural adaptations occurring in the first decades of the century. While the movement's eschatology was a resounding

---

[81]Goff, *Fields White Unto Harvest*, 11—12.

[82]Charles Edwin Jones, 'The Beulah Land and the Upper Room: Reclaiming the Text in Turn-of-the-Century Holiness and Pentecostal Spirituality,' a paper presented at the 22nd Annual Meeting of the Society for Pentecostal Studies (Springfield, MO: November 12–14, 1992).

[83]Bloch-Hoell, *The Pentecostal Movement*, 12.

[84]Grant Wacker, 'Planning for the End, the Enduring Appeal of Prophecy Belief,' *Christian Century*, 19 January 1994, 48–52.

rejection of the existing world, it is clear that adherents generally experienced a sense of dissonance toward the world. On the one hand they demonstrated a desire to live peaceably within the existing order to the extent that it provided for their immediate needs, on the other hand they demonstrated a capacity to critique the prevailing existing order as sinful in nature. The frequency with which Pentecostal preachers pointed to their rise 'from plow to pulpit' mirrored the experience of the large proportion of rural Americans who were coming to terms with a changing America— in transition from villages, farms, and family-owned businesses to a more urban, industrial, and economically integrated nation.

As other illustrations of the forward thrust of the movement, one may observe the important role given to demonstrative music in Pentecostal churches. Their music was apparently not unlike evolving musical styles—jazz, soul, gospel—that emerged as major contributions of popular culture despite their humble origins, as well as promptly using commercial radio to advance their movement.[85] These and other tendencies tended to place Pentecostals in a historical framework that belies some of their alleged otherworldliness and demonstrates how their spiritual posture had practical, immediate consequences.[86]

It is to be noted, moreover, that far from remaining isolated from contemporary thought and developments, Pentecostalism gained its defining characteristics from the main currents of national life. While Pentecostalism quickly found a place in a variety of cultures, the movement initially was culturally specific, having had its origins in the American religious development, a cultural setting that was itself distinct from any preceding national religious tradition. 'Whatever factors may have ushered in the Pentecostal Movement', notes Bloch-Hoell, 'it now seems clear this movement is characteristic of certain elements of American Christianity, and that, at the same time, it has absorbed and

---

[85] Aimie Semple McPherson was one of the first to receive a radio frequency in the United States.

[86] As Grant Wacker points out, these competing impulses in Pentecostal identity between 'heavenly minded pilgrims, spiritual wanderers, pursuing other-worldly satisfactions' and a this-worldly 'pragmatism of pushing toward results in changing the world and its future' were not self-consciously recognized and therefore not problematic. For Pentecostals these two worlds did not exist in a 'means to an end' relationship, but rather these two worlds represented the reality implicit in the Pentecostal experience. Grant Wacker, 'Character and Modernization,' 8–21.

intensified many of the features typical of religion at the turn of the century.'[87]

These features, common to the modernizing process, included heterogeneity, resulting from the many traditions that made up the American people; the free church tradition; tolerance; voluntarism; proselytism; emotionalism; individualism; optimism and pragmatism, by which Bloch means demonstrable proof in experience. This final characteristic, in a world where verifiable proof was demanded, regulation was increasingly rational and administration was increasingly centralized, saw Pentecostals, despite their other-worldly spirituality, insisting on a tangible sign like physical healings and the gift of tongues. Thus Pentecostalism, despite its novelty, should be considered an outgrowth of its times. 'In short', concludes Bloch, 'the special circumstances in the U. S. A. at the turn of the century had established a mentality which facilitated the birth of a primitive religious mass-movement like the Pentecostal Movement.'[88]

In similar fashion, the movement's democratizing tendencies were not out of step with the turn-of-the-century political and cultural developments. Bloch finds the movement's support of low-church principles and practices especially instructive:

> There is no doubt from one point of view that the Pentecostal Movement is a link in the democratizing of society. The Pentecostal Movement was, and to a certain extent still is, a class movement, the primitive Christianity of the less educated.[89]

Seen as a system bent on increasingly widened influence, however, Pentecostalism, by its democratization of religious life, its promise of physical and social healing, its compassion for the socially alienated and its insistence that all human ills were at root a consequence of moral evil, addressed the concerns of the disinherited, frustrated and assertive persons who in large part made up the

---

[87]Bloch Hoell, *The Pentecostal Movement*. 12.
[88]Ibid., 10. Jean-Daniel Plüss makes this same point in slightly different terms. Plüss notes that 'the first generation of Pentecostals was influenced by dualistic positivist objectivism.' Accordingly, within the first decade after the Azusa Street Revival, Pentecostals had formulated a doctrine that made glossolalia the 'initial physical evidence' of Spirit baptism. Plüss observes: 'They might just as well have called it "basic empirical proof".' Jean-Daniel Plüss, 'Azusa and Other Myths: The Long and Winding Road from Experience to Stated Belief and Back Again,' *PNEUMA: The Journal of the Society for Pentecostal Studies* 15 (Fall 1993): 190–191.
[89]Ibid., 11.

movement. The Pentecostals' potential for taking action appropriate to the needs of constituents, rather than being wedded to a specific ideology, constituted the movement's social philosophy. Ultimately, by empowering people who were previously denied a voice, the movement acquired a revolutionary potential.[90]

While most scholars agree that the beliefs of the Pentecostal groups were essentially those of the Holiness movement, the two most prominent features of the movement—tongues and healing—deserve special consideration, since they are considered the universal religious phenomena among Pentecostals of all types. According to psychological theory both involve the 'invasion and control of the individual', with healing offering the personal wholeness and well-being and tongues providing psychic escape through ecstasy.[91]

This analysis, far from being hostile to Pentecostal beliefs, suggests the first of two important distinctions between Pentecostals and the preceding revival moments to which they were indebted, namely, validation of the worth of the individual adherent. Even though Pentecostals were allegedly 'other-worldly', their message was essentially one of immediate personal help. Healing, a mark of personal worth and power, was not deferred and was not considered essentially spiritual,[92] but rather remarkably down-to-earth, gratifying and practical. If the Holiness movement considered divine healing to be an indication of divine presence, and healing remained in those ranks largely a token of inner grace, spiritual transcendence and symbolic of future restoration, for Pentecostals, healing had immediate practical results. It was, along with tongues, a credential of the practitioner's New Testament apostolic power, as well as his or her seeking divine healing as a form of medical attention instead of seeking help from the medical profession. Pentecostals were matter-of-fact about healing

---

[90]David Martin, *Tongues of Fire*, 108.

[91]David Edwin Harrell, Jr., *All Things are Possible: The Healing and Charismatic Revivals in Modern America* (Bloomington, IN: Indiana University Press, 1975) in his study of the Healing Movement in America notes the entrepreneurial side to the Pentecostal healing evangelists. The healing ministries that succeed and/or emerge do so by pragmatic adaptation and innovation.

[92]For Pentecostals, divine healing was not part of the natural order of things but resulted from God's direct and miraculous intervention to change the natural course of an illness, handicap or affliction. Although divine healing could be gradual in its effects, the overwhelming emphasis among early Pentecostals was instantaneous healing. From 1916 forward the Assemblies of God declared in its 'Statement of Fundamental Truths,' article 12: 'Divine healing is an integral part of the gospel. Deliverance from sickness is provided for in the atonement, and is the privilege of all believers' (Isa. 53:4,5; Matt. 8:16, 17; James 5: 14—16).

as they were about other miracles. For them power shifted from symbolic promise to fulfilment, from the purely spiritual to the demonstrable. Thus, the participants' sense of being empowered by the Holy Spirit was often expressed in music and singing that was boisterous, strident, provocative and insistent, and in testimonies that emphasized boldness, aggressive evangelism and personal conviction.

According to Goff, 'Pentecostalism differed little in the expression of these themes from evangelical Protestant religion in general, except that the emphasis on such divine intervention was unusually high. The one unique plank of the Pentecostal message [Spirit baptism with the evidence of tongues] demonstrated that intensity.' Goff further explains, that in the Pentecostal worldview

> Conversion absolved the guilt of past shortcomings; sanctification promises an assurance of one's rightness with God. Divine healing, perhaps more than all the others, symbolized God's approval of an individual and his power over the uncertainties of mortal life. Premillennialism provided the knowledge that God's chosen people would hold a special place in the fulfilment of divine justice.[93]

There is some suggestion that the apparent passivity of Pentecostalism was less a matter of conflict avoidance than of strategy. Luther P. Gerlach has argued that Pentecostalism in the 1960s underlay the activism of some black congregations. 'While many "Negro" Pentecostal churches did preach resignation in the face of white power,' he notes, 'most were quick enough to move to the offensive and press for change once Black Power gathered momentum.' 'It is clear', according to Gerlach, that 'resignation and acceptance of the status quo was a function of survival requirements, not an intrinsic characteristic of the Pentecostal religion itself.'[94] Pentecostalism showed itself to be a movement capable of generating an experiential spirituality and a pragmatic and practical temperament among its adherents.

Tongues, the other major innovation made by early Pentecostals, with its essential universality, suggests the inclusiveness of all the participants in the common experience of Spirit baptism. While Roman Catholicism has never realized the ideal of a unified church, not since the Reformation had the faith been so divided by sectarian exclusivity as in late nineteenth century America. The American

---

[93] Goff, *Fields White Unto Harvest*, 12.
[94] Gerlach, 'Pentecostalism: Revolution or Counter Revolution,' 679.

experience that democratized the faith, also tended to fragment it. Pentecostalism perpetuated, and even accelerated, this American tendency toward democratization of the faith. At the same time the movement so diffused charismatic authority that recognition was given by Pentecostals to virtually anyone who could gather a following. While sectarian groups proliferated, none could claim superiority by apostolic succession, moral excellence or spiritual enlightenment. Pentecostalism quickly became reproducible and was easily networked in the popular religious market, where groups vied for prospective members and support for their particular brand of belief or form of association. Not a few observers of the movement have noted the irony of a sectarianism so particularistic that it became generic. Thus, the *Dictionary of Pentecostal and Charismatic Movements*, published in 1988, lists from A to Z Christian traditions of significance, ranging from the American Baptist Charismatic Fellowship, the Anglican Renewal Ministries and the Apostolic Overcoming Holy Church of God to the now defunct (Pentecostal) Zion Evangelistic Fellowship.

PENTECOSTALS AS PRODUCERS OF SOCIAL CHANGE

While religious movements have generally been considered to be expressions of popular sentiment or cultural tensions from a functionalist perspective, sociologist of religion Luther P. Gerlach has depicted Pentecostalism quite differently as primarily a 'producer' of social change.[95] His investigation of Pentecostalism in the 1960s and 1970s, when the movement made inroads into groups as diverse as the counterculture 'Jesus people' to the Lutheran, Episcopal and Roman Catholic denominational establishments, provided opportunity to view the movement's organizational structure from a new perspective. Gerlach's analysis, which abstracted the reproductive process from these culturally varied associations, demonstrated that traditional Pentecostalism, far from being primarily an expression of frustration and resignation, was a movement that created ingenious mechanisms for extending its influence.[96]

In contrast with the time-honoured corporate model of ecclesiastical organization as a highly rationalized, pyramidal structure

---

[95]Ibid., 671—673.
[96]Ibid., 675—676.

with central authority and a clear channel of command, Gerlach found Pentecostal groups to have diffused leadership and flexible, resilient structures. These features he referred to as 'segmentary', 'polycephalous' and 'reticulate', a kind of organization that he identified as well in other movements that incorporate some of the motivational features of a sect, including the revolutionary 1960s Black Power movement and the ongoing ecology movement.[97]

In the Gerlach paradigm, a typical Pentecostal movement is composed of semi-autonomous 'cells or segments'. Gerlach identifies the following three characteristics of movement organization, such as that embodied in Pentecostalism, to show how these 'cells' produce movement growth.

1. New cells are formed by a splitting of ongoing cells, by the formation of entirely new units, or by a combination of these two. Cells frequently overlap and intertwine in complex fashion so that movement participants are often simultaneously members of several cells. An individual cell is encouraged to do its own thing, perform according to its own special capabilities afforded by the qualities of its members.

2. A second characteristic of movement organization is that it is *decentralized* and *polycephalous*, or 'many-headed'. Movements do not have a single paramount leader who rules through a coordinated bureaucracy. Each cell may have its own temporary head, but such a man is no more than a *primus inter pares*, or first among equals. He can retain such leadership only by proving his worth. Any member of a small group is a potential leader and many indeed strive to be actual leaders since they feel that they have a duty to help the group succeed. If any ongoing leader falters or fails, or appears to sell out to the establishment, he will quickly be replaced by another.

3. A third characteristic of movement organization is that it is *reticulate*. Reticulate means 'network'; that the individual cells of a movement are tied into a loose and informal network of reticulate structures by the personal interaction of 'cell' leaders, by overlapping membership as noted above, by the sharing of a common ideology, common cause, and common opposition. Traveling spokesmen or 'evangelists' move across the network, contributing to its cohesion and ideological unity. This network also provides a very effective grapevine communication system and logistical financial support system.[98]

---

[97] Ibid., 680.
[98] Ibid., 680–681.

Gerlach explains the versatility of such a system by noting that it defies efforts to rationalize organization and, in the process, creates a system 'highly adapted for exponential growth and for generating and promoting revolutionary change'. He identifies the following from factors in movement organization that lead to growth and change.

> First, it promotes coping in new environments, maximizing cellular variation, innovation, entrepreneurship, and trial-and-error experimentation and problem solving. . . . Second, it permits a movement to penetrate and recruit from a broad societal range. An individual who is attracted by what he perceives to be the general purposes of the movement can find within the myriad of movement cells a group of peers whose goals, tactics, personal life styles, and backgrounds appeal to him. Third, it prevents effective suppression or co-optation of the total movement through its redundancy, multiplicity of leadership, and self-sufficiency of local groups. Fourth, it generates an escalation of effort and forward motion through the rivalry and competition among its various segments and leaders.[99]

Unlike observers such as Christian Lalive d'Epinay who considered Pentecostalism in Latin America as primarily a retrograde reaction to despair, a 'Haven of the Masses', Gerlach concluded that the religious confidence unleashed by Pentecostal emphases—a feeling of worth and power and a radical world view—gave adherents extraordinary purpose in facing the future. 'Such ideology encourages individual and group persistence, risk taking, sacrifice for the cause, identifies an unjust opposition, strong enough to challenge but eventually overcome, and bridge-burning acts that set the participant apart from the established order and often from past associations.'[100]

Gerlach observes that Pentecostals thus violate convention and tend to change their converts into religiously radical persons, apparently, according to popular wisdom, because the movement tends to attract individuals open to such conversion because of pre-existing defects. He suggests rather that the movement turns 'normal' persons into 'abnormal' ones and 'ordinary' persons into 'extraordinary' ones. Repeatedly, he reports, he and his associates

---

[99]Ibid., 681.
[100]Ibid., 682.

observed the 'positive fatalism' which produced personal transformation and had implication for change.[101]

> The very characteristics of ecstatic religious behavior—ceremonial dissociation, decentralized structure, unconventional ideology, opposition to established structures—which might appear to be makers of a sect of misfits and dropouts, are indeed the features which combine to make Pentecostalism a growing, expanding, evangelistic religious movement of change. It is a movement which is likely to disturb those who wish religion to maintain established ways and values. Among our Pentecostal case studies are examples of men and women who certainly did open their neighborhoods, places of work, and churches to the winds of change—radical religious change.... We have examined Pentecostalism as an example of a religious movement which, in spite of conventional interpretations of its seemingly bizarre features, is in fact a movement for change, not a collection of sects, an opiate, or an anchor for tradition.[102]

Pentecostalism thus provided for its early twentieth century adherents both an elevated estimation of the individual's worth and a means of mobilizing human resources to achieve their claims to a better life. Long before the movement gained recognition as a force in Latin American popular culture, it possessed the social dynamics of a movement organization potentially capable of generating social change.

---

[101]Ibid., 683.
[102]Ibid., 685—686.

Chapter 2

The Formation of Popular, National, Autonomous Pentecostal Churches in Central America

THE PENTECOSTAL FOREIGN INVESTMENT

In tracing the emergence of Pentecostalism as a social as well as a religious phenomenon, the focus of this work shifts from the movement's origins in the United States to the specific case of Central America, one of three regions, in addition to Brazil and Chile, where the movement has experienced rapid development.[1] It is the intent of this chapter to demonstrate that although the Pentecostal paradigm described previously was exportable, the churches identified with the Assemblies of God in Central America, led by the movement in El Salvador, came into existence largely through indigenous efforts with little external assistance or foreign control. Religiously inclined persons contextualized Pentecostalism, adapting features appropriate to their circumstances, to make their churches not only the region's largest expression of Protestantism, but also one of its most important grass-roots social movements.[2]

---

[1] Sociologists of religion, as well as theologians, have largely ignored the Pentecostal religious movements in Central America. A survey of the literature will demonstrate that the majority of scholars studying the religious phenomena taking place in Latin America, particularly with Pentecostals, has concentrated on the massive groupings found in Brazil and Chile. The research published by the Departamento Ecuménico de Investigaciones (Editorial DEI) and Luis E. Samandú, *Protestantismos y Procesos Sociales en Centroamerica* (San José, Costa Rica: Editorial Universitaria Centroamericana, 1991) are among the few serious investigations of Pentecostalism in Central America.

Central America, nevertheless, offers a superb contemporary context in which to study and analyze Pentecostalism as a religious and social phenomenon. Pentecostalism, the largest representative of evangelical Protestantism, comprises a significant segment of the Central American peoples. Furthermore, the Isthmus provides, precisely because of its relative smallness, a unique opportunity to observe the interplay between socio-economic and political transition with the emerging and exponentially-growing Pentecostal movement among the masses.

[2] Based upon the statistical data of several research organizations there were an estimated 1,500,000 communicant evangelicals in Central America in 1988 (table 5). Non-Pentecostal scholars are in agreement that 75 per cent of these evangelicals are of Pentecostal persuasion (see Appendix I: Statistics. Because *Las Asambleas de Dios* has the largest denominational membership in each of the Central American republics they provide a suitable prototype for analysis and evaluation of historical Pentecostal characteristics. This study considers 'historical Pentecostalism' to be the groups that have an existence for at

For the purposes of this study, Pentecostalism refers not only to characteristic beliefs and practices (e.g., glossolalia and faith healing), but to essentially popular, self-sustaining churches of this *genus* that owe little to foreign influences beyond their inducement of religious insurgency. In this contextual respect, Pentecostals were essentially different from other Protestants, both in the traditions introduced by immigrant communities and in those established by transcultural missionaries as overseas extensions of their own denominations. Pentecostalism, with its emphases on freedom of expression in worship and the affirmation of the individual's worth within the community, provided a versatile mechanism easily adapted to a variety of cultures, social classes and age groups.[3] Moreover, there has been increasing scholarly support for viewing Latin American Pentecostalism as essentially a social movement provoked by the disruptive conditions of life experienced by the common people, thus making social or personal crisis—and its solution—one of its distinguishing features.[4]

Pentecostalism in Central America, as elsewhere, was often marked in its early stages by strong, determined personalities whose influence was more catalytic than institutional, providing models for Latin Americans who applied Pentecostal beliefs and practices

---

(footnote 2 continued)
least several decades and whose total membership accounts for the greatest proportion of Pentecostals in Latin America. For aggregate totals of the Assemblies of God, see table 1. Classical Pentecostalism designates those Pentecostal churches and denominations which had their origin in the United States at the beginning of this century in the events surrounding Charles Parham's Bethel Bible College in Topeka, Kansas and William Seymour's Azusa Street Mission in Los Angeles, California. At first the churches with these origins were known simply as 'Pentecostal'. They were designated 'classical' during the 1970s to distinguish them from the 'charismatic' Pentecostals in the Roman Catholic Church and the 'neo-Pentecostals' in the mainline Protestant churches. According to Vinson Synan, 'By 1980 the classical Pentecostals had grown to be the largest and fastest-growing family of Protestant Christians in the world.... In 1987 David Barrett estimated the world constituency of the classical Pentecostal churches at 146,906,306.' H. Vinson Synan, 'Classical Pentecostalism,' *DPCM*, 219—222.
[3]Concerning the impact of the church community upon individual personal confirmation see the discussion in chapter 3.
[4]Including David Martin, *Tongues of Fire: The Explosion of Protestantism in Latin America*, 1990; Barbara Boudewinjse, Andre Droogers, and Frans Kamsteeg, eds., *Algo más que opio: Una lectura antropológica del pentecostalismo latinoamericano y caribeño* (San José, Costa Rica: Editorial DEI, 1991); David Stoll, 'A Protestant Reformation in Latin America?' *Christian Century*, 17 January 1990, 44–48; Jean-Pierre Bastian, 'The Metamorphosis of Latin American Protestant Groups: A Sociohistorical Perspective,' *Latin American Research Review* 2 (1993): 33–61.

to their own situations without becoming dependent or subordinate. Only Latin Americans, because of their familiarity with popular Latin American cultures, were capable of implementing radical programmes on any significant scale among common people. Ultimately, what North American missionaries conveyed to Latin Americans was not their institutions, which were not in any event transferred intact, but rather encouragement to Latin Americans to become assertive in taking control of their own personal and community affairs.[5]

It is important to bear in mind that during the entire period of Pentecostal institutional development in Central America, from about World War I to at least the 1950s, the Pentecostal foreign missionary presence was minimal. In the 1930s, when the movement was established in Latin America, the North American Pentecostals who were still relatively small, isolated and working-class groups, were hardly able to promote overseas work with strong financial and personnel resources. The pioneer Assemblies of God missionary in El Salvador was forced to withdraw from the mission field intermittently during his initial efforts at the height of the Depression, while two of his missionary colleagues in Nicaragua died during their first term of service, one in the 1920s and the other in the 1930s.[6] Prior to World War II, there were never more than two North American Assemblies of God missionary families, most of whom had a short tenure, in any Central American country at a given time. The Assemblies of God, the region's largest Pentecostal affiliation with nearly 4,000 self-supporting congregations and a combined membership of as many as a million adults in 1992, even now supports only ten North American missionary families in the seven republics of the isthmus (including Belize and Panama)—an average of fewer than two per republic in general missionary work, apart from superannuated and administrative personnel.[7]

---

[5]The conscious and deliberate efforts of North American missionaries to utilize indigenous church methodology is modelled clearly in the life and work of Ralph Williams and described in this chapter.

[6]Bartolomé Matamoros Ruiz, *Historia de las Asambleas de Dios en Nicaragua* (Managua, Nicaragua: Editorial Vida, 1984).

[7]'Ministers and Missionaries of the General Council of the Assemblies of God,' rev. to September 25, 1992 (Springfield, MO: Gospel Publishing House). In 1992 there were 38 appointed Assemblies of God missionary units in the seven countries of the isthmus, including Belize and Panama. Of these, 12 were specialized administrative or support personnel, 12 were language-school students or relatively inexperienced persons in their

A further circumstantial indication of the sparse influence of the North American mission over these national churches is given by David Stoll. He pointed out that with a combined adult membership of about 10 million (roughly 1:40 of the entire regional population) and a total annual expenditure of $20 million for all of Latin America (the vast majority of it for missionary salaries—many of them paid for staff work in the United States—and capital projects like schools), the Assemblies of God was hardly able to account for its growth with an investment of $2.00 per year per member. 'A mere $20 million a year cannot explain these kind of results. If evangelical [Pentecostal] churches were really built on handouts, they would be spiritless patronage structures, not vital, expanding grass-roots institutions,' Stoll observes.[8]

Despite this lack of foreign involvement by 1992 each of the national churches had a well-organized, entirely self-supporting and nationally directed administrative system consisting of legally recognized constitutions, elected executive officers, salaried staff members to oversee expansion and the operation of specialized youth, women's, children's, missions and educational programmes, a network of elective regional representatives which had authority to make policy decisions between annual plenary meetings of the pastors and congregational delegates, annual national budgets exceeding in several cases $100,000 and combined assets of at least $150 million in real estate and improvements.[9] The number of accredited national pastors had grown to more than 4,500 in the seven countries to serve almost as many churches, plus more than eight thousand preaching points or satellite churches. These national organizations were themselves supporting dozens of overseas personnel in a variety of missionary

---

(*footnote 7 continued*)

initial term of service, and 4 were superannuated or were serving what was expected to be their final term of service, leaving only 10 families for the general work of the seven countries.

[8] David Stoll, *Is There a Protestant Reformation in Latin America?*, 46. In 1992 the Assemblies of God estimated the adult membership in Latin America to be over 22 million. Information obtained from a compilation of various reports issued by the national Assemblies of God Conferences. Chapter three provides an analysis of Pentecostal community and church life.

[9] Information obtained from the archives of the national Assemblies of God Conferences in Central America. My estimate is 4,000 churches and properties estimated conservatively to have a value of $100 million. Additional institutional properties such as Bible institute facilities and *colegios* (over 200) are estimated at another $50 million.

projects both within and beyond Latin America.[10] Clearly, these groups had acquired a life of their own that had developed out of the experience and needs of the constituent members.

SOCIAL CIRCUMSTANCES IN CENTRAL AMERICA

Pentecostals in Central America during the movement's formative years were, with few exceptions, drawn from the rural sectors who were suffering from dislocation. The demographic profiles of these republics establish circumstantially the plight of large proportions of the population and imply, moreover, that the substantial religious changes that occurred were related to social concerns. Specifically, groups of people who had enjoyed a measure of security and personal contentment in previous years found themselves victims of sweeping economic changes that not only adversely affected their livelihoods but also offended their sense of self-worth and morality. The course of the movement's development, in fact, roughly corresponds to the successive social crises within the region. Besides natural disasters and civil conflicts, these were the secular deterioration of the *campesinos* and the beginnings of large scale migrations to the cities.

A review of several conventional criteria of social development indicates that the percentage of the population in 1980 considered to be in either 'extreme poverty' or 'without basic necessities' in Guatemala was 71.1: in El Salvador, 68.1: and in Honduras, 68.1.[11] In contrast, the proportion of the population considered to be in the middle and upper classes in Guatemala, El Salvador and Honduras in 1950 was, respectively, 7.7, 10.5 and 5.1.[12] Likewise, in 1960, life expectancy in four of the republics where Pentecostalism took early root, Guatemala, El Salvador, Honduras and Nicaragua, was respectively, 45.6, 50.5, 46.5 and 47.0 in 1960.[13]

---

[10]Country reports of the *Consejo ejecutivo latinoamericano de las Asambleas de Dios* (CELAD), (Panama City, Panama: November 25–29 1992). CELAD is a group that convenes every three years for the purpose of coordinating efforts and identifying achievements and concerns. This body consists of the elected leaders of each of fourteen autonomous Assemblies organizations. CELAD has no authority over any of its member national churches.

[11]Instituto Interamericano de Cooperación para la Agricultura (IICA), *Centroamérica en cifras* (San José, Costa Rica: Facultad Latinoamericana de Ciencias Sociales (FLASCO, 1991), 121.

[12]*Cifras*, 152.

[13]Population Division of the United Nations, Human Development Report 1992 (New York, NY: Oxford University Press, 1992), Table 3. [Division de población de las Naciones Unidas, Desarrollo Humano 1992].

Available labour statistics document more precisely the misery and hopelessness of the majority of these peoples ground down by poverty and existing under the shadow of short life-expectancy. In countries where agricultural labour is typically tenuous and poorly remunerated the proportion of the total population in the agricultural sector in 1950 was 69 per cent in Guatemala, 68 per cent in El Salvador, 81 per cent in Honduras and 69 per cent in Nicaragua.[14] Bringing the same issue into clearer focus are the statistics regarding family members who are unremunerated for their labour (as a percentage of the economically active population), which in 1950 was 18.4 per cent in Guatemala, 12.9 in El Salvador, 38.0 in Honduras (the comparable figure in Costa Rica was only 9.5).[15] The percentage of children gainfully employed (boys and girls aged 10 to 14 years who are considered to be economically active) in these republics, as recently as 1970, ranged from 15.6 per cent in Guatemala to 18.3 and 18.6, respectively, in El Salvador and Honduras.[16] The rapid recent growth in the Latin American republics of the 'informal' or 'parallel' economy, with its notorious fortuitous risks and insecurities for both operators of small, highly entrepreneurial production and also for service workers outside the protection of labour codes suggests a further index of vulnerability to which the recent immigrants to the cities are subjected. Regarding health and adult literacy, the per capita calorie intake reported for Guatemala, El Salvador and Honduras all fell below the minimal daily requirements in 1970, while the number of doctors per 100,000 inhabitants in 1970, was only 27 in Guatemala, 24 in El Salvador, 26 in Honduras, although rising to 62 in Costa Rica.[17] Rural illiteracy in 1970 for Guatemala was 65.9 per cent (51.8 per cent for the entire population), for El Salvador, 55.3 per cent (40.3 per cent total), for Honduras, 54.4 (47.5 per cent total), for Nicaragua, 68.7 per cent (46.9 per cent total), and, by way of comparison, for Costa Rica, 14.7 (10.2 per cent total).[18]

In respect to education, in Guatemala in 1965 only 49 per cent of

---

[14] *Cifras*, 143.
[15] Ibid., 152.
[16] Ibid., 142.
[17] Ibid., 161. The percentage of rural population with access to health services in Guatemala, El Salvador, Honduras and Nicaragua, in 1987–90 was, respectively, 25, 40, 65 and 60. Human Development Report 1992, Table 10.
[18] Ibid., 165.

students of primary school age were in attendance, while in El Salvador in 1962, somewhat typical of the rate of academic failure in these republics, only 58 per cent of the students were promoted to the following grade.[19] Even though a large proportion of students traditionally drop out of school, at that time 20 per cent were repeating classes. Moreover, in El Salvador in 1963, of 2,621 public primary schools, only 803 (30.6 per cent) offered the full six years of primary instruction. The corresponding figure for rural schools was 91 out of 1,678 (5.4 per cent).[20] Because Pentecostal membership was drawn overwhelmingly from the poorer sectors of the society their adherents were extremely vulnerable to the negative economic and social consequences indicated in these various statistics.

DETERIORATING CONDITIONS OF CENTRAL AMERICAN PEASANTRY

Historians have generally attributed this tragic waste of human resources in Central America to the liberal economic policies adopted by the ruling classes in each of the republics in the latter decades of the nineteenth century, when neither tradition nor a paternalistic state was permitted to interfere with the operation of a free market. By 1929, as the export economy in El Salvador and Costa Rica displaced traditional crops and systems of production to attain a value in both countries of $18 million, $12 million in Costa Rica and $17 million in El Salvador came from coffee. Meantime, almost 80 per cent of Guatemala's $25 million export trade came from coffee, and 80 per cent of Honduras' $25 million in exports came from bananas. In Guatemala at the time, almost all of the railroad mileage, the utilities company, the leading bank and 7 per cent of the total land area of the country were controlled by foreign fruit companies.[21] In assessing the impact of the development of these corporate activities on Honduras, Walter LaFeber concludes that 'If Honduras was dependent on the fruit companies before 1912, it was virtually indistinguishable from them after 1912.'[22]

---

[19]George R. Waggoner and Barbara Asbton Waggoner, *Education in Central America* (Lawrence, KS: The University Press of Kansas, 1971), 59.
[20]Ibid. See table 3, p. 245 for statistics on education in 1992.
[21]Walter LaFeber, *Inevitable Revolutions, The United States in Central America* (New York, NY: W. W. Norton and Company, 1983), 61.
[22]Ibid., 45.

'Clearly, if the prices of coffee and bananas suddenly dropped on international markets, all Central America would plunge into disaster.'[23]

In El Salvador, as elsewhere in Central America where Pentecostalism would soon take root, contemporaries clearly saw the implications for land ownership, land use and labour practices of these revolutionary changes in production, despite the wealth that flowed into the country to the privileged few. The net increase in exports, with some better distribution of wealth, investment in the social infrastructure and access to representative government could potentially have benefited the popular groups, but the hierarchical, authoritarian traditions of the Central American elite classes with the partial exception of Costa Rica—and the rationalization and impersonalization of production with absentee ownership and professional management—generally deprived the labouring sector of even the modest security and dignity that they had traditionally enjoyed. The Salvadoran newspaper *Patria*, in articles published throughout the 1920s, protested that many small agriculturists had been replaced with large estates producing only for the export economy.

> The conquest of the territory by the coffee industry is alarming. It has already occupied all the high land and is now descending to the valleys, displacing corn, rice and beans. Like the conquistadors, it is spreading hunger and misery, reducing the old proprietors to the worst kind of conditions. While one can demonstrate with figures that the country is becoming richer, [these changes] really are bringing death! Can the income of the peasant who has lost his land now buy corn, rice, beans, clothes, medicine? What good does it do to increase sales of coffee when it leaves so many people in misery?[24]

The phenomenon of reduced buying power in a rich country, where we find millionaires, wrote another contemporary, 'is explained by the pitiable wages of the workers, who, in the majority, are employed in agriculture'.[25] A U.S. Army officer's assessment in 1931 was one of impending disaster.

---

[23]Ibid., 61.
[24]'La crisis del maíz,' *Patria*, January 18, 1929.
[25]'Al margen de la implantación en El Salvador del impuesto sobre el capital y la renta y del proyecto de contribución territorial,' *Revista Económica*, 12 (November 1924): 19.

There appears to be nothing between these high-priced cars and the oxcart with its barefoot attendant. There is practically no middle class. Thirty or forty families own nearly everything in the country. They live in almost regal style. The rest of the population has practically nothing.[26]

The demoralization of the rural workers was complete, in the opinion of a national writer. 'In the countryside where most of our people live, conditions are unacceptable. There people are plagued by alcoholism, gambling and other vices. They are unable to get medicines or decent housing. They are devoured by terrible sicknesses like tuberculosis and malaria.'[27] Sorghum (*maicillo*), considered animal fodder in the neighbouring countries, was consumed in large quantities by human beings, while the consumption of pork and beef, much higher in Guatemala and Honduras, was in El Salvador significantly less.[28] Historian Walter LaFeber, assesses the general effect of these structural changes, commenting that 'the rapid expansion of coffee had torn apart Indian villages and their communal lands which provided the food supply. Peasants and Indians became little more than a hungry, wandering labour force to be used by the oligarchy.'[29]

The moral loss suffered by the popular groups was made more poignant, in the opinion of various observers, by their former conditions of life. As early as 1852 a Prussian consular report described El Salvador in idyllic terms. 'Land tenancy is widely distributed, and there are no great estates. In all of Central America, El Salvador's agriculture is the most intensive and its people are the most industrious.'[30] In 1918, Dana G. Munro ventured that 'the prosperity of the republic, with its fertile soil and hardworking population, seems certain,' and Munro continued his laudatory comments by comparing the workers of El Salvador with those of

---

[26]Quoted in LaFeber, *Inevitable Revolutions*, 71.

[27]Eduardo Alvarez, 'Vialidad, moralidad,' *Actualidades* VII (February 1926): 457.

[28]'Impresiones de un sabio alemán sobre El Salvador; notas de viaje del doctor Sapper,' *Pareceres* I (December 1, 1926): 3; Everett A. Wilson, 'La Crisis de integración nacional en El Salvador,' in *El Salvador de 1840–1935; Estudiado y Analizado por los Extranjeros*, eds. Rafael Menjivar y Rafael Guidos Vejar, (San Salvador: Universidad Centroamericana José Simeon Canas, 1978), 163.

[29]LaFeber, *Inevitable Revolutions*, 70.

[30]Quoted in David Alejandro Luna, *Manual de historia económica de El Salvador* (El Salvador: Editorial Universitaria, 1971), 204.

Guatemala and Nicaragua, who, though they offered 'a striking contrast to their opulent and Europeanized superiors, nevertheless, are in a much better position than [workers] in the neighbouring republics, except Costa Rica'.[31] 'The Salvadorans,' comments LaFeber, 'the most industrious people in Central America, were awarded for their efforts by being among the poorest fed and most exploited in the hemisphere.'[32]

Beyond the circumstantial evidence of decline implied by economic monopolies and dismal social statistics, specific indicators marked the deterioration of the popular groups. The changing status of traditional trades, artisans and small entrepreneurs, was captured in a communiqué made by W. H. Franklin, the United States consul in El Salvador in 1920, who reported that every truck and trailer imported to replace traditional transportation in the coffee industry displaced 80 oxcarts and their drivers.[33] While few trucks were imported before 1918, the numbers increased to several hundred a year during the 1920s, disrupting the employment of as many as 60,000 workers in a total labour force of 600,000. The shoemaking trade, like other handicrafts that had traditionally been important in the small towns and villages, was similarly in decline because of competition from imported shoes—and a large, mechanized factory. 'Whole families migrate,' wrote a contemporary, 'they sell their oxcarts and even the homes their families had acquired, often at great sacrifice.'[34] By the end of the 1920s, an estimated 10 per cent of the entire labour force had emigrated to the north coast of Honduras.[35]

As Alistair White points out in his analysis of the deeply rooted social problems of El Salvador, liberal theories of labour provided

---

[31]Dana G. Munro, _The Five Republics of Central America_ (New York, NY: Oxford University Press, 1918) 117, 118. Similar assessments were made by W. H. Koebel, _Central America: Guatemala, Nicaragua, Costa Rica, Honduras, Panama and Salvador_ (London: T. F. Unwin Ltd., 1917), 275, and by Wallace Thompson, _Rainbow Republics of Central America_ (New York, NY: E. P. Dutton and Company, 1926), 108. See also George Palmer Putman, _The Southland of North America_ (New York: G. P. Putman's Son, 1913), 191, and Agnes Rothery, _Central America and the Spanish Main_ (Boston: Houghton Mifflin Company, 1929), 79.

[32]LaFeber, _Inevitable Revolutions_, 70.

[33]Bureau of Foreign and Domestic Commerce. Daily Consular Reports, 23 (October–December, 1920), 1259.

[34]J. Alberto Herrera, 'La Emigración salvadoreña,' _Isidro Menéndez_ 2 (May–June 1925): 11–14.

[35]Wilson, 'La crisis de integración,' 198.

no recourse for displaced artisans and agricultural producers, given the relative shortage of land in the densely populated country.[36] Some wage earners on the coffee farms (*fincas*) could recall the preceding era when their families had claimed a share in communal lands, and saw the growth of sprawling estates of the small privileged class based on the domination of the well capitalized export economy. Visitor Arthur Ruhl was told by his wealthy Salvadoran host in the mid-1920s that 'Bolshevism' was drifting in. 'The people hold meetings on Sundays and get very excited. They say, "We dig the holes for the trees! We prune the trees! We pick the coffee! Who owns the coffee, then? We do!" '[37] While the *campesinos* received few material benefits beyond some health services and wage-paying, labour-intensive public works projects, vagrancy laws and land policies for a half century prior to 1930 suggested the growing tensions as the wealthy (known in Salvadoran social history as the 'Fourteen Families') bought up small parcels with their previously accumulated assets or with the help of banking connections. In 1912 the Salvadoran government, apparently concerned with tensions caused by increasing disparity in wealth and the social deterioration in the countryside, introduced a rural constabulary patterned after the Spanish Guardia Civil. In Honduras and Guatemala in 1919 and 1920, respectively, strikes that were of sufficient intensity to overthrow the two governments graphically demonstrated the common people's reaction to changing conditions and their ability to mobilize in response to their increasingly precarious position.[38]

PRECEDENTS OF CENTRAL AMERICAN GRASS-ROOTS ORGANIZATION

The Salvadoran popular groups, however, had never long remained passive. Previously, according to Alistair White, in national politics 'the masses had few spokesmen; their dissatisfaction with their poverty, when it attained political expression, took the form of sporadic revolts.' The growth of a strong labour movement throughout the 1920s, however, demonstrated the workers' capacity for initiating

---

[36]Alistair White, *El Salvador* (New York, NY: Praeger Publications, 1973).
[37]Arthur Ruhl, *The Central Americans: adventures and impressions between Mexico and Panama* (New York, NY: C. Scribner's Sons, 1929), 202.
[38]LaFeber, *Inevitable Revolutions*, 70.

popular action.[39] With the highest population density (600 persons per square mile in the 1980s, equal to that of India) of any country in the hemisphere except Haiti, El Salvador became a leader in the Latin American labour movement after the Central American Congress of Workers convened in San Salvador in 1911.[40] Participants mostly represented self-help societies whose intention was to benefit their members by promoting mutual aid, savings, education, charities and sobriety. In 1918 a workers' convention met in the town of Armenia where 200 delegates of the leading organizations formed a national labour federation.[41] In addition, the *cofradias*, local lay religious organizations responsible for maintaining parish activities, still brought together the surviving remnants of the traditional Indian communities. Not until the late 1920s did a clear rupture appear between labour groups that promoted structural changes and those that supported the moralistic, gradualist approaches of the highly regarded newspaper publisher, Alberto Masferrer.[42]

However, after the economic crash in 1929, which was accompanied by a decline in wages of more than 50 per cent, the revolutionaries were able to organize an estimated 80,000 agricultural labourers, mainly coffee workers in western El Salvador, into militant unions. A series of strikes and, in May 1930, a mass march ensued in San Salvador.[43] As the protests continued into 1931, repression began that climaxed with an abortive peasant uprising on the night of January 22nd-23rd, 1932. Within three days an estimated 30,000 Indians and peasants had been murdered, and in a paroxysm of fear and revenge the ruling groups cut off the rural working classes from the recourse previously opened to them, taking labour and political representation from the sectors whose land ownership and supportive communities had already been lost.

'The revolt,' according to Alistair White, 'included many *ladinos* [Europeanized mestizos], as well as Indians.'

It was concentrated in the western coffee-growing areas, where coffee

---

[39]White, *El Salvador*, 95.
[40]Wilson, 'La Crisis de integración,' 173.
[41]Ibid., 174.
[42]Ibid., 175. See Alberto Masferrer, *Qué Debemos Hacer?: cartas a un obrero* 5 ed. (San Salvador: Dirección General de Cultura, Dirección de Publicaciones, 1968) and *El Rosal Deshojado* 2 ed. (El Salvador: Ministerio de Educación, Dirección General de Publicaciones, 1965).
[43]White, *El Salvador*, 99.

had already spread to cover most of the ground in the areas of suitable altitude, and the rural population was already almost completely dependent on seasonal wage labour on the coffee plantations; there was no space left for them to plant subsistence crops. This process had not gone so far in the eastern coffee-producing zone where there was no revolt.[44]

Adopting draconian, paternalistic policies, the recently established regime of Maximiliano Hernández Martínez began what was to become the longest succession of military governments in Latin American history. It remained Martínez's policy until his overthrow in 1944 to prevent any political activity by advocates of structural reform. Under Martínez, all popular organizations other than his official party were banned.[45]

Against this backdrop, Pentecostalism, in contrast with such still small traditional Protestant groups as the Baptists, the Methodists, the Adventists and the Central American Mission, acquired a popular, indigenous character. The traditional Protestant groups were found mainly in the capital and in the towns among those of the middle class. These elements, because of their access to opportunity and resources, had hope for a secure future. The first Pentecostals, however, were decidedly rural and traditional, persons more generally affected by spreading latifundia, social disabilities and repressive governments.

The general social statistics of the Central American countries, which as in the case of El Salvador, indicate continuing human neglect and cultural deprivation of large proportions of the population, suggest that Pentecostalism took root among the most deprived sectors. In Guatemala, the earliest Pentecostal converts, received into the Church of God (Cleveland, TN), were ethnic Indians, who continue to constitute one-half of the national population and are the groups with the least access to the benefits of national life. In Honduras and Nicaragua, where the movement had less impact initially, growth occurred notably among the small landholders, tenant farmers, small merchants and artisans whose conditions, with the rise of the export sector, were in relative decline. The inherent contrast between the landed elements and the labourers was illustrated by an incident reported by Samuel Purdie, the first Protestant missionary in El Salvador,

---

[44]Ibid., 101.
[45]Ibid.

who complained in 1896, soon after his arrival, that people attended his services simply to register their protest at established religion, but even the few persons who seemed genuinely interested were threatened by their employers with reprisals if they attended the meetings.[46]

Sectarian Protestantism, however, did not become a recognized alternative in El Salvador even as evangelical churches appeared elsewhere in Central America. By the early 1960s the republic had received fewer Protestant foreign missions and missionaries than had any other Latin American republic.[47] Moreover, the groups that had come into existence with foreign support did not flourish. Protestants in El Salvador in 1939 constituted only one per cent of the national population.[48] Nevertheless, against a backdrop of deteriorating social conditions, the Pentecostal groups in El Salvador, and increasingly in the adjacent republics, grew rapidly, having established themselves during the previous decades through grass-roots initiative.

Against the backdrop of social deterioration and the failure of the non-Pentecostal evangelicals to make as rapid gains as did the popular Pentecostals, Pentecostalism emerged as a movement with its own character, rooted in the social needs of sectors that swelled its ranks.

In spite of Pentecostals' phenomenal growth, and their distinctive and unique characteristics, the movement in Central America is generally evaluated and analyzed as an expression of evangelicalism and/or protestantism. For an adequate understanding of the movement, however, it is important to distinguish Pentecostalism from the other forms of non-Roman Catholic Christianity.

LATIN AMERICA AND HISTORICAL PROTESTANTS

Protestantism, the broadest term generally applied to Pentecostals, derives from its sixteenth-century Reformation origins and finds its expression in the mainline or historic European and North American denominations. These groups established themselves in Latin America first by migration in the nineteenth century and only later by denominational and 'faith missions' intended to establish their

---

[46]James Purdie Knowles, *Samuel A. Purdie: his life and letters* (Plainfield, IN: Publishing Association of Friends, 1908), 230.

[47]Damboriena, *Protestantismo*, 2:96.

[48]Joseph I. Parker, ed., *Interpretative Statistical Survey of the World Mission of the Christian Church* (New York, NY: International Missionary Council, 1938).

evangelicalism overseas. Many of the first type, Lutherans and Anglicans in Brazil, Argentina and Chile, Mennonites in Paraguay and Uruguay, Plymouth Brethren in Argentina, for example, had little interest in proselytism, and rather focused on the religious maintenance of their own communities, sometimes referred to as 'transplanted churches,' which were the institutions reconstituted at the core of foreign communities with educational and social welfare as well as spiritual functions.[49]

Other Protestant groups, also promoted by means of immigration, more generally established their influence by means of foreign missions programmes. In this way missionary Protestantism was directed at least in part to extending its influence among Roman Catholics, although even these groups tended to justify their intrusion on the basis of the alleged needs of aboriginal or neglected groups. The formation of the Committee on Cooperation in Latin America in 1916 represented the legitimization of such missions, which by the 1920s were well established in most of the republics. In Central America the Protestant presence had begun in Belize at least by 1835, when British Baptists built a place of worship and in Nicaragua in 1849, when Moravian missionaries arrived on the Miskito Coast.[50] By 1884 there was a Methodist missionary in Panama, and a Baptist church in Puerto Limón, Costa Rica by 1894. Methodists and Anglicans had also organized churches in Costa Rica by 1894 and 1896, respectively. Wilton Nelson does not find the arrival of Protestant missionaries intent on proselytism until 1882 in Guatemala and in 1891 in Costa Rica, maintaining that previous activity should be considered 'foreign protestantism'.[51]

---

[49]Waldo Luis Villapando, ed., *Las Iglesia del Transplante: Protestantismo de Immigración en la Argentina* (Buenos Aires: Centro de Estudios Cristianos, 1970) offers a complete bibliography for that country.

[50]Wilton N. Nelson, *Protestantism in Central America*, 19.

[51]Ibid., 21. Several of the earlier books on Protestantism reflected a subjective and sectarian bias, see, for example, José María Ganunza, *Las sectas nos invaden* (Caracas, Venezuela: Ediciones Paulinas, 1978); or Mildred Spain, *And in Samaria: A Story of Fifty Years Missionary Witness in Central America, 1890–1940* (Dallas, TX: Central American Mission, 1940). Two classic works from the 1960s that do not view Pentecostals as forms of 'foreign protestantism' are Christian Lalive d'Epinay, *Haven of the Masses: A Study of the Pentecostal Movement in Chile*, 1969 and Emilio Willems, *Followers of the New Faith*, (1967). Both books concentrate on the Pentecostals from a sociological perspective. An older standard review of Protestant missions in Latin America is William R. Read, Victor M. Monterroso, and Harmon A. Johnson, *Latin American Church Growth* (Grand Rapids, MI: Wm. B. Eerdmans Publishing Co., 1969).

When most writers refer to Protestantism they are generally referring to a brand of Protestantism that entered the Latin American context within the framework of neocolonialism during the period of 'modernization' that occurred after the mid-nineteenth century and continued in some republics until at least World War I.[52] Protestant missionaries during this era basically targeted immigrants and peasants who had been uprooted from their rural regions and thrust into the urban cities. Thus, the emerging Christian communities were neither among the poor of the traditional society nor from the elites of higher society. According to José Míguez Bonino, 'The new Protestant communities had no sense of belonging, no strong ties with traditional Latin American societies [and] not infrequently the country of the missionary was idealized as sort of an earthly paradise: the land of Protestantism, honesty, freedom, and progress.'[53] Further, states Míguez Bonino, the religious ideologies proclaimed by these Protestant missionaries were 'conscious or unconscious expressions and agents of a world view in which the Protestant faith was integrated with a political philosophy (democracy in its American version), an economic system (free enterprise capitalism), a geopolitical/historical project (the United States as champion and centre of a "new world" of progress and freedom), and an ideology (the liberal creed of progress, education, and science).' As a result, contends Míguez Bonino, 'both from the perspective of the general historico-political framework in Latin America and in the world, on the basis of the ethos of the American missionary enterprise and in terms of the

---

[52]Much of contemporary scholarship on Protestantism is committed to the premise that missionary endeavour was directly tied to the cultural, historical, political and theological positions of the Western European nations in general and to the United States in particular for the simple reason that most of the missionaries that worked in Latin America came from these countries. See Ganunza, *Las sectas nos invaden*; Antonio Quartanciono, *Sectas en América Latina* (Guatemala City, Guatemala: Consejo Episcopal Latinoamericano, 1981); and Spain, *And in Samaria*. Though candidly admitting that early Protestant missionaries were closely aligned to the neoliberal governments in Central America, Wilton Nelson, a missionary in Costa Rica, contends that Protestant expansion was not an expression of 'cultural imperialism' but rather a sincere desire on the part of the missionary to proselytize. See Nelson's *Protestantism in Central America*.

[53]José Míguez Bonino, 'How Does United States Presence Help, Hinder or Compromise Christian Mission in Latin America,' *Review and Expositor* 74 (Spring 1977): 174–177. For an insightful discussion of Protestantism in Latin America see Míguez Bonino's classic work *Doing Theology in a Revolutionary Situation* (Philadelphia, PA: Fortress Press, 1975).

ideals, mentality, and interests of the new Protestant communities which were created, Latin American Protestantism grew up in intimate relation to the interests and influence of the United States in Latin America.'[54] Even when the Latin churches endeavoured to emerge from this context and commenced some form of indigenization they were thwarted, claims Míguez Bonino, because they had to confront the 'power structure' in which the missionaries controlled plans for growth and directly or indirectly governed institutions. Such structures, he argues, prevent any meaningful relationship between the church and its people.[55]

Therefore, the Protestant Church in Latin America that emerged was dependent both economically and theologically upon the sending church in the United States. This allegiance became so deeply entrenched that Latin American Protestants could not distinguish between their conservative theology and political ideology. Míguez Bonino further argues that such dependence upon the United States and the North Atlantic countries paved the way for the apparent political passivity and, at times, allegiance by Protestants to regressive governments. Such dependency, according to the Argentine theologian, was characteristic of Latin American Protestantism.[56] Similarly, Juan-Pierre Bastian, an ecumenical Protestant theologian, agrees that there is a tie that inextricably binds Latin American Protestantism to the United States. Bastian, however, contends that Latin Americans, especially in rural areas, appropriate certain aspects of North American Protestantism and contextualize them to their own indigenous models and thus produce a home-grown version that is somewhat compatible with their own culture.[57]

It has been difficult for these Protestant groups to avoid the appearances of foreignness, not because they have utilized foreign

---

[54]Míguez Bonino, 'How Does United States Presence,' 176. However, Míguez Bonino makes a clear distinction between the idea of Protestant missions in Latin America as partners in 'a USA imperialistic conspiracy'—which he rejects—and the recognition of the influence of North American origins of many missions in their methods, organization, theological and even social ideas. José Míguez Bonino, *Protestantismo y Liberación* (Buenos Aires, Argentina: Nueva Creación, forthcoming).

[55]José Míguez Bonino, 'Confrontation as a Means of Communication in Theology, Church and Society,' in *The Right to Dissent*, eds. H. Kung and J. Moltmann (New York, NY: Seabury Press, 1982): 86.

[56]José Míguez Bonino, *Protestantismo y liberalismo en América Latina*, 91.

[57]Jean-Pierre Bastian, *Protestantismo Y Sociedad en México* (Mexico City, Mexico: Casa de Publicaciones Unidas, 1983), 91.

personnel or failed to make necessary accommodations to national cultures, but because their governance, their polities, their funding and their styles have relied unduly on the sending agencies. The payment of the pastors with foreign dollars, the training of many personnel in the United States, concern with retaining the theological dogmas and prescriptions of the overseas denomination, and styles and values of North American culture all tend to separate these groups from the popular masses of Latin America. Above them has always been the shadow of foreign faith.

Míguez Bonino distinguishes between this brand of Protestantism and Latin American Pentecostalism. Contrary to his thesis that traditional Latin American Protestantism is a direct legacy of its North American counterpart, Míguez Bonino identifies Latin American Pentecostalism as an authentic expression of the very ethos of the Latin American culture and context.[58] According to Míguez Bonino, the allure of Pentecostalism for modern Latin Americans can no longer be satisfactorily explained within the older traditional theories that espoused that Pentecostalism was 'foreign' or 'a penetration of something that came from outside'.[59] The growth of Pentecostal churches, notes Míguez Bonino, has resulted in an authentic religious expression of the Latin American peoples from within their own cultural context, not as a result of an association with the denominational sending body of the missionaries.[60] Pentecostalism can be interpreted, he states, as a movement that gives expression to a 'Christian and human protest against the condition of life in the world.... The ethos of that process has not only theological and spiritual elements, but a social dynamic which you find also in the movements which underlie liberation theology.'[61] Míguez Bonino's position correctly asserts that Pentecostalism, though having early foreign influences, quickly became indigenous and emerges as an authentic religious and social expression within the Latin American context. Consequently, Pentecos-

---

[58]José Míguez Bonino, interview by author. Tape recording, Buenos Aires, Argentina, 17 January 1993.

[59]Ibid. It is Míguez Bonino's opinion that serious scholarship no longer emphasizes the impact of foreign assistance or the penetration of foreign invasion in reference to Latin American Pentecostalism. Such evaluations are generally found in 'journalistic approaches' or in Catholic apologetics as evidenced in the document prepared for the CELAM conference in Santo Domingo.

[60]Ibid.

[61]José Míguez Bonino, 'The Pentecostal Movement,' *International Review of Mission* 66 (January 1977): 77–78.

talism cannot be adequately understood within the rubric of the historical projects of the traditional Latin American Protestant movement. Neither can Pentecostalism be understood strictly within the framework of evangelicalism.[62]

EVANGELICAL MISSIONS AND CHURCHES IN CENTRAL AMERICA

If Protestantism in Central America should be viewed primarily in terms of the religious institutions of the immigrant communities or of missions that grew essentially by the incorporation of detached, deculturated individuals, the missionary investment in Central America since World War I represents a different current of evangelical Protestantism that envisioned the transplanting of North American churches and institutions overseas. These churches more generally targeted the lower middle class and were generally urban. The Evangelicals established churches on the basis of their theology. Even more important were the resources that they had at their disposal. Following the decline of missionary interest in the mainline denominations during the years of the Modernist-Fundamentalist conflict, Protestant missions were promoted primarily by groups of Fundamentalists within, primarily, the Baptist and Holiness branches of the Protestant denominations, as well as the faith missions (non-denominational groups that often directed their efforts at the specific area or population or identified its goal in its organizational name).[63] Fired with a desire to

---

[62]The Spanish word *evangélico*, a literal translation of 'evangelical,' is used often interchangeably with the term Protestant (as well as Pentecostal). However, church life and theology are quite distinctive in each of the traditions. Protestant would be the term most appropriately used when treating the older mainline churches related to the conciliar ecumenical movement. *Evangélico* refers to that grouping of those Protestants that hold a high view of Scripture and who emphasize a commitment to personal faith, conversion and evangelism. Though the term *evangélico* is shared by most Pentecostal communities, this study distinguishes certain differences between Evangelicalism and Pentecostalism.

[63]The term 'fundamentalist' is used in a way to identify the American 'evangelical' Christian movement that emerged from the Fundamentalist-Modernist struggle of the early part of the twentieth century and which subsequently broadened its agenda to include the engagement of Christian faith with American politics and social life. For a watershed work which facilitated this movement from fundamentalism to evangelicalism, see Carl F. H. Henry, *The Uneasy Conscience of Modern Fundamentalism* (Grand Rapids, MI: Wm. B. Eerdmans Publishing Co., 1947). For an analysis of the Fundamentalist-Modernist controversy and the subsequent development of evangelicalism out of the fundamental wing of the debate, see George C. Bedell, Leo Sanden, Jr., and Charles T. Wellborn, eds., *Religion in America* (New York, NY: Macmillian Publishing Company, 1975); and

evangelize, these groups paid little attention to forming national churches overseas in their efforts to establish their influence, often in forms that were not particularly appropriate to the receiving countries. These groups also invested heavily in support and auxiliary programmes that often left few traces of their efforts.

Although churches were in most cases eventually 'nationalized,' their foreign origins, doctrines and practices gave them a distinctive character. Quite often missionaries planted churches that were considered to be part of the North American denomination. Pastors regularly received subsidies and in a real sense a dependent structure of church government was established. Emilio Núñez and William Taylor articulately demonstrate the resulting problems that emerged in the attempt at the process of 'indigenization' within these evangelical churches.

> Some missions terminated the salary subsidy rather abruptly as a result of the Great Depression, others tapered it off gradually, and yet others today still pay part or all of their national pastors' salaries. The indigenization issue... basically revolved around the questions: Who controlled the churches? Who controlled the foreign missions and the missionaries? Who controlled the purse strings? Who controlled the institutions? Who controlled the agenda, discussion, and decisions?[64]

When, in the 1970s and 1980s, conservative elements in the United States seemed to promote evangelical churches in Latin America as centres of North American influence, the assumed foreignness of these groups became pronounced. As a result, liberationists and Marxists loudly protested against North American evangelical influence in Latin America, labelling all evangelicals by the same criteria.[65]

Excessive foreign control in Latin America's evangelical churches is implicit when Núñez and Taylor call for Latin American involvement in 'the forms and structures of evangelical churches and

---

(footnote 63 continued)
Augustus Cerillo, Jr., and Murray W. Dempster, eds., *Salt and Light: Evangelical Political Thought in Modern America* (Grand Rapids, MI: Baker Book House, 1989).
[64]Emilio A. Núñez C. and William D. Taylor, *Crisis in Latin America: An Evangelical Perspective* (Chicago, IL: Moody Press, 1989), 156.
[65]'The Salvation Brokers: Conservative Evangelicals in Central America,' *NACLA Report* 18 (January/February 1984): 3. This entire issue is dedicated to reporting the impact of the fierce attack by conservative evangelical groups upon the people and culture of Central America.

institutions which have come from abroad. Latins do not want to toss the institutional baby out with the bath water. But they do respectfully request permission to make decisions as Latin evangelicals.'[66] Such statements clearly indicate that even though there may be a different theological commitment between non-Pentecostal evangelicals and traditional Protestants their missiological strategy was surprisingly similar. Both approaches tend to assume, paternalistically, that ultimately decisions will be made by foreigners.

Although Pentecostals are certainly evangelical in belief, they have been traditionally marginalized by other evangelical groups as being unreliable, theologically suspect and unsophisticated. The evangelical groupings often viewed their Pentecostal 'cousins' with disdain, often because of the latter's lack of educational training and financial support, their excessive emotionalism. and undue emphasis on the ecstatic personal experience of speaking in tongues and receiving gifts of healing and prophecy. The Pentecostal movement is still evaluated and analyzed within this narrower 'evangelical context' by both critics and sympathizers. Pentecostalism, however, needs to be understood on its own terms.

PENTECOSTAL BEGINNINGS IN CENTRAL AMERICA

While Latin American Pentecostalism in many ways corresponds to these Protestant and evangelical groupings, it is in other respects quite different, especially in beliefs and practices as well as in social origins and cultural appropriateness to the popular groups. Unlike other Protestant groups, Latin American Pentecostals have emerged almost without foreign assistance. Initially, personnel consisted of relatively few overseas missionaries, whose work was undertaken with few resources, little preparation for the enterprise and without a coherent strategy to develop a church. The extraordinary growth of the movement, without adequate institutional explanation, can be found in the experience of the Latin Americans themselves.

Clearly the differences between Protestants, evangelicals and Pentecostals are not easily distinguished as long as one looks only at the fact that all are forms of Protestantism. Yet, the identification of the Pentecostal groups with other forms of evangelicalism obscures certain important differences. While it was natural that

---

[66]Núñez and Taylor, *Crisis in Latin America*, 175.

interpreters of Latin American Pentecostalism assumed that a direct correlation would exist between growth and foreign investment, observers failed to recognize that these groups functioned in quite different ways. At its extreme, Pentecostalism may be viewed as a creation of Latin American popular culture, an authentic expression of its ethos. As has already been pointed out, according to Míguez Bonino, theories applicable to missionary Protestantism do not adequately explain Pentecostalism.[67] Despite early foreign influences, Pentecostalism became indigenous and emerged as an authentic religious and social expression within the Latin American context.

One authority estimates that Pentecostals represent 75 per cent of the total Protestant aggregate in Latin America.[68] According to Wagner, one member of this group, the Assemblies of God, has become the largest or second largest in denominational membership in Argentina, Bolivia, Brazil, Costa Rica, Cuba, Dominican Republic, El Salvador, Guatemala, Honduras, Nicaragua, Panama, Peru, Puerto Rico, Uruguay, Venezuela or 13 (excluding Puerto Rico and Portuguese-speaking Brazil) of the 18 Spanish-speaking republics of Latin America.[69]

For the Assemblies of God, the number of foreign personnel, as well as the ratios between national members and missionaries, has put the issue of dependence into clear perspective (table 1). In 1951 the five republics of Central America registered 17 missionaries[70] and 7284 members and adherents.[71] In 1992 the proportions were 29 missionaries and 729,620 members and adherents (table 2) for a ratio of 1 missionary per 25,159 members and adherents (table 3).[72] A comparison between the ratio of Assemblies of God missionaries to communicant membership and evangelical missionaries to com-

---

[67]Míguez Bonino, 'The Pentecostal Movement,' 78.

[68]Núñez and Taylor, *Crisis in Latin America*, 159.

[69]Wagner, 'Church Growth,' *DPCM*, 185.

[70]Missionaries couples or singles are both referred to as 'one unit' throughout this study.

[71]Data on members and adherents is taken from the archives of the national Assemblies of God in the five Central American Republics of Guatemala, El Salvador, Honduras, Nicaragua, and Costa Rica. Note that the figures for members and adherents do not include estimates of the Assemblies of God 'community' as is often done in computing the size of religious communities. Because the Assemblies of God is the largest classical Pentecostal movement in Latin America, it provides a suitable prototype for the analysis and evaluations of its social issues.

[72]The statistics for the number of members and adherents does not include children of the adherents nor does it include an estimate of the size of the 'Pentecostal community.' See Appendix I: Statistics.

municant membership further underscores the differences. While the Assemblies of God in 1988 had only one missionary for every 18,586 members, the evangelical churches had one missionary for every 1108 members (table 4).[73] In the meantime, in 1951 the number of fully accredited national pastors was 148, while the number had grown in 1992 to 4330, with an additional 8753 *obreros* (the term used for apprentice pastors), giving an aggregate total of 13,083 (table 2). Thus in 1992 the ratio of missionaries to accredited ministers was 1:451 (table 5).[74] Moreover, these fields had already gained a reputation for developing without external assistance, as was illustrated with the publication in 1953 of Melvin Hodges', *The Indigenous Church*, an analysis of the indigenous methodology (decidedly sensitive to the initiative of the national church), employed by Pentecostals in El Salvador, Honduras and Guatemala.[75]

The reports of the growth of a church with hardly a missionary presence resulted in various non-Pentecostal groups seeking to emulate or gain the advantage of such methods. Publications like The Evangelical Alliance Mission report of 1970; the 1969 *Latin America Church Growth* study and Peter C. Wagner, *Look Out! The Pentecostals Are Coming* all emphasized such autonomy of operation.[76] By 1990, when David Martin published *Tongues of Fire*, it

---

[73]The contrasts in ratios is even more apparent when it is noted that the evangelical ratios include Pentecostals.

[74]Unfortunately, adequate data is not available to make a comparison between the ratio of missionaries to national workers between Pentecostals and non-Pentecostal evangelical groups in Central America. However, from the evidence that is available it is likely that the same dramatic difference in ratios would exist.

[75]The Division of Foreign Missions of the Assemblies of God in the United States subscribed to the missiological doctrines of the 'indigenous church' as presented by Roland Allen, *Missionary Methods: St. Paul or Ours?* (Grand Rapids, MI: Wm. B. Eerdmans Publishing Co., 1962). The work in each Central American country, from its initial stages of formation, was completely autonomous from its United States counterpart, with only a fraternal relationship existing between them. The Division of Foreign Missions was careful to adhere to the philosophy that the emerging Assemblies of God church in a country must have a grass-roots constituency and an authentic contextual structure in order to have any hopes for the work to grow. For a thorough study of Assemblies of God foreign mission's theology and strategy, see Melvin A. Hodges' widely heralded work, *The Indigenous Church* (Springfield, MO: Gospel Publishing House, 1953), as well as his two subsequent missiological releases, *A Theology of the Church and Its Mission* (Springfield, MO: Gospel Publishing House, 1977), and *The Indigenous Church and the Missionary* (Pasadena, CA: William Carey Library, 1978).

[76]Norman Chugg and Kenneth Larson, 'Chugg-Larson Report to TEAM's 1970 Conference on Their Church Planting Study Trip to Central America,' *Evangelical Alliance Mission*, Wheaton, Illinois; Wm. R. Read et al., *Latin America Church Growth* (Grand Rapids, MI: Wm. B. Eerdmans Publishing Co., 1970); C. Peter Wagner, *Look Out! The Pentecostals Are Coming* (Carol Stream, IL: Creation House, 1973).

was clear that whatever the origins of the Latin American Pentecostal churches, their rapid growth—exceeding any correlation to the resources of the sending agencies—further indicated that these groups were essentially autochthonous.[77] National leaders, whatever their relationship doctrinally and denominationally with foreign churches, are clearly the only ones who can take the initiative in the development of the Pentecostal movements.

Not all observers, however, view every Pentecostal movement as intrinsically Latin American. The taxonomy of Manual Gaxiola-Gaxiola, of the Iglesia Apostólica de la Fe en Cristo Jesus, recognizes several groupings, including the autochthonous Pentecostals, denominations founded by foreign churches, and special kinds of churches that resemble the messianic-prophetic independent churches of Africa.[78] The first, in his taxonomy are movements formed with little or no foreign influence, whose practices derive directly from the traditions of the people among whom they have grown.[79] The second are, generally, highly 'indigenized,' but retain relationships that compromise the churches' autonomy and the third are groups like the *Luz del Mundo* movement based in Guadalajara, Mexico.[80]

Other writers, including Carmelo Alvarez, a non-Pentecostal ecumenist, agree that these denominations founded by foreign churches are not to be included among the spontaneous Pentecostal movements of the first category, identifying them with the 'electronic church' and foreign evangelists like Jimmy Swaggart, whose overpowering wealth and popular influence strongly, if often indirectly, impose North American values on their Latin American

---

[77] Autochthonous is usually related to presence or absence of foreign leadership. Taken from the Greek autochthon auto=self chthon=the earth, the word literally signifies one of the aboriginal inhabitants of a country or a dweller who is original to a particular country. Missions use has evolved to mean that religious expression which arises from the aboriginal members of a country without foreign control.

[78] Manuel J. Gaxiola-Gaxiola, 'Latin American Pentecostalism: A Mosaic within a Mosaic,' *PNUEMA: The Journal of the Society of Pentecostal Studies* 13 (Fall 1991): 107.

[79] Ibid., 115—118. Gaxiola-Gaxiola designates the Assemblies of God of Brazil in this category but indicates that after their establishment (three years prior to the founding of the Assemblies of God in the United States) they 'later joined or signed working agreements with a foreign church'. (116). It should be noted that no formal agreements of any kind have ever been established between the Assemblies of God in the United States and any national Assemblies of God fellowship. The relationship has always been strictly fraternal.

[80] Ibid.

organizations.[81] Alvarez is far more strident than Gaxiola-Gaxiola in his critique of these churches when he states that, 'They commissioned missionaries to plant churches, to produce materials (mostly translations), to organize evangelistic campaigns and to establish biblical institutes. To this day, these churches conduct their strategy from the USA with an important emphasis on the so-called "electronic church". Jimmy Swaggert (sic) is part of that strategy.'[82]

Generally, Gaxiola-Gaxiola argues, there are certain characteristic patterns that surface in these indigenous Pentecostal churches. In many cases, missionaries retain some degree of control as heads

---

[81]Carmelo E. Alvarez, 'Latin American Pentecostals: Ecumenical and Evangelicals,' *Catholic Ecumenical Review* 23 (October 1986): 93. Alvarez includes the Assemblies of God and the Church of God (Cleveland, TN) in this 'missionary church' category. The German theologian, Heinrich Schäfer, *Protestantismo y crisis social en América Central* (San José, Costa Rica; Departamento Ecuménico de Investigaciones [DEI], 1992, 190) divides the Pentecostals in Central America into two main categories. In the first group are the traditional Pentecostals comprised of the large denominations, with international connections such as the Assemblies of God, the Church of God, (Cleveland, TN), and the Church of the Foursquare Gospel as well as numerous small churches of the same type. These make up over 50 per cent of all Protestants. These Pentecostals, according to Schäfer, are found almost exclusively in Central America's poorest barrios. In a second category or in the the the group Schäfer calls neo-Pentecostals he places the churches of both international or local origins such as Guatemala's El Verbo, Elim, Shekinah, El Shaddai, Fraternidad Cristiana, etc. This group more commonly known as the charismatic-Protestants comprises only 1 – 2 per cent of the aggregate Protestant believers and members are generally to be found in the middle-upper and upper classes. It is not clear where Schäfer includes the 'indigenous-autochthonous' churches to which Gaxiola-Gaxiola and Alvarez refer.

[82]Alvarez, *Latin American Pentecostals*, 93. Hugo Assman, *La Iglesia Electrónica y su Impacto en América Latina*, 17–24, a Brazilian Catholic liberation theologian, writes a scathing attack against the importation of a North American brand of Protestantism particularly as it relates to the impact of televangelists. In his polemic work, Assman argues that the television programming from the United States is an expression of religious imperialism. Such programming serves to legitimate the socio-economic and political system of North American capitalism. A characteristic of 'fundamentalism' in the United States, argues Assman, is that it serves to provide a theological underpinning for the status quo of the ideological mindset of capitalism. Assman contends that the message promulgated by these television preachers in Latin America serves only to deaden the conscience and distract attention from the struggle that the Church should have on behalf of the poor. Although Assman is undoubtedly correct in his assessment of most televangelists, it must be noted that Pentecostalism had a huge following years before the emergence of the televangelists such as Jimmy Swaggart and Jim Bakker. There are millions of rural Pentecostals who have never seen nor heard of any televangelist, and Pentecostalism has continued its unprecedented growth after the disappearance of the most famous of these preachers. Assman and Alvarez are right, however, when they contend that many television evangelists and the movements associated with them, with their impressive economic, technological, even theatrical deployment, emulate the cultural, political and theological norms of those North Americans drawn toward this type of religious expression.

of the Pentecostal unit in the country, even though they may have turned over the pastorship of the local congregation they have founded to a national pastor. Though the local church claims to be autonomous, the national pastor is hesitant to assert himself for fear of missionary reprisal. Gaxiola-Gaxiola makes a drastic statement when he writes that 'there are now in Latin America thousands of churches that belong to American denominations'.[83] Missionaries, he contends, may still maintain a kind of ideological control through the preparation of literature and hymnbooks by the sponsoring mission. He does admit that the financial support for these churches and pastors is sustained by national resources.[84]

While some of these arguments are incontrovertible, they widely miss the mark by their assumptions about the exercise of control, the source of funding, the inherent attractiveness of Pentecostal beliefs and practices for Latin Americans and the energies put into

---

[83]Ibid., 118. Gaxiola-Gaxiola does not identify these American Pentecostal denominations.

[84]Ibid., 118–119. Probably, 75 per cent of all Pentecostals in Latin America fall into this grouping (see table 4). Though Gaxiola-Gaxiola does not specifically list groups like the Assemblies of God and the Church of God (Cleveland, TN) in this category, such a designation is implicit. Schäfer is explicit in his declaration that ideological and hierarchical control from the United States is intentional. According to Schäfer, the Assemblies of God, for example, exercises manipulation through its Sunday School literature. He contends that because the literature is written in the United States and later distributed in Latin America a 'magnificent possibility' is available for the 'Central Office' to influence directly national churches with 'political/religious manipulation' that presents a 'procapitalist' position that supports 'right wing Reaganism' and at the same time, is opposed to popular movements in Central America. See Schäfer, *Protestantismo y crisis social*, 221. Schäfer's accusation of North American control over Latin America Pentecostal churches in the area of church literature simply because he sees 'a magnificent possibility' for the 'Central Office' to do so must be questioned. The author has read carefully Schäfer's study and cannot find any evidence that he uses to support his assertion. It should be noted that although the Sunday School literature is printed in the United States it is written by Latin Americans and distributed only in Latin America. Though Chilean ecumenical Pentecostals, Marta Palma and Juan Sepúlveda are more measured in their evaluations of classical Pentecostals in Latin America, they both adhere to the position that such Pentecostals are inextricably linked to their North American counterpart. Palma notes that 'toward the middle of this century more and more Pentecostal denominations from North America . . . linked conversion very closely with the adoption of the "American way of life".' 'A Pentecostal Church in the Ecumenical Movement,' *The Ecumenical Review* 37 (April 1985): 225. Similarly, Sepúlveda echoes the same sentiments when he refers to the Pentecostalism that entered Latin America as a result of missionary activity as a movement that 'manifests a greater financial, cultural and theological dependence on its churches of origin, and therefore, a much weaker rootedness in the autochthonous culture'. See 'Reflections on the Pentecostal Contribution to the Mission of the Church in Latin America,' *Journal of Pentecostal Theology* 1 (October 1992): 27.

proselytism, especially among converts' families and friends. Gaxiola-Gaxiola also makes too many assumptions about the influence of hymnbooks which few Pentecostals seem to use.[85]

Of even greater importance, the extent to which Latin American Pentecostals of various 'indigenized' movements realize their aspirations to take advantage of opportunity should not be underestimated in light of their rapid growth and institutional autonomy. Rather than viewing denominational labels as marks of submission, many Pentecostal denominational leaders apparently view the internal discipline, the respectability and the access to wider networks that result from affiliation as desirable. They are thereby raised, in effect, above the parochial restrictions of self-appointed leaders who are apparently more concerned with maintaining their positions within their closed circles than to embracing a wider view of the church. Ultimately, however, the character of the Latin American Pentecostal churches is itself the best way to determine whether they represent, as asserted by Míguez-Bonino, authentic impulses of Latin American culture.[86]

THE ESTABLISHMENT OF PENTECOSTALISM IN CENTRAL AMERICA

In analyzing the characteristics of indigenous churches in Latin America, Eugene Nida notes that, in most cases, even a 'fully indigenous church' which grew exclusively with Latin leadership, has had at least, an indirect link to some type of missionary endeavour.[87] In some cases the national indigenous church may have resulted from an early split from the sending church, as is the case with the Chilean Pentecostal Methodist churches. These churches were begun in 1909 by W. C. Hoover, an American Methodist missionary, who was expelled from the Methodist Church and initiated the Pentecostal work in that country.[88] In

---

[85]The author is generally in agreement with Gaxiola-Gaxiola's taxonomy of Pentecostal groupings in Latin America. However, his contention that Latin American Pentecostal movements, such as the Assemblies of God, that had original ties to missionaries, do not represent authentic indigenous churches is contradicted by the evidence presented in this chapter.

[86]See the discussion of Pentecostal activities as authentic cultural expressions within Latin American culture in chapter 3.

[87]Eugene Nida, 'The Indigenous Churches in Latin America,' *Practical Anthropology*, 97.

[88]The standard account of Hoover's work is found in Willis C. Hoover, *Historia del Avivamiento Pentecostal en Chile* (Valparaíso, n. p., 1948).

other cases, the indigenous churches may be one 'spiritual generation' removed from missionary influence or the doctrines and practices themselves may ensure a church's autonomy and integrity.[89] The evaluation of these Central American Assemblies of God groups later in the chapter demonstrates this process.

Pentecostalism was introduced into El Salvador early in the century by Frederick Mebius, a Canadian whose own religious experience, healing from tuberculosis while confined to a sanitorium, inspired an evangelistic mission to Latin America.[90] His association with Herbert Bender, the respected leader of the Central American Mission, as well as an adventurous Bible distribution expedition to Bolivia, preceded his taking up permanent residence in El Salvador. There, apparently during Bender's absence in about 1914, Mebius gathered a small group of believers who had previously identified with the CAM and certain Baptist groups to form a congregation in the remote community of Las Lomas de San Marcelino, a community of coffee workers located among the *fincas* (farms) on the slopes of the Volcano of Santa Ana.

Mebius is portrayed as a kindly but impetuous personality of limited leadership ability who nevertheless exerted a mesmerizing influence over his followers. By 1927, when some members of the community contested his spiritual and administrative leadership, a cluster of two dozen congregations with a combined membership of several hundred adults had come into existence. Isabel Navas de Paredes has girlhood recollections of groups of people gathering for prolonged, noisy meetings, sometimes lasting for several days, as the expressive features of Pentecostalism established the identity and reason for being of the group that despite their fanatically religious orientation, had much in common with other self-help associations familiar to Salvadorans.[91]

From these origins, at the initiative of Central Americans, emerged the two leading Pentecostal denominations in the republic, *las Asambleas de Dios* de El Salvador and la Iglesia de Dios, associated with the Church of God (Cleveland, TN), as well as

---

[89]Nida, 'Indigenous Churches,' 97–98.
[90]Roberto Domînguez, *Pioneros de Pentecostés* (San Salvador: Literature Evangelica, 1975), 2:221.
[91]'The Salvation Brokers: Conservative Evangelicals in Central America,' *NACLA*, 3. This entire issue is dedicated to reporting the impact of the fierce attack by conservative evangelical groups upon the people and culture of Central America.

several remaining Pentecostal groups that owed their denominational existence to internal schisms rather than to outside influence. In the case of the Assemblies of God, the group's origins resulted from the urging of some members who, having lost confidence in the founder's leadership, organized a mission to the United States to acquire the assistance of a foreign missionary. After two attempts in the late 1920s proved fruitless, the group's emissary, Francisco Arbizú, succeeded in persuading Ralph Darby Williams, a missionary whom he met in Mexico, to take up residence in El Salvador.[92]

The role of Arbizú and Williams, for the next decade or more, became decisive in the group's subsequent development.[93] Arbizú, the proprietor of a small shoe-making establishment, experienced the same aspirations and disadvantages experienced by other persons then living through the country's disruptive economic changes.[94] Commissioned by the congregation to find someone to assist the group in its further development, he travelled at his own expense and, on a second voyage with help from other Pentecostals, to San Antonio, Texas, where, in accordance with literature that had fallen into his hands, Henry Ball had established a Pentecostal training school for Hispanic leaders whose work was flourishing in Mexico and the Southwestern United States. Arbizú proved to be a practical, dedicated leader who gave the movement credibility and, who with other members of the group, directed it toward more specific objectives.

Though in many respects quite different from his Salvadoran counterpart, Ralph Williams demonstrated by his comments and conduct over several years of collaboration that he had affection and respect for his Central American colleague.[95] Williams was patient, precise and tenacious. At the time he was carrying a British passport, having only in 1924 gone to the United States from his native Wales with his older brother Richard. The brothers had been mentored by

---

[92]For a denominational history of the Assemblies of God missionary movement in Central America see, Louise Jeter Walker, *Siembra y Cosecha* (Springfield, MO: Gospel Publishing House, 1992).

[93]A first-hand account of the early formation of the Assemblies of God is extant in Ralph Williams' unpublished memoirs in the possession of his widow and cited in Everett A. Wilson, 'Identity, Community, and Status,' in *Earthen Vessels: American Evangelicals and Foreign Missions, 1880–1980*, eds. Joel A. Carpenter and Wilbert R. Shenk (Grand Rapids, MI: Wm. B. Eerdmans Publishing Co., 1990): 135–136.

[94]Domínguez, *Pioneros*, 225–230.

[95]Wilson, 'Identity, Community, and Status,' 143–146.

Alice Luce, a former Anglican missionary, who had become Pentecostal as a result of her experience with the Mukti revival in India in 1905. Williams had with his brother Richard helped to establish churches among the Spanish-speaking community in Southern California. Richard, who had aspired to extending the Pentecostal work to Peru, died of fever shortly after Ralph's arrival in El Salvador.

THE LATINIZATION OF PENTECOSTALISM IN CENTRAL AMERICA

Prima facie evidence of the process of the early latinization of Pentecostalism particularly within the Assemblies of God in Central America is easily adduced.[96] The role the pioneer missionary, such as Ralph Williams, fulfilled was primarily and essentially motivational. Everett Wilson correctly notes that missionaries succeeded in establishing an efficient prototype of a church that extended beyond their own personal energies, abilities, and resources. They immediately shared the responsibilities of church life with the fledgling national leaders, thus guaranteeing that the work would be extended into the future indefinitely. Even the Pentecostal churches that originated as denominational missions resulted from missionaries having reproduced their churches overseas than of their having incited Latin Americans to find their own compelling faith.[97] Ralph Williams, who was well acquainted with the missiological principles promulgated by Roland Allen, the Anglican author of *Missionary Methods: Saint Paul's or Ours?*, recognized the situation in El Salvador as an opportunity to implement Allen's indigenous missions theories in assisting an already existing church. Within a few months he had accompanied Arbizú in a survey of the existing churches and had with him drafted a set of principles which came to be known as the *Reglamento local*. The *Reglamento* contained the basic doctrinal statements of Pentecostal beliefs concerning the Bible as the inspired and infallible Word of God, the baptism of the

---

[96]In each of the Central American republics the Assemblies of God comprises the largest aggregate of all Pentecostals (table 1). Franz Damen, a Belgian Catholic missionary in Bolivia, makes the observation that evangelical Pentecostal groups 'that grow faster are either indigenous to the continent, or, if they had an origin in North America, they have quickly become "Latin-Americanized" in both leadership and financing'. *Christianity Today*, 6 April 1992, 30–31.

[97]Wilson, 'Identity, Community, and Status,' 135–136.

Holy Spirit, divine healing, sanctification of the believer, and the Second Coming. The document gave considerable emphasis to church order. The responsibilities of the membership, the function of the pastor and the duties of the lay officers are outlined. The congregations, each being autonomous within the structure of the conference, were to be governed by a *cuerpo oficial* (church board) comprised of both deacons and deaconesses.[98] The *cuerpo oficial* was to be responsible for all of the activities and the spiritual development, including discipline of the members, for the congregation. They were to hold monthly meetings in which they would treat pertinent church issues, present detailed financial reports and record all of their decisions in the official minutes. The *cuerpo oficial* could also extend a 'license to preach' to aspiring members who demonstrated leadership ability in the formation and pastoral care of the church's *campos blancos*.[99] The churches were also granted representation at the annual conference comprised of all the churches of *las Asambleas de Dios*.[100] The *Reglamento* concludes with a pact of membership that required a pledge to respect civil authority and refrain from political involvement.[101]

Within a few months Arbizú and Williams convened a meeting in the western town of Ahuachapán for the purpose of addressing the issues that the men felt to be unbiblical and the adoption of a statement of faith and conduct. The process of adopting a mutually acceptable constitution for the movement is recorded in Williams' unpublished memoirs, as well as in surviving comments of the two men recorded in the late 1970s. Having been an acknowledged leader of the movement before Williams' arrival, and having spent

---

[98]The *Reglamento local* specified that the number of women on the *cuerpo oficial* was not to exceed the number of men. Given the subservient position of women in Latin American culture in the 1930s when the document was drafted, the allowance for women to serve in this leadership capacity was truly exceptional. The opportunities for women to develop their leadership skills in Pentecostal churches is further treated in chapter 4.

[99]*Campos Blancos* are treated in chapter 3, note 30.

[100]*Manual de doctrinas y práticas de las Asambleas de Dios: Reglamento local*. The influence that the document 'Reglamento local' had upon the burgeoning Pentecostal movement, especially upon the Assemblies of God in Latin America is treated in Everett A. Wilson, 'Sanguine Saints: Pentecostalism in El Salvador,' *Church History* 52 (June 1983): 186–98.

[101]It must be remembered that the *Reglamento* was drafted shortly after the political massacre of 30,000 El Salvadorans in 1932. Any political involvement during this historical period by a member would have struck a mortal blow to the fledgling movement. Undoubtedly, the position of political neutrality would have a long term impact upon the political aspirations of the *Asambleas de Dios*.

several months under the influence of Henry Ball, the still young Arbizú was more than simply an assistant to his colleague. He actively participated in gaining support for the programme and continued for half a century to hold the respect of the Pentecostal community. Moreover, given the recentness of Williams' arrival, his limited experience with the people among whom he worked, and the demands that the ensuing constitution and the *Reglamento* made on the Pentecostal community, he obviously relied on Arbizú to gain acceptance for his proposals, depending ultimately on a consensus of support among the rank-and-file members to make the virtually spontaneous movement 'biblical' in its operation.

Williams' description of the meeting that adopted the constitution statement reveals the proprietary nature of Central American Pentecostalism from the outset.[102] 'The kind of decisions we entered upon were new to most of our people,' he reported. 'By means of "many questions and arguments" the representatives "tried to understand, but did not always find agreement".' Williams and Arbizú urged them to come to 'an understanding of doctrine and church order to which all could agree'. But the questions persisted: ' "What if the Holy Spirit shows us something different?" and "Who is to say who is right?" "What if I want to preach, who is to stop me?".' Williams recalled 'some less spiritual moments' when outbursts erupted because most lacked the patience to hear out the opinions of others. 'Opposing views were judged carnal or of the devil. Frequently the loudest speaker thought that his greater volume was proof that he was right. I heard someone shout, "That man is only a *campesino* (farmer); he knows nothing. I'm the one in charge,".' But, concluded Williams, they finally completed a 'constitution . . . which provided for amendments as the work developed'. The document was not a ' "hand-me-down," ' for these brethren had a major part in its making, so they understood it and defended it'.

The estimated one-half of the Pentecostal community that had boycotted the organizational meeting referred to themselves thereafter as 'free brethren' (*hermanos libres*) and remained under the nominal leadership of Frederick Mebius for several years. In 1940 Mebius, then aged seventy and in declining health, accepted the offer of the Church of God organization in Guatemala to assume

---

[102]Selections from the unpublished memoirs of Ralph Darby Williams are in Wilson, 'Identity, Community, and Status,' 133–151.

oversight of his churches.[103] This grouping has grown to the present to include about a quarter of all the Pentecostal churches and congregants in the country. For the most part, the other Pentecostal groups that came into existence resembled the two largest groups in their manner of operation and in appealing to the humble classes. All of these groups mobilized the entire membership and developed the leadership potential of the members by placing promising lay persons in charge of local meetings referred to as '*campos blancos*' ('whitened fields-ready for harvest'). The development of a rudimentary training programme for prospective pastors, the rapid extension of the movement with the opening of the new *campos blancos*, and the mobilization and training of the membership with the adoption of the *Reglamento local* provided an effective formula for the group's continued growth.[104]

When Williams left El Salvador in June of 1934 because of his wife's ill health, 26 organized congregations adhered to the regulations that he and Arbizú had sponsored. Although he returned from April, 1936 to July, 1939, and retained nominal oversight of the church in Central America for more than a decade thereafter, the church continued to expand rapidly in the absence of a resident missionary. A North American colleague, Melvin Hodges, who was briefly associated with Williams in El Salvador before continuing on to Nicaragua, was impressed with the independence and viability of the church and in 1953 published an analysis of its development and operation entitled *The Indigenous Church*.[105] In view of the church's success and independence, a number of evangelical missions leaders investigated its operation in the ensuing years.[106]

In the meantime, El Salvador became the staging area for the spread of the movement elsewhere in Central America, as Salvadoran evangelists visited Honduras and Guatemala, opening churches in homes until a national leadership emerged to organize a congregation. The network expanded from Jutiapa, in lowland

---

[103]Charles W. Conn, *Where the Saints Have Trod: A History of the Church of God Missions* (Cleveland, TN: Pathway Press, 1959), 143.

[104]Everett A. Wilson, 'The Central American Evangelicals; From Protest to Pragmatism,' *International Review of Mission* 77 (January 1988): 98.

[105]Bibliographic information for Hodges, *The Indigenous Church*, is found in note 75.

[106]See Norman Chugg and Kenneth Larson, 'Chugg-Larson Report' cited previously in note 76.

Guatemala, to the highlands, retaining the character and flavour of traditional, popular social organization.[107]

PENTECOSTALISM AND SOCIAL CRISIS IN CENTRAL AMERICA

A profile of the churches in the Central American republics in the mid-1950s indicates that they retained both their organizational autonomy and their popular character. The more than 300 churches of the Salvadoran Assemblies of God were with few exceptions rural and were most often found among populations where social dissolution was advanced. Moreover, later observers are generally in agreement that the formation of these churches corresponded to the civil war, natural disasters, forced migrations and other disruptive events of the 1970s and 1980s.[108] In 1981 Garry Parker reported in *Christianity Today* that 'Evangelicals Blossom Brightly amid El Salvador's Wasteland of Violence.'[109] One of the best assessments of the essentially popular and independent character of the Salvadoran Pentecostal, however, is the unintended commendation given by the Jesuit scholar, Prudencia Damboriena, in his two-volume study of Latin American Protestantism. After observing 'that the group that is the most developed and most efficient [in leadership preparation] is the Pentecostals,' Damboriena argues that 'We are obliged to accept with extreme caution the claim that between 1957 and 1961 [the Asambleas de Dios de El Salvador] have ordained 479 pastors, which would make El Salvador among the leaders of all the Latin American republics in producing national (autochthonous) pastors.'[110] However reluctantly accepted, Pentecostalism in Central America, led in its institutional development by the church in El Salvador, is the product of national initiative and directly related to the deterioration of peoples who have

---

[107]*Origen y desarrollo de las Asambleas de Dios en Guatemala* (Guatemala: Concilio Nacional de las Asambleas de Dios de Guatemala, 1987). The investigations of social scientists such as Sheldon Annis, *God and Production in a Guatemalan Town* (Austin, TX: University of Texas Press, 1987) and Bryan S. Roberts, 'Protestant Groups and Coping with Urban Life in Guatemala,' *American Journal of Sociology* 73 (May 1968): 747 demonstrate the functionality of the social format provided by the Pentecostals in that country.

[108]Wilson, 'Central American Evangelicals,' 104–105.

[109]Garry Parker, 'Evangelicals Blossom Brightly amid El Salvador's Wasteland of Violence,' *Christianity Today*, 8 May 1981, 34.

[110]Prudencia Damboriena, *El Protestantismo en América Latina*, 2:96.

historically demonstrated their ability to organize in response to overwhelming social problems.[111]

If the Pentecostal churches of Central America are in some appearances and practices indistinguishable from other evangelicals in the region, they nevertheless from the beginning developed within the context of their own circumstances and reflected the needs and aspirations of their own members. Ample opportunity was given for national leadership and local control.[112] Not only did their movements—characterized by freedom of individual expression and of human aspiration—grow almost entirely at their own initiative but from the beginning they operated and expanded with the voluntary and often sacrificial financial support of their members. In this respect the Pentecostals of Central America differ intrinsically from other emergent evangelical churches that operate within the considerably less flexible ecclesiastical programmes of a given church or foreign mission or that have acquired patterns of financial and administrative dependency.[113]

In addition, these groups, having emerged from sectors that had experienced the effects of dislocation and the frustrations of a national system that deprived them of social and economic opportunity, have from the beginning harboured at least an implicit social agenda. Concerned with their own problems and vulnerabilities, they have found in their Pentecostal faith, as this work will demonstrate in the following chapter, a promise of a better life, beginning with a sense of worth and purpose and including access to providential health and assistance. If Pentecostals have been willing to forego some minor rewards and pleasures (especially the common vices, conviviality and peer acceptance) for the sake of realizing their vision of establishing a radically separate pattern of life, they have nonetheless been remarkably realistic in functioning in the temporal world. Having at considerable effort and sacrifice established mechanisms for addressing their own concerns, the Pentecostals have increasingly acquired the institutional strength and resources to address the human needs of the societies in which they live.

In order to maintain high levels of credibility and to develop

---

[111]Stoll, *Protestantism*, 45.

[112]See discussion on the leadership apprentice system utilized by Pentecostals in chapter 4.

[113]See earlier discussion of this point in this chapter.

institutionally, all of these groups are required to face the same problems of legitimization, structuring, adaptability and moral accountability. If Pentecostal success in Latin America is in some senses assured, it is also precarious. As improbable as these movements were for gathering large followings several decades ago, they must now demonstrate continuing leadership in the resolution of severe human problems. In the leadership vacuum that the Pentecostals have attempted to fill, only appropriate and effective application of the groups' energies and resources at strategic intervals can sustain their dynamic structure.

Pentecostals derive their recognizable character largely from their origins among the socially marginal populations and from the protean formula that enables individuals and like-minded groups to satisfy their yearnings for legitimacy, realization, recognition and power. This working definition of Pentecostalism, as will be described in the following chapter, is consistent with what observers have often considered adherents' presumption, audacity, opportunism, faith, naïvety, dedication, obstinacy, and other similar expressions of assertiveness. This root tendency finds application in Latin American life in the generation of Pentecostalism's dynamic movements.

Table 1: Assemblies of God Growth Rates in Central America, 1951-1992

Country	Year	National Ministers	Christian Workers	Total	Churches	Preaching Points	Total	Members & Adherents	Missionaries
Guatemala	1951	31	–*	31	32	–	32	1,553	3
	1961	406	–	406	165	370	535	8,601	4
	1972	501	–	501	875	nr*	–	32,731	7
	1982	1,017	1,375	2,392	875	1,456	2,331	84,444	5
	1992	1,826	2,202	4,028	1,541	2,326	3,867	234,717	6
El Salvador	1951	70	–	70	65	–	65	3,692	6
	1961	929	–	929	240	780	1,020	11,322	6
	1972	nr	–	–	808	nr	nr	81,600	4
	1982	350***	385	735	730	2,200	2,930	180,000	3
	1992	1,240	5,000	6,240	1,096	5,020	6,116	263,195	8
Honduras	1951	20	–	–	21	–	–	691	3
	1961	63	–	–	37	25	62	2,212	4
	1972	97	–	–	92	nr	nr	5,000	4
	1982	235	192	427	360	150	510	26,806	5
	1992	429	326	755	442	374	815	52,931	8
Nicaragua	1951	24	–	–	28	–	–	1,123	3
	1961	77	–	–	38	40	78	1,595	6
	1972	115	–	–	230	nr	nr	10,480	6
	1982	361	320	681	425	320	745	16,650	0
	1992	520	465	985	401	507	908	100,000	2
Costa Rica	1951	3	–	–	3	–	–	225	2
	1961	80	–	–	18	50	68	958	6
	1972	74	–	–	56	nr	nr	2,841	7
	1982	120	100	220	100	105	205	12,466	6
	1992	315	760	1,075	186	444	630	78,777	5

* Statistics for these catagories not kept until a later date.

** Statistics for these catagories not reported in these years.

*** There is an opportunity for error in the number of ordained ministers reported by El Salvador in 1992.

Table 2: Aggretate Totals: Assemblies of God in Central America

Date	Ordained	Christian Workers	Total Credentialed Workers	Churches	Preaching Points	Member & Total	Adherents	Missionaires
1951	148	–	148	149	–	149	7,284	17
1961	1,555	–	1,555	498	1,265	1,763	24,680	26
1972	2,126*	–	2,126	2,061	500***	2,561	132,652	28
1982	2,083**	2,372	4,455	2,446	4,231	6,677	320,366	19
1992	4,330	8,753	13,083	3,666	8,671	12,337	729,620	29

* El Salvador did not have the number of ordained ministers on file for 1972. The number of ordained ministers reported for 1974 was used.
** There is an apparent error in the umber of ordained minidters reported by El Salvador in 1982 (see Table 1).

Table 3: Ratios: Missionary to National Membership

	Year	Ratio
Guatemala	1992	1:39,120
El Salvador	1992	1:32,899
Honduras	1992	1:6616
Nicaragua	1992	1:50,000
Costa Rica	1992	1:15,755
Average:		1:25,159

Table 4: Comparisons of Evangelical Community and The Assemblies of God in Central America (missionary to membership ratio)

Evangelical Community Central America 1988			Assemblies of God Central America 1988		
	Year	Ratio		Year	Ratio
Guatemala	1988	1:1586	Guatemala	1988	1:29,703
El Salvador	1988	1:5357	El Salvador	1988	1:23,333
Honduras	1988	1:435	Honduras	1988	1:6473
Nicaragua	1988	1:2500	Nicaragua	1988	0:64,000
Costa Rica	1988	1:470	Costa Rica	1988	1:5666
Average:		1:1108	Average:		1:18,586

Note: #1: Emilo Núñez and William Taylor estimate that their 1988 statistics, based upon Read, Monterroso, Patrick Johnstone and the Atlas de COMIBAM; as well as their own information could have an error rate of twenty per cent. They are confident that their figures are conservative. They estimate the Central America 'evangelical community' to be 4,308,000 and the number of actual communicants to be 1,436,000 (using a coefficient of 3 to 1). See Núñez and Taylor, *Crisis in Latin America,* p.158. They grant that 75 per cent of this number is Pentecostal, resulting in a Pentecostal communicant population of 1,077,000. In 1988 the Assemblies of God alone had a communicant membership of 501,827. I do not have statistics for other large Pentecostal groupings such as the Church of God, but the available evidence would confirm Núñez and Taylor's estimation of Pentecostal membership to comprise conservatively an aggregate total of 75 percent of all evangelicals. Further, the available statistics would seem to confirm that 'classical Pentecostalism' forms the overwhelming majority of all the Pentecostal groupings.

Note #2: Read and Monterroso estimations of ratios of missionaries to national membership further underscore the dramatic difference between Pentecostals and non-Pentecostal evangelical groups.

Group	*Proportion of Missionaries (%)*	*Proportion of Communicants (%)*
Faith Missions	33.0	1.5
Protestant	44.8	25.5
Newer Denominations	10.0	3.4
Adventists	2.7	6.3
Pentecostals	9.8	63.0
	100	100

Undoubtedly, the numbers have changed significantly since Read's study in 1969, but the trend in contrast in ratios of missionaries to national workers (Table 5) was firmly established.

Table 5: Ratios: Missionary to Pastors
and Christian Workers

	Year	Ratio
Guatemala	1992	1:671
El Salvador	1992	1:780
Honduras	1992	1:94
Nicaragua	1992	1:493
Costa Rica	1992	1:215
Average:		1:451

Chapter 3

The Practical Outworking of Doctrinal Confession in Latin American Pentecostalism

A PENTECOSTAL HERMENEUTIC

Any attempt to define Pentecostals according to a specific confession of faith is a challenging task. Theological sophistication has been regarded with considerable suspicion by the adherents of the movement. In spite of the substantial divergencies in specific confessions, however, Pentecostals hold to certain conservative evangelical doctrinal positions including 1) an absolute acceptance of the Bible as the authoritative rule for faith and practice; 2) a commitment to orthodoxy, including belief in the doctrine of God and the Trinity, the salvific work of Jesus Christ in his death and resurrection, the regenerative power of the Holy Spirit, and the second coming of Jesus Christ to judge the quick and the dead; 3) a fundamental affirmation of justification by faith; 4) a personal pursuit of holiness in daily living; and, 5) a participation in the church and its mission and ministry in the world. Pentecostals consider themselves to be evangelicals in their identification with these beliefs and practices. However, Pentecostals especially emphasize the work of the Holy Spirit in empowering believers to participate in the truths encapsulated in doctrine. Pentecostals wholeheartedly believe that the Holy Spirit enables a believer to translate creed into conduct, faith into practice, and doctrine into daily living.

This Pentecostal commitment to the Holy Spirit's work in connecting doctrinal confession with practical living can be illustrated in the Pentecostal approach to hermeneutics.[1] Pentecostal theologian

---

[1]For a comprehensive description of a Pentecostal hermeneutic, see Gordon Fee, *Gospel and Spirit, Issues in New Testament Hermeneutics* (Peabody, MA: Hendrickson Publishers, 1991); Russell Spittler, ed., *Perspectives in the New Pentecostalism* (Grand Rapids, MI: Baker Book House, 1976); J. Rodman Williams, *Renewal Theology*, 3 vols. (Grand Rapids: Zondervan Publishing House, 1990); Roger Stronstad, 'Pentecostal Experience and Hermeneutics', *Paraclete* 15 (Winter 1992): 14–30; Roger Stronstad, *The Charismatic Theology of St. Luke* (Peabody, MA: Hendrickson Publishers, 1984); and the recent dialogue between Roger Stronstad, 'The Biblical Precedent for Historical Precedent,' and Gordon Fee, 'Response to Roger Stronstad's "The Biblical Precedent for Historical Precedent" ', *Paraclete* 27 (Summer 1993): 1–14. Also, the Fall 1993 issue of *PNEUMA: The Journal of the Society for Pentecostal Studies* was devoted to the theme of Pentecostal hermeneutics.

Gordon Anderson understands the basic elements of an evangelical approach to biblical hermeneutics. He contends that Pentecostals utilize the same historical-grammatical methods as do other conservative evangelicals. Because questions of 'personal and historical experiences along with theological biases' must be handled apart from method,[2] Anderson emphasizes that competent Pentecostal exegesis must follow the same canons of historical criticism that non-Pentecostals utilize.[3] A Pentecostal interpreter does not have a special 'pneumatic' interpretation. Neither do Pentecostals claim an additional pneumatic dimension to interpretation. However, Anderson argues that a Pentecostal hermeneutic 'incorporates different but legitimate methodological, personal, historical, and theological presuppositions in its interpretative work'.[4]

Fundamental to Pentecostal doctrine, according to Anderson, is that the account of God's actions, as recorded in Scripture, should be considered as normative in the continuing manner in which God has acted 'from the time of the Resurrection to the Second Coming'.[5]

Therefore, the belief that God's actions are continuous and normative throughout history influences much of Pentecostal thought. A Pentecostal hermeneutic is informed not only by the personal experience of salvation, but by 'the charismatic experience

---

[2]Exegetes invariably bring personal presuppositions to their work on the biblical text. An excellent and honest example of this process is utilized by theologians Christopher Rowland and Mark Corner in their sympathetic description of the manner in which the Bible is used in liberation theology. They rightly assume that it is 'difficult if not impossible' to approach the biblical text from a 'position of studied neutrality(3)'. Rowland and Corner admit that 'detachment' from one's own 'social and political preferences' is . . . an unavoidable part of the complex process of finding meaning in texts—what we call exegesis. A recognition by exegetes that personal agendas are inevitable, suggest that two theologians, 'will enable one another to be aware of the various kinds of exegesis which we practise in all their subtlety and sophistication' (5). Their book is a refreshing approach to 'liberating exegesis' understanding that their 'method' is and must be coloured by their biases. See Christopher Rowland and Mark Corner, *Liberating Exegesis: The Challenge of Liberation Theology to Biblical Studies* (London: SPCK, 1990).

[3]Gordon Anderson, 'Pentecostal Hermeneutics', *Paraclete: A Journal of Pentecostal Studies* 28 (Spring 1994): 13–14. Though interpreters may have certain personal and theological 'presuppositions', the basic method of exegesis, discovering what the words meant, should follow the same approach. Krister Stendahl underscores this position when he declares that the 'descriptive task [exegesis] can be carried out by believer and agnostic alike'. Krister Stendahl, 'Biblical Theology, Contemporary,' *Interpreter's Bible Dictionary* (New York, NY: Abingdon Press), 1:422.

[4]Anderson, 'Pentecostal Hermeneutics,' 13.

[5]Ibid., 21.

that is unique to Pentecostals'.[6] Pentecostals contend that the biblical text cannot be fully understood apart from personally experiencing the events that the Bible describes. God does miracles today and the believer is empowered to participate as God's agent by way of the Baptism in the Holy Spirit.[7] How exactly does this work? Anderson responds:

> It is in this vein that Pentecostals include personal experience in the hermeneutical process. They are willing to admit that their understanding of Scripture is formed, in part, by what they have experienced. That does not elevate experience above the text. It simply means that as an expression of Christianity which emphasizes and appreciates the personal and experiential dimension of a relationship with God. Pentecostals rather unabashedly admit they reflect upon their own experiences as they study the text. . . .
>
> The difference between Pentecostals and others is that they use real life experience with an awareness and admission of the fact and the belief that it is an appropriate step in a legitimate hermeneutic.[8]

The approach that Anderson outlines for Pentecostal hermeneutics is typical of the way in which Pentecostals address areas of doctrine across the board, and illustrates the way doctrine has functioned in the emergence of Latin American Pentecostalism. The emphasis has been on the process of living out the truth rather than on historical or structural analysis alone.[9] Walter J. Hollenweger is on target in his observation that a description of Latin American Pentecostal theology cannot start with only its doctrinal concepts.[10] Likewise, Eugene Nida has correctly noted that the theological descriptions of doctrines, though important, are not as crucial for Pentecostals as they are in other evangelical/Protestant churches. Pentecostals have always emphasized experiential Christianity as the way to validate the authenticity of their doctrinal confession. Doctrinal concepts such as redemption and atonement are explained not so much in technical terms as they are in an

---

[6]Ibid., 18—19.
[7]Ibid., 21.
[8]Ibid., 19.
[9]Dr. Everett A. Wilson's published and unpublished research on Latin American Pentecostalism has had considerable influence upon the author in the construction of this chapter.
[10]Walter J. Hollenweger, 'The Religion of the Poor is not a Poor Religion,' *The Expository Times* 87 (May 1976): 228.

interpretation of one's personal relationship with God that produces a radical transformation of life.[11] Pentecostal churches are intent on demonstrating how their fundamental doctrines work their way out practically in the lives of the people.

When appraising this Pentecostal approach to doctrine, it is important to recognize the various characteristic dimensions of Pentecostal faith that provide the necessary motivation and reward to sustain the individual members' high level of commitment. Pentecostals invest extraordinary amounts of time, personal resources and even relinquish old relationships.

For most Pentecostals, these dimensions appear to include first, a time of crisis or vulnerability resulting in conversion when Pentecostal beliefs and practices become especially appropriate; second, acceptance into a church life with accompanying emotional support; third, a subjective experience of Spirit-baptism and a sense of the presence of the supernatural that follows conversion; fourth, the empowering that accompanies these intense post-conversion experiences that are encouraged by Pentecostals such as healing; fifth, the emotional security and satisfaction that derives from the groups' moralistic demands of personal holiness; and sixth, a dynamic tension between the present and the future, demonstrated in its practice of organizational and cultural adaptability which enables its members to overcome restrictive internal and external conditions in order to ensure ongoing personal and institutional development. These six practices can be identified in Pentecostal groups, in their collective beliefs and practices, as well as in the formation of individual members.[12]

CONVERSION AND TRANSFORMATION

While Pentecostals constitute only a small proportion of Latin America's poor, these social elements are characteristically drawn from the groups most affected by changing conditions of life. The modernization process has tended to break up the traditional social

---

[11]Eugene Nida, 'The Indigenous Churches in Latin America,' *Practical Anthropology*, 105.
[12]The role that the doctrinal dimension in Pentecostal thought plays in giving shape and direction to the processes of Pentecostal experience in the ethos of practical life is explored in this chapter. In chapter six, a coherent Pentecostal theology of social action will be developed to add intellectual rigour to the experiential aspects of doctrinal confession discussed in this chapter.

structures, including the extended family, the village community and the patrón system that formerly provided the region's masses with a stable world view and a supportive social system. This vulnerability is not only the backdrop for the introduction of Pentecostalism, but it also demonstrates the applicability of the movement for the masses in general, even for the individuals who for various reasons have not or would not opt for a new faith.

Moreover, since identification with a new religion often results in the convert's exclusion from some traditional social rewards, characteristically the denial of full acceptance in the family or work group, the conversion process requires deliberation, assertiveness, and, presumably, strength of character. To the extent that this description holds true, Pentecostals may not be simply responding to changing circumstances, but may well be a group of resilient individuals prepared to break away from tradition in order to participate in something novel. Eugene Nida has adopted this view in his description of 'indigenous Protestants' as led by a 'creative minority'. 'The Protestants have directed their appeal to the masses, not only because they were the most numerous,' he argues, 'but because they were the most concerned with change and responded to the hope of a better chance.'[13]

When a person decides to convert, their testimony almost invariably follows the pattern of contrast between their old life 'in the world' and their new life 'in Christ'. Once they were 'lost' and now they are 'found'. They have opted to choose between two alternatives—for this 'world' or for God. Sepúlveda observes that when converts testify that 'they cease to be of this world,' they do not mean they have opted out of the world, because for Pentecostals there are always two worlds—'two worlds of life, two ways of living. . . . in a Pentecostal testimony, "a world" is not an objective category such as society or history. It is strictly a way of life: "World," then is "my life" before accepting a "new life" through conversion.'[14]

José Míguez Bonino in addressing the broad Protestant constituency aptly describes this 'new life' that Pentecostals believe must also take place for the Latin American who experiences the conversion event:

---

[13]Eugene Nida, *Understanding Latin Americans* (Pasadena, CA: William Carey Library, 1974): 94.
[14]Juan Sepúlveda, 'Pentecostalism as Popular Religiosity,' *International Review of Mission* 78 (January 1989): 82.

> In our particular Latin American situation . . . people experience their
> existence (both individually and collectively) as artificially blocked, as
> captive due to structural and ideological factors which block their
> material and social fulfillment. The Christian message . . . dare not offer
> an escapist, substitutive way out . . . The goal of conversion is not just
> the reception of a conceptual message or the formal acceptance of a
> doctrinal formula, but the 'creation of a new creature'.[15]

Míguez Bonino is not reciting a mere reiteration of theoretical
conversion but calls for a conversion that results in a radical
transformation of both individual and corporate actions.

> The call to conversion is a call to discipleship. . . . Consequently, it
> involves a community committed to an active discipleship in the
> world.[16]

Similarly, Juan Sepúlveda describes the 'militancy' of Pentecostal converts when he implies that any convert who 'ceases to
"militate," to participate in the life of the community, and
abandons the duties of evangelization, in reality has "gone astray"
or "lost the way".'[17]

In anthropological terminology this convert is a change agent or
a 'culture broker,' the independent, the entrepreneurial, the aspiring, in short, the taker of initiative. Costa Rican pastor Eric Lennox,
in his Sunday morning sermon, vividly describing the initiative,
risks and costs of publicly sharing one's conversion experience
strikes the same note:

> They say we are the people of *aleluyas*—of tambourines; that we clap
> our hands and tremble. Do you have the courage to go to work, to the
> university, plaza or the colegio and declare without shame that 'Jesus
> Christ is Lord'?
>
> Your friends will deny you, your family may forsake you . . . if they
> accuse you, it is for the gospel, it is for Jesus Christ—say, 'Glory to
> God!' Many die for a few acres of land, others for gold or silver but we
> are willing to die for the gospel! Your faith will take you into the fire.[18]

---

[15]José Míguez Bonino, 'Conversion, New Creature and Commitment,' *International Review of Mission* 72 (July 1983): 330–331.
[16]Ibid.
[17]Juan Sepúlveda, 'Pentecostal Theology in the Context of the Struggle for Life,' in *Faith born in the struggle for life: a rereading of Protestant faith in Latin America today*, ed. Dow Kirkpatrick, trans. L. McCoy (Grand Rapids, MI: Wm. B. Eerdmans Publishing Co., 1988), 304.

Eugene Nida observes that though Pentecostal preaching is often criticized for its lack of theological content, it is, nonetheless, preaching directed to the needs of the people. It challenges people to make a crisis decision, it is person-centred and it is the *kerygmatic* proclamation. Such power of preaching, avers Nida, provides a personal participation and a psychological identification that cannot be equalled in the traditional churches.[19]

The rapid growth of Pentecostalism strongly suggests that the movement has emerged with the active participation of assertive personalities, in effect, people with personal reasons to reject the *status quo* and who are in search of change.[20] The description of evangelical converts in the slums of Guatemala City provided by Byran Roberts indicates that they are characteristically young, detached, disillusioned or uncommitted to tradition, perhaps with tendencies to individualism. Many became evangelicals following a personal crisis or natural disaster that left them deprived of an identity and security.[21] However, their coming to faith is not simply a way to cope with insecurity. Their activity in Pentecostal churches reflects their unwillingness to accept passively their lot in life, especially as they are regularly thrust into positions that require the assumption of leadership, rationalization of conduct and creativity in confronting the church's problems.

Whether Pentecostals should be considered as the undifferentiated, passive masses who are simply victims of modern life—as they have been represented by writers such as Deborah Huntington—is doubtful.[22] Acquaintance with their personal accounts of enduring hardship, ostracism and tenacity leads to a judgement that these are

---

[18]Eric Lennox is the associate pastor of 'Oasis de Esperanza' an Assemblies of God congregation in San José, Costa Rica. Excerpts were taken from his sermon by the author on May 23, 1993. Such preaching is typical of sermons that the author has heard hundreds of times.

[19]Nida, 'Indigenous Churches in Latin America', 102.

[20]See chapter two for a description of 'popular, autonomous Pentecostal churches'.

[21]Bryan Roberts, 'Protestant groups and coping with urban life in Guatemala City', *American Journal of Sociology* 73 (May 1968): 753–767. During the civil wars of the late 1970s and 1980s 80,000 people were killed in Guatemala, 75,000 in El Salvador and 100,000 in Nicaragua. During approximately this same period of civil war the Assemblies of God registered growth in members and adherents in Guatemala from 84,444 (1982) to 234,717 (1992), in El Salvador from 180,000 (1982) to 263,195 (1992) and in Nicaragua from 16,650 (1982) to 100,000 (1992).

[22]Deborah Huntington, 'The Prophet Motive,' *NACLA Report* 18 (January/February 1984): 2–11.

men and women of commitment and determination.[23] José Comblin, a Catholic liberation theologian, candidly admits that Pentecostals have been looked down upon prejudicially by the 'higher churches' predominately because they are part of lower-class society. 'Pentecostal churches,' he writes, 'are denigrated by their class. . . . They have been accused of being alienated, removed from the world, conservative, but a more sympathetic examination would show these accusations to be exaggerated and even baseless.'[24] Unquestionably, Pentecostals in general have displayed tenacity, persistence, inner strength and determination in the process of establishing their influence. Ostracism and abuse occurred with enough frequency in the early stages after conversion to suggest that these people were either very determined or masochistic.[25]

Pentecostals appear to be characteristically determined and assertive persons. The word 'audacious' has sometimes been applied to them. Perhaps the term 'boldness,' used by St. Luke in the Acts of the Apostles, appropriately applies to them. Pentecostals seem to have hope for the future. They hold aspirations for themselves and their families and apparently see opportunities that remain obscure to many Latin Americans who

---

[23]Converts almost immediately after conversion, often within a few days, may be seen publicly sharing their testimony of new found faith with their family and friends as well as in the parks, plazas, buses-anywhere and to anyone who will listen.

[24]José Comblin, *Holy Spirit and Liberation* (Maryknoll, NY: Orbis Books, 1989), 8–9. Such polemical attitudes as described by Comblin are often seen as a reflection of Pope John Paul II's attitude in his attacks upon 'sects' and other religions. At the Fourth General Conference of Latin American Bishops (CELAM) held in the Dominican Republic in 1992 the statements of John Paul II were also clearly indicative of the position of CELAM as can be seen in the final report from the Santo Domingo Conference. Edward Cleary, a respected scholar and Catholic priest, decries the Pope's polemical rhetoric when he reports that the Pope, in an obvious reference to Pentecostal groups, warned the faithful that 'sects were like "rapacious wolves" devouring Latin American Catholics and "causing division and discord in our communities".' Edward L. Cleary, 'John Paul Cries "Wolf": Misreading the Pentecostals,' *Commonweal* 7 (November 20 1992). Cleary cites the final document [22]. The Pope further describes the 'fundamentalist sects' in paragraphs 139–142 of the final approved document from the IV Conferencia General Del Episcopada Latinoamericana held in Santo Domingo, Dominican Republic, Oct. 12–28, 1992. *Nueva Evangelización, Promoción Humana, Cultura Cristiana* (México: Ediciones DABAR S.A., 1992), 107–108.

[25]A mother-in-law from a staunch Catholic tradition remarked to her newly converted daughter-in-law that she would prefer that her son become a drug addict or a criminal rather than convert to Pentecostalism. Ironically some of the most devout practitioners of Pentecostalism confess that before their conversion they were ardent Catholics who held utmost disdain for Pentecostals because they considered them to be a fanatical sect. Such testimonies are typical of what one can hear in the testimony time during the *culto*.

share their circumstances. As observers like Sheldon Annis and Bryan Roberts have recognized, in a society where there are few options, agents of change who project new social alternatives acquire a strategic importance.[26]

The conversion experience is critical for the establishment of a solid basis for the development of the Pentecostal community. Pentecostals have grown especially among Latin America's popular society. Populations that have not been integrated into national life, including ethnic minorities, rural groups, peasants dispossessed of their land, urban immigrants, the young, women and recent foreign immigrants have become active participants.[27] In a society where few alternative social programmes exist, Christian converts may channel their aspirations and creative energies for change into the promotion of an alternative religious movement.

CHURCH LIFE

Wilson correctly notes that general approaches taken to the study of Pentecostalism have tended to neglect one of the most characteristic features of the movement, that is the formation of congregations.[28] Stereotypes of the revivalists such as portrayed by Hugo Assman in his polemical book *La Iglesia Electrónica y su Impacto en América Latina* misdirect the attention of readers from the grassroots, individual dynamics of the movement to the highly visible personalities of the mass media.[29] While the latter reflect the enthusiasm of the masses, the media personalities are hardly capable of generating the interest that sustains their influence. The strength of the movement is achieved at the level of the local congregation, where small groups of congregants regularly have not only organized themselves into stable, often growing associations,[30] but have

---

[26]Bryan Roberts, *Organizing Strangers* (Austin, TX: University of Texas Press, 1973) and Sheldon Annis, *God and Production in a Guatemalan Town,*(1987).

[27]See chapter one for a description of the personal origins and components of Pentecostals.

[28]Everett Wilson, 'Dynamics of Latin American Pentecostalism,' in *Coming of Age: Protestantism in Contemporary Latin America*, ed. Daniel R. Miller (Lanham. MD: University Press of America, 1994), 100.

[29]Assman, *Iglesia Electrónica*', 1987. See chapter two, note 82.

[30]City-wide crusades held in huge stadiums often offer the prevailing stereotypes of Pentecostal evangelism in Latin American. However, by far the greatest degree of evangelism and growth results from Bible Studies (*campos blancos*) which begin in the home of a church member. These *campos blancos* have some similarities to ecclesial base communities. They are begun in the home of a local church member, usually initiated by the pastor of the 'mother church,' whenever there are two or three church families living in close proximity to each other. These 'home services' are fashioned after the style

invariably acquired land, support a pastor and undertake social programmes.[31]

Pentecostal congregations are characteristically small in size, generally with an average attendance of 80-90 people and an even smaller nucleus of believers who are responsible for the inner operations of the group.[32] The church building is usually located on a small lot, not centrally placed, and often still in some stage of construction. It is normal for a congregation to begin construction on their *templo* with minimal resources, proceeding to build as they are able. The com-

---

(footnote 30 continued)
of a home Bible study. Persons demonstrating leadership ability, under the mentorship of the pastor, are given opportunity to develop their gifts as leaders of the group. There is a time for praise and worship, sharing testimony, reading and studying the Bible. Neighbours are invited to attend. As soon as the group grows to approximately a dozen families, the mother church will begin the process of organizing the *campo blanco* into an official congregation. A *campo blanco* is considered strong enough to be independent of the mother church when there is a pastor in place, the church is self-supporting, self-governing, and has secured a piece of property in order to construct a church building. By far the major part of church expansion within the Assemblies of God follows this pattern. There are obvious similarities, along with significant differences, between the *campos blancos* and the *comunidades de base* (ecclesial base communities or CEBs) within the Catholic church. The literature on CEBs is substantial. For some insightful articles comparing and contrasting the two from a Pentecostal perspective see Adoniram Gaxiola, 'Poverty as a Meeting and Parting Place: Similarities and Contrasts in the Experiences of Latin American Pentecostalism and Ecclesial Base Communities,' *PNUEMA: The Journal of the Society for Pentecostal Studies* 13 (Fall 1991): 167–174 and Charles E Self, 'Conscientization, Conversion, and Convergence: Reflections on Base Communities and Emerging Pentecostalism in Latin America,' *PNEUMA: The Journal of the Society for Pentecostal Studies* 14 (Spring 1992): 59–72; from a sociological perspective see Rowan Ireland, *Kingdoms Come: Religion and Politics in Brazil* (Pittsburgh, PA: University Press, 1991) and John Burdick, 'Rethinking the Study of Social Movements: The Case of Christian Base Communities in Urban Brazil,' in *The Making of Social Movements in Latin America: Identity, Strategy and Democracy*, 1992, 171–184. The entire issue of *Transformation: An International Evangelical Dialogue on Mission and Ethics* 3 (July–September 1986) deals with CEBs. The primary work on ecclesial base communities has been written by Guillermo Cook, *The Expectation of the Poor: Latin American Basic Ecclesial Communities in Protestant Perspective* (Maryknoll, NY: Orbis Books, 1982).

[31]See chapters four and five for a description of various social programmes established by Central American Pentecostals.

[32]The average Assemblies of God congregation, in Central America, not including their *campos blancos*, has a following comprised of members and adherents of less than 100. There are several large churches in the region, with attendances that exceed 1,000, that because of their large facilities and obvious visibility attract considerable attention when observers analyze Pentecostalism. The author, who has been integrally involved with several of these 'mega-churches,' would argue that certain Pentecostals characteristics described in this chapter, particularly those of personal militancy, community and participation, as well as discipline are not nearly as apparent within these churches as they would be within the more numerous smaller groups.

pletion of the building could, and usually does, take several years. In all, the Assemblies of God in Latin America, including Brazil, with an aggregate of 15,782,150 members and adherents, consists of as many as 11,939 organized churches and an additional 98,671 preaching points, totalling at least 110,610 groups.[33]

It would be difficult to overemphasize the importance of property ownership that inheres in these churches. Members submit to the discipline of the group, accept rigid standards of conduct, regularly tithe or otherwise systematically support the programme, exhibit a high degree of loyalty and freely exercise their rights to express themselves regarding policies. Few Latin Americans of the popular levels have such an opportunity for expression and recognition,[34] and having acquired a place in their local groups they hold tenaciously to their benefits.

In contrast to the Pentecostal practice, particularly of pastors, of endeavouring to incorporate new communicants immediately into active participation in society, Juan Luis Segundo, the Uruguayan liberation theologian, critiques the Catholic Church for its resistance to reaching out to the common people. Though written almost 20 years ago, *The Liberation of Theology*, which is a revised amplification of a course he taught at Harvard Divinity School in the Spring semester, 1974, is significant for this study for at least two reasons. First, Segundo's main thesis is that in the historical evolution of the Catholic Church, it became an ideological captive of the social, political, and economic forces supporting the privileged classes of the world, and this fact could be observed most poignantly in Latin America.[35] Particularly significant for this section is his assertion that the pastoral agents of the Catholic church are unwilling and unable to respond positively to the lower classes.[36] Segundo elaborates upon

---

[33]Aggregate statistics taken from the Division of Foreign Missions Annual Statistics for Year Ending 12/31/92.

[34]See socio-economic and educational tables for Central America in chapter 5.

[35]José Míguez Bonino in his classic *Doing Theology in a Revolutionary Situation*, reached a similar conclusion as do the majority of Catholic liberation theologians. For further discussion on the theological underpinnings that certain Catholic tenets, considered to be sacred, provide for the legitimation of social and economical activities of the elites see chapter 4, note 34.

[36]The encouragement for the formation of ecclesial base communities (CEBs) as a strategy to give voice to and include the popular masses in religious life within the Catholic Church has been utilized to combat the marginalization of massive groups of people not only from society but from their church as well.

this resistance in his *Hidden Motives of Pastoral Action*, which provides a stinging critique of the Catholic response to urbanization and the mushrooming class of the urban poor, who are unable to negotiate the literacy-centred communication system of the bustling cities. As a consequence, the move to the cities by rural peasants means that the cities are surrounded by homeless squatters with no hope of becoming assimilated into an urban way of life. The hidden motive behind the church's pastoral inaction to help the poor in their dire straits, Segundo charged, is the recognition that the church by spiritualizing the meaning of life can keep the poor 'in the fold'. The poor would continue participating in the sacraments and the traditional church liturgy because they provided the only touchstone they had with the reality of their rural roots.[37]

Pentecostal church life and pastoral practice in these marginal *barrios* functions in striking contrast to the church described by Segundo. The following story is familiar:

I came to San José from Guanacaste [province in Costa Rica] with hopes of making a better life for myself and my family. I had saved a little bit of money with hopes that it would last until I could find work. Unfortunately, I could not read or write. It was not long before my savings were gone and we were forced to move into *Los Guido* [one of the *tugurios*—city slum dwelling on the outskirts of the city]. Our home was made up of cardboard and zinc. During the rains our 'house' would fill up to our ankles with water. I could find work only as a *peón* (day labourer) and there was seldom adequate money to buy food for my family much less clothes or the opportunity to buy school uniforms or school supplies for our children. Our situation was desperate.

One evening as I left our little shack I heard singing from a small church—a building with just a dirt floor, roof and a lean-to type wall on one side and the other sides of the building were open to the air—that had just begun to hold services in this community. Out of interest I entered the service. I enjoyed the testimonies and especially the music. After the service was over the pastor, as well as several other people, came to greet me. The following day the pastor came to our house and told us about how the Lord could change our lives. He told us that his church was opening a school and all the children in the community would be able to attend.

---

[37]Juan Luis Segundo, *The Hidden Motives of Pastoral Action: Latin American Reflections*, trans. John Drury (Maryknoll, NY: Orbis Books, 1978).

I felt drawn in my spirit to this small group of people that showed such joy and compassion. The Lord has changed my life and now I am grateful that I have opportunity to be a part of this church.[38]

Sociologist Emilio Willems has pointed out that local organizations are familiar to traditional Latin Americans. Arrangements for reciprocal labour, for example, are widespread in Brazil and elsewhere.[39] Moreover, with the breakup of the patron-client relationship of the traditional hacienda (plantation) and the breakdown of the extended family, some observers have porported to find large numbers of Latin Americans vulnerable to Pentecostalism because they offer surrogates for the associations they have lost.[40] It is precisely this tendency to group formation that distinguishes Pentecostals from historic Protestant denominations even though in their early origins they may have had similar characteristics to those one finds today in Pentecostal groups.[41]

The church building (*templo*) itself plays an important role in the group's operation. To social elements of the lower and aspiring lower middle sectors, the building provides a location where members find security and recognition. Congregations hold services (*cultos*) virtually every night,[42] creating a literal sanctuary for the entire family as commonly, different age or gender groupings (youth, women, men) assume the responsibilities of a given meeting. Thus, people who may

---

[38]Member of the congregation of *Las Asambleas de Dios de Los Guido*, interview by author, San José, Costa Rica, June 13, 1992. Los Guido is a slum community of approximately 20,000 people on the outskirts of San José, Costa Rica.

[39]Willems, *Followers of the New Faith*, 28—29.

[40]This concept first put forth by Lalive d'Epinay, *Haven of the Masses*, 178–179 and followed up by several, including most recently, Jean-Pierre Bastian, 'The Metamorphosis of Latin American Groups,' 42.

[41]Wilson, 'Dynamics of Latin American Pentecostalism', 101.

[42]A most insightful and fruitful survey studying Protestantism in El Salvador has been conducted by four professors of the University of North Carolina at Chapel Hill. Their research analyzes the sociological and political implications of Protestantism on a random sample of 1,065 respondents from five different social strata. The survey entitled '*La religión para los salvadoreños*' was taken between June 11 and 26, 1988. Their survey data revealed that Protestants attend church on an average of 9.3 times a month, twice as frequently as practising Catholics, and that an amazing 12.6 per cent attend daily. Further, congregational intimacy enjoyed by Pentecostals was supported by the findings from the survey that showed that 77 per cent of all Pentecostal followers had received a pastoral visit in their home by contrast with only 28 per cent of practising Catholics who had ever had a priest make a home visit. See Edwin Eloy Aguilar, et. al., 'Protestantism in El Salvador: Conventional Wisdom versus Survey Evidence,' *Latin American Research Review* 28 (1993): 127–128.

have little hope of owning real estate contribute to the purchase and maintenance of a substantial material asset. The emotional support of a Pentecostal congregation consequently goes beyond the fervour of an expressive religious service. It is grounded in the ownership of property and the conferred status of membership.

Such benefits also impose demands on the membership. While lower-class Pentecostals may enjoy a number of benefits generally not available to their non-Pentecostal counterparts, they also assume responsibilities which the latter may be reluctant to accept. Thus membership in a congregation may differ substantially from other kinds of voluntary organizations which, presumably, could provide the same advantages to their members.

EXPERIENCE AND WORSHIP

Pentecostals are further differentiated from other groupings by their encouragement of expressiveness. While at times this feature may appear to non-Pentecostals as irreverence and uninhibited emotionalism, for the participants the experience provides a profound sense of personal confirmation. Beyond simply endorsing such doctrines as Spirit baptism and the exercise of tongues, Pentecostal groups encourage lay individuals' participation in the same kinds of peak experiences as their pastoral leadership.[43] The pastor encourages the new convert to take a first step into spiritual blessing by experiencing the baptism of the Holy Spirit. Such an experience will result, one is told by the pastor or other church leader, in victory over sin and complete transformation of life. This unique experience in one's life is convincing evidence that one has had a real and direct contact with God. Such a peak experience is expected to affect the seeker profoundly. Those 'tarrying' for the experience are taught that old habits and vices will be purged away, a new enthusiasm will permeate their testimony, and they will be uniquely empowered to witness to others the reality of God's saving grace. The power of the baptism of the Holy Spirit is to be demonstrated in all of their actions.[44] The experience has happened personally

---

[43]Wilson, 'Dynamics of Latin American Pentecostalism', 102.

[44]Eugene Stockwell is undeniably correct when he writes that the 'baptism of the Spirit' focuses on individual experience. However, it is a mistake to understand the experience, as Stockwell does, as exclusively individual and that 'community and collective experience is generally omitted from important consideration'. The Pentecostal experience regularly takes place within the structure of the community. Eugene Stockwell, 'Editorial: Responses to the Spirit; pt. 2: Charismatics,' *International Review of Mission* 75 (April 1986): 114.

to the seekers and they will know what they are speaking about. They must become participants. Pentecostals have no hesitation in taking part in and expounding upon an experience that sounds confusing and mystical to the outsider.

Analyses of Latin American Pentecostalism that focus on descriptive rather than dynamic features may fail to appreciate the importance this personal experience has for one's self-esteem, motivation and moral strength. A decisive break with one's past, especially if the subject's personal history is remembered in negative terms,[45] provides the incentive for personal discipline and the motivation to rise above the frustrations and discouragements that have destroyed constructive action. Moreover, the renewal of periodic climactic experiences ensures the prolongation of such benefits.

Typically in the format of the *culto*[46] in most Pentecostal churches there is a time when believers are invited to the front of the church where they wait on the Lord for a supernatural enduement of power. Additionally each month a Friday night is selected for an all-night prayer service known as a *vigilia*. But most importantly the believer is encouraged to experience the reality of the baptism of the Holy Spirit (with speaking in tongues) on a daily basis during the personal devotional time of reading the Bible and prayer.[47] The believer is encouraged to experience baptism in the Holy Spirit,

---

[45]David Wilkerson, noted for his work among drug addicts in New York and the establishment of Teen Challenge centres throughout the United States and in many parts of the world, strongly believed that unless a drug addict who had converted received the baptism of the Holy Spirit, he or she would have little hope of recovery from drug addiction. According to Wilkerson, 75 per cent of all converted and recovered drug addicts had received the experience. See David Wilkerson, *The Cross and the Switchblade* (New York, NY: Dell Publishing Co., 1958) or in Spanish *La cruz y el puñal* (Miami, Florida: Editorial Vida, 1976).

[46]The Pentecostal *culto* in Central America is an assembly of believers that almost invariably includes a time of singing and worship, testimony sharing, the preaching of the Word, and an invitation for conversion followed by a corporate time of prayer for healing or some other supernatural intervention for the personal or collective needs of the assembly.

[47]Although the subject is outside the parameters of this book, there is a new tendency in Pentecostal movements in Latin America to escalate the emotional experience such as 'falling under the Spirit', sometimes in a mass experience and 'being drunk in the Spirit', actions that in one sense are similar to past spiritual ecstasies but in another sense are really very different. Though the difference is not always apparent to the outside observer of Pentecostalism, for the insider these new experiences appear to be similar to current practices of certain North American televangelists. The desire or need for emotional satisfaction by Latin American Pentecostals who participate in these exhibitions could become destructive. Professor Quentin J. Schultze aptly notes that this type of ministry influenced by certain North American televangelists may 'transform worship into

not only in an initial peak experience but on a sustained basis
through times of prayer in corporate worship, daily devotionals,
Bible reading and personal prayer.

A number of observers of Latin American Pentecostalism have
identified music as an important catalyst for the experiences men-
tioned above.[48] The greater freedom Pentecostals have given to use
of popular instruments permits ready adaptation of familiar musical
styles to worship. This appropriation, an essential aspect of Pentecostalism, has facilitated Latins' natural cultural expression in music
and has been a vehicle for the movement's growth. While other
Christian groups typically curtailed the use of certain popular
instruments such as drums and tambourines, Pentecostal freedom
of expressiveness not only permitted their use, but readily composed
or adapted tunes whose singing conformed to the rhythms and
phrasing based on these instruments. Similarly, while established
churches continued to use organs, pianos and the classical musical
structures utilizing the more traditional instruments, Pentecostals
unashamedly utilized the acoustical and electronically amplified
instruments used by performers of popular music. The electronic
keyboard or synthesizer has thus emerged as the standard musical
instrument of Pentecostal groups, if not yet for all Protestants.[49]

Music goes beyond merely facilitating expression. The repetitive
use of phrases and expressions present themes that are essential to
Pentecostal beliefs and practices. Analysis of these songs and choruses
(*coritos*) especially points up the frequency with which they confirm
self-worth, the adequacy of divine grace and the accessibility of divine
power.[50] Although this music, often loud, prolonged, vigorous and
repetitive, may appear to be largely spontaneous, excessive emotional
displays and individual expressions that cannot be appreciated by the

---

(*footnote 47 continued*)
entertainment and turn congregations into audiences'. Quentin J. Schultze, 'TV Religion
as Pagan-American Missions', in *Transformation: An International Evangelical Dialogue on
Mission and Ethics* 9 (October/December 1992): 2. The style of Pentecostalism described
in this note is a brand quite different from the indigenous Pentecostalism being described
in this thesis.

[48] Wilson, 'Dynamics of Latin American Pentecostalism', 103.

[49] Though such musical artifacts have been characteristically utilized in Pentecostal groups
for many years, within recent years such musical practices can also be seen in some more
traditional congregations.

[50] Many songs composed by El Salvadorans in the 1940s found in *Himnos inspirados selectos*
demonstrate the above.

group are usually restricted in public services. Outbursts that are unusual (even for Pentecostals) may, however, be tolerated in special settings like retreats or other intimate meetings where emotional extremes are not especially disruptive. According to a writer familiar with Latin American Pentecostal practices, persons who have 'tasted' such experiences may have such an integrating sense of their own spiritual self that they are not likely to be satisfied thereafter by more formalistic, liturgical or stylized expressions. In practice, Pentecostals tend to find a level of emotion consistent with their own experience and expectations.[51]

HEALINGS, MIRACLES AND DIVINE INTERVENTION

Stereotypes of Pentecostals as 'otherworldly,' pathological or fanatical also obscure an important 'feature' of the movement's strength. Practicality and effectiveness are characteristic of these Pentecostal groups, who appear pragmatic more often than mystical or passively withdrawn. Tangible indications of power, consequently, figure largely in their beliefs and practices. Healings, the resolution of unpleasant circumstances, the availability of employment or resources may all be taken as indications of divine favour, or sometimes simply provide the inner strength to endure difficulties.

These attitudes and values, of course, are not unlike those frequently found in Latin American popular culture, where nonscientific cures and magical powers are common-place. Distinctions between the living and the dead, generally pronounced in North American culture where death represents finality, are less absolute in Latin American belief systems. Inner resources and acceptance of the reality of the transcendent have traditionally been a recourse of Latin Americans who have resorted frequently to *curanderos*, spiritualist mediums and African religious traditions for emotional support.[52]

---

[51] Wilson, 'Dynamics of Latin American Pentecostalism', 102.

[52] Among the numerous writings dealing with popular religions in Latin America we single out Roger Bastide, *The African Religions of Brazil* (Baltimore, MD: John Hopkins University Press, 1970) and more recently Diana D. Brown, *Umbanda: Religion and Politics in Urban Brazil* (Ann Arbor, MI: University Microfilms International Press, 1986); Lawrence Eugene Sullivan, *Ichanchu's drum: an orientation to meaning in South American religions* (New York, NY: Macmillan Publishing Co., 1988), as well as Rowan Ireland, *Kingdoms Come*, (1991). Though focusing on South America and particularly Brazil, these works help the reader understand the constructs of religious life and culture far beyond Brazil's borders.

The rapid spread of religious alternatives among the Latin American popular groups must be viewed in the context of social upheaval. According to Everett A. Wilson, 'In a culture that draws simultaneously from modern, rationalized economic and political concepts and from traditional African, medieval Christian, and indigenous notions of the spirit world, millions of people have turned to Pentecostalism.'[53] These new followers of Pentecostalism have not converted in order to withdraw from their reality or to escape into a mystical world, but rather to recreate their world into an acceptable social existence. While Pentecostalism was initially introduced in Latin America by North Americans and Europeans, it was immediately appropriated by Latin Americans without the taint of foreignness. The spiritual benefits of the beliefs and practices found application in the lives of deprived, aspiring persons who found the teachings appropriate to their desire for control of their lives. The continuing growth of the movement simply testifies to its cultural relevance to large numbers of the Latin American poor.

The concern of Latin American Pentecostals is primarily with forms of personal power. Although the desire for control of their lives may be expressed in other ways, including political expression, concern with physical healing and similar personal and immediate exercise of power has been a reason to which the growth of the movement has been frequently attributed.

MIRACLES OF HEALING

The deterioration of public health care throughout the Latin American continent has left millions of people without any

---

[53]Everett A. Wilson, 'Dynamics of Latin American Pentecostalism', 103. There is considerable research on the similarities of Pentecostal movements with indigenous folk religions. Specifically, the common beliefs shared between the two which are usually identified, are an embracing of a spirit world, acceptance of the supernatural and mysticism and an overt expression of emotionalism. In Central America, the research of Luis E. Samandú has led him to assert that Pentecostalism is a restoration of some of 'the profound roots in the popular culture' such as 'demons, spirits, revelations, and divine cures'. Luis E. Samandú, 'El pentecostalismo en Nicaragua y sus raíces religiosas populares,' *Pasos* 17 (May–June, 1988): 1–10. Bastian goes even further when he suggests that there are grounds to consider Pentecostalism as a 'syncretic religious movement.' Bastian, 'Latin American Protestant groups,' 45, 53. For a similar notion see also Ireland, *Kingdoms Come*, especially chapter eight. However, it should be abundantly clear that these same Pentecostal characteristics demonstrated by Latin Americans are also all found and practised within the New Testament church. For Pentecostals the Bible serves as the authority upon which the validity of all spiritual experiential practices must be based.

possibility of receiving medical care. Sickness in the new economic models becomes an everyday experience for large sectors of the population. Healings and other putative demonstrations of divine favour in such a context are taken at face value. Latin American Pentecostals make little distinction between God's providence and sovereignty and his acts of healing or miracles. The consequences of such confidence in immediate access to divine power, for whatever reason, are easily extended to every area of life. Identification with a group that verifies such occurrences becomes the basis for recognition of God's empowerment. There is a new sense of personal worth and access to the group's collective tangible and intangible resources. Belief that circumstances can be altered by prayer and divine intervention gives personal confidence often lacking in traditional culture which is considered generally to be inclined to fatalism. A Pentecostal worldview that does not make a division between miracles of providence, natural healing and supernatural, forms an important plank in the base for the euphoric confidence that sustains Pentecostals.[54]

A testimony distributed by the *Programa integral de educación de las Asambleas de Dios (PIEDAD)* illustrates the acceptance of God's actions very clearly:

> Joseph Poveda Céspedes is an elementary student enrolled in the *Escuela Cristiana de las Asambleas de Dios* in Torremolinos [a suburb-slum area in San José, Costa Rica]. Joseph was diagnosed with a serious bone problem, particularly in his spine and hip. This illness forced Joseph to have a childhood different from other children his age—he could not run, jump or play with his classmates. Joseph's health steadily worsened. By doctor's orders he was completely immobilized in a body cast for 90 long days to avoid fractures and to enable the painful medical treatment to be successful.
>
> When the doctors did everything humanly possible to make Joseph a normal child the entire *Escuela Cristiana* united together to make

---

[54]Nida underscores the relevance that divine healing has in Latin America given the people's 'preoccupation with psychosomatic disease, especially the "evil eye" and the *susto* "fright" or "shock" '. Nida, 'The Indigenous Churches in Latin America,' 102. The evil eye (*mal de ojo*), resulting from superstition, is thought to be an illness that adults indirectly can give to children. It causes fever and nausea in the child. It is popularly believed to be cured through wrapping the child in the clothing of the person who gave the child the 'eye'.

something supernatural possible. The teachers and students, especially his classmates, began to pray for a miracle. Simultaneously something was happening in the lives of Joseph's parents because they had never seen such love demonstrated towards their family and their son. So many teachers and students came to their home to see Joseph and pray with him that before long they were converted at the same church that was such a church of prayer, praise and hope for Joseph.

In spite of the prayers and the preaching of the Word of God that Joseph received he still required difficult operations, that far from weakening his faith, strengthened his confidence that God, in his time, would perform a miracle in his bones. Everything had a purpose because his parents and other members of his family were converted; the time clock of God worked perfectly and God was miraculously glorified. Joseph is now completely healed! Today Joseph is doing well in his studies and his teacher, Carmen Lía Pérez, confirms that Joseph is running and jumping and glorifying God together with his parents who attend the church located beside the *Escuela Cristiana*.[55]

Though it would appear from the evidence available that Joseph was healed through successful medical treatment, it is apparent that Pentecostals are unconcerned with the method. God is the one who is actively in charge of all events. However, as with the 'miracle' of Joseph, Pentecostals are fortified by the experience of a documented healing, although the documentation for them would not be a critical factor. The healing of Sara Rodríguez, though far more dramatic, provides similar joy to the miracle with Joseph.

Sara was a third-grade student who had become ill while attending the *Escuela Cristiana de los Cuadros* (a marginal housing community in Costa Rica). Her teacher noticed that each week Sara was becoming a little sicker until the child was unable to attend school. The teacher suggested to Sara's mother that she be taken to the *Hospital de Niños* for a medical examination. The X-rays showed that Sara had been infected with a parasite in her liver and already the liver had abscessed to the point where a portion of the liver had been destroyed. The doctor declared that there was little medically possible that could be done. Sara would undoubtedly die.

---

[55]'Joseph es sanado de sus huesos,' *Noti-PIEDAD: Un Noticiero de las Escuelas de las Asambleas de Dios* (setiembre 1993). Hollenweger also notes that prayer for healing and available medical help work hand in hand for many Latin American Pentecostals. Hollenweger, 'The Religion of the Poor,' 330.

Several weeks passed and Sara's condition subsequently deterio-
rated. After several stays in the hospital, the doctor suggested that
the mother take her home so she could die peacefully in the familiar
surroundings of her own house, comforted by the care of her family.
The *Escuela Cristiana* at Los Cuadros immediately upon hearing of
the seriousness of Sara's condition began to pray for a miracle of
healing. Sara had been taught at the *Asambleas de Dios* school that
because she had been created in the image of God she was God's
child and therefore had dignity and worth.[56] Furthermore, her
teachers had instructed her that God loved all those he had created
so much that he would perform miracles for his children. Sara
wanted a miracle for herself and announced to her mother, 'I'm
not going to die because "*Dios me va a sanar*" (God is going to heal
me)'. Within days the child improved. Her mother returned with
Sara for further medical examinations and X-rays. The X-rays, in
contrast to those taken earlier, clearly indicated that Sara's liver was
completely normal. In 1992 Sara was a healthy child and was still
attending the *Escuela Cristiana*. Because of the miracle of healing
Sara's mother was converted and is a member of the Assemblies of
God church located beside the *Escuela Cristiana*.[57]

The verifiable healing of Sara Rodríguez provides a dramatic
depiction of a miracle that serves to undergird and sustain a family
as well as an entire group of Pentecostal believers. This testimony
gives insight into the ethos of the experience of supernatural healing
and makes the connections between miracle, conversion and
church belief imminently clear.

SUPERNATURAL INTERVENTIONS

Pentecostals regularly share with each other the concerns of life in
their meetings and look to supernatural intervention to resolve
seemingly impossible problems. The day-to-day health, financial,
relational and morale needs become the objects of prayer and, when
they are satisfactorily resolved, the subjects of testimonies that
attribute any improvement to divine intervention. Such focus on
the individual's needs and the support, sympathy and approval
they may invoke appear to function in a manner which gives a

---

[56]The concept of the *Imago dei* and its importance to the pedagogical approach of the
Escuelas Cristianas will be presented in chapter 5.
[57]Carmela Rodríguez, mother of Sara, and Rev. Carlos Bermudez, Sara's pastor, interview
by author, September 25, 1990.

psychologically verifiable response that enables the individual to perform well because of the sense of support and approval.

The rapid spread of Pentecostalism in Latin American popular culture quite obviously has much to do with its relevance to the aspirations and frustrations of the adherents. Rather than viewing the movement as the result of foreign-induced proselytism, it should be recognized as a grassroots organization which has arisen in response to the unsatisfied demands of the common people for a more secure, fulfilled existence. Beyond their own desires, Latin American popular groups are usually concerned with providing greater opportunities for their children than they have experienced. In these senses, Pentecostalism cannot be separated from the popular urge for power.

PENTECOSTAL REACTION WHEN GOD DOES NOT RESPOND MIRACULOUSLY

That Pentecostals claim to experience the power of the miraculous in almost every aspect of their daily life is obvious. However, Pentecostals, though anticipating the miraculous, interpret theologically the silence of God when he chooses not to intervene as his right to sovereignty. There are countless times when God does not miraculously heal, the ardent prayer is not answered and God is silent. Dramatic illustrations of the inactivity of God in response to prayers for miraculous interventions can be seen in the reaction of evangelical Pentecostals in Peru to the terrorist activities of the Maoist-guerrilla group 'The Shining Path' (*Sendero Luminoso*). The goal of the *Sendero Luminoso* is to intimidate and terrorize the civilian population through sabotage, kidnappings, bombings and murder. The terrorists will often enter a village to kill all of the men who refuse to follow them, burn the houses and the crops, leaving the women and children to starve to death. Evangelical pastors and lay people have been specific targets for the *Sendero Luminoso*. Pastor Lucas Muñoz, a former Superintendent of the *Asambleas de Dios* in Peru, explains the personal attacks upon Pentecostals as a consequence of their faith. 'You must understand that these groups [*Sendero Luminoso*] are atheists and very militant in their beliefs. We have found that they are antagonistic towards the *Asambleas de Dios* because we continue to testify of Jesus Christ and we are simply not afraid to die.'[58] The testimony of Pastor Elizabeth López from Tingo

---

[58]Video tape with Lucas Muñoz, *The Church Goes On* (Peru: Mandate Magazine 1991).

María, Peru demonstrates the faith that Peruvian Pentecostals exhibit in the midst of the persecution.

> On a Saturday night at about 9:00PM we had between 600–800 people in the church for the evening service. The service was just concluding when the *Sendero Luminoso* came and threw sticks of dynamite into the church. After the explosion there were more than 300 people hurt. . . . The truth is it was difficult to go back [to church] wondering if it would happen again and if it did would I live through it. But I went back because I knew the Lord wanted me there.[59]

The Peruvian pastors and lay people are given a simple choice by the terrorists. They must either deny their faith in Jesus Christ or suffer the consequences. Pastor Isaac Díaz defied the warnings of the Sendero Luminoso to cease his preaching. One Sunday they came and found him preaching. They told him, 'You have not obeyed us, now you are going to die.' Pastor Díaz responded that he preferred to die and be with Christ rather than to stop preaching. Without a struggle or a fight they took him outside the building, the congregation knelt to pray and Pastor Díaz was shot down and killed in the street.[60]

The stories abound, some of miraculous divine intervention, but many others of God's apparent silence. Since 1980 more than 945 pastors and lay people of the *Asambleas de Dios* have died for the sake of the gospel. In that same time period of intense persecution, the *Asambleas de Dios* has more than doubled its membership.[61]

Pentecostals have understood that God's non-intervention in response to their prayers is also an opportunity to testify to the faithfulness of God in their lives despite all opposition. Pentecostal Christians regularly testify, 'How can I deny the Lord who has bought me with his blood?' It is evident that the persecution suffered by Pentecostals has not hindered their growth. Such persecution may well be a significant impetus for authentic evangelism and radical conversion because of the high cost of active discipleship.

Although the failure of Pentecostals sometimes to receive a

---

[59]Ibid.

[60]Ibid.

[61]In 1980 the *Asambleas de Peru* reported 102,000 members and adherents while in 1992 they had an aggregate membership of 204,750.

desired answer to their prayers (for healing, employment, the resolution of conflicts, for example) may appear as a major problem, with accompanying disappointment not unlike unfulfilled prophecies of a personal nature, the Pentecostal is not simply manipulating the deity, he or she is maintaining a dialogue which may progress even without concrete results to one's prayers.

While such beliefs and practices of putative healings and miracles require a great deal more interpretation than they have received, there is little reason to doubt the sincerity of such testimonies or their wide-ranging effects. The theme of power, belief in one's access to power, allegations of supernatural intervention and the fear of others' power are all part of the emotional and cultural life of Latin Americans. Far from offering alternative, 'nonscientific,' explanations of natural and social phenomena to Latin Americans, Pentecostals simply use the idiom to which most Latin Americans are accustomed. Pentecostalism, it might be said, is not effective because it introduces such considerations, but rather because it addresses the real-life historical situation with an effective power.

HOLINESS

While many of the community needs of Pentecostal adherents may possibly be satisfied in other ways, Pentecostalism (as well as some other religious groups) is distinguished by its moralism. According to Bryan Roberts, who studied the evangelical churches of Guatemala City, these groups 'are effective social communities [that] stress the importance of their moral code; offenders are disciplined.'[62] Roberts observed similarly that 'As they see it, a person's Christian quality . . . is certified by changes which occur in his moral life, rather than by his doctrinal loyalties.'[63] The Pentecostal view of reality, invested as it is with a pervasive sense of the sacred, imposes moral sanctions on its adherents. Rather rigid rules of conduct tend to separate adherents from the easygoing, permissive attitude toward marital infidelity, gambling, excessive drinking and misrepresentation found often in Latin American culture. Given the somewhat democratic features of the Pentecostal groups' organization, however, these sanctions are largely reduced to peer pressure,

---

[62]Bryan Roberts, 'Protestant Groups and Coping with Urban Life in Guatemala City,' 765.
[63]Ibid., 767.

threat of expulsion and are necessarily internalized by most of the membership.

Pentecostals must necessarily find mechanisms for restoring members who have lapsed.[64] In fact, while each congregation may appear to be a largely undifferentiated group adhering to similar standards, members themselves are viewed as being spiritually mature or immature, committed or superficial. After an initial declaration of commitment (usually evidenced by a change of attitude or lifestyle), the convert may progressively be permitted or encouraged to fulfil functions within the church programme. Depending on demonstrated integrity, perseverance and transparency of motive, the person may gradually be recognized as a leader, with corresponding respect within the group. Persons who fail in various ways to show such commitment, may find a measure of acceptance, but will find only commensurate confidence among their peers.

While these standards of conduct often appear to be arbitrarily defined, they are hardly out of character with the purposes of the group. In large measure they are features of traditional Latin American popular culture that are respected and even venerated. Consequently, the undistinguished member of the greater community who asserts oneself by assuming a disciplined personal life, may be highly respected, even by persons who dislike the implied criticism of contrary conduct. Honesty, loyalty, reliability and compassion, for example, are respected ideally by virtually everyone even when they are not practised. Thus, Pentecostals, in large part found among the popular groups, often find an ambiguous acceptance in Latin American life. In contrast with past decades, being an evangelical in Latin America now often brings as many benefits as liabilities.

In spite of the Pentecostals' emphasis upon corrective discipline some observers have correctly detected a 'revolving door process' among certain Pentecostals.[65] It should be noted that growth is based on net rather than absolute increases. Undoubtedly many

---

[64]The purpose of discipline, according to the *Reglamento local*, is, on one hand, to correct and restore the member that has violated the code of behaviour and, on the other hand, to maintain and protect the testimony of the other members and the local congregation. A detailed process of the manner in which the rules of discipline are to be applied can be found, in brief, in the *Reglamento local*.

[65]Roger S. Greenway, 'Protestant Missionary Activity in Latin America', 175–204.

initial converts have lapsed or have failed to go beyond an initial statement of faith and, accordingly, remain marginal within the congregation. The rather robust growth of many congregations suggests that the life of the church is probably best measured by the proportion of highly committed individuals to the size of the group rather than by the proportion of neophytes whose faith fails to develop in keeping with the groups' beliefs.

ESCHATOLOGY

An attempt to understand Pentecostal practice doctrinally is particularly open to misunderstanding in the area of eschatology. Doctrinal categories that do not take into account the dynamics of Pentecostal experience and real life will inevitably be misunderstood in the function they play. Theology comes into play as a rationale for the experience, but it is not so intrinsically connected with the experience itself. The teaching of eschatology in Pentecostal churches vividly demonstrates this reality. Latin American Pentecostals have traditionally taught a premillennenial eschatology that in more fundamentalist congregations would place great import on the future and have little to say about the present.[66] Juan Sepúlveda observes that it is precisely the penchant that scholars have, in their study of Pentecostalism, to place emphasis solely on doctrine, without observing practice, which creates 'the impression that Pentecostalism proposes an otherworldly salvation,' when often quite the contrary is the case.[67] Similarly, sociologist Andrés Opazo Bernales, assumes that because the Pentecostal churches have a fervent, apocalyptic message they 'naturally do not take interest in earthly things,' the typical observation given by most appraisers of the movement.[68] NACLA, a journal reporting on Latin American affairs, demonstrated this same misunderstanding when it categorized Pentecostals as merely a church of 'hallelujahs' which systematically ignored the real and physical poverty of Latin America's marginalized masses. They

---

[66]For a discussion of James Darby and the influence of dispensationalism upon Pentecostalism see notes 37 and 38 in chapter 1.
[67]Juan Sepúlveda, 'Reflections on the Pentecostal Contribution to the Mission of the Church in Latin America,' *The Journal of Pentecostal Theology* 1 (October 1992): 101–102.
[68]Andrés Opazo Bernales, 'El Movimiento Protestante en Centroamérica: Una Aproximación Cuantitativa,' in *Protestantismo y Procesos Sociales en Centroamérica*, ed. Luis Samandú (San José, Costa Rica: Editorial Universitaria Centroaméricana, 1991): 15.

accused Pentecostals of presenting a message damaging to Latin American life because the message ignored the present and offered only eternal hopes for the future which NACLA categorized as simply 'pie in the sky for the sweet by and by'.[69] Even sympathetic evangelical scholars like Emilio Núñez and William Taylor erroneously assume that 'they [Pentecostals] have not been so concerned with life on this planet; and that is understandable if we remember the socio-economic strata from which most of these believers have come—the lower ranks.'[70]

However, Pentecostals are exceptionally optimistic about both their present and future existence. Their theological conviction that the God who performed mighty works in the New Testament continues to act in miraculous ways through the empowerment of the Holy Spirit provides the great majority of Pentecostal believers with a sense of hope for the present.[71] Certainly they have been uprooted from their social contexts, seen their world view, values and social norms break down—they have been alienated from traditional society.[72] These 'nonpersons' are exceedingly familiar with unnecessary death, illness, unemployment, prejudice, repression, war, perhaps even torture. But it is within this context that they receive the testimony of the Word and are converted. In this context of tragedy it is quite clear that the eschatological certainty of eternal life gives freedom to risk one's present life. The Pentecostals' personal relationship with a caring

---

[69]Deborah Huntington, 'The Prophet Motive,' *NACLA*, 2–11.

[70]Núñez and Taylor, *Crisis in Latin America*, 168.

[71]In the sense that Pentecostals hold to the continuity of God's power from the time of the New Testament through to the present, they cannot be considered to be dispensational. See Gordon Anderson, '*Pentecostal Hermeneutics*,' 21. Professor Gerald Sheppard, 'Pentecostals and the Hermeneutics of Dispensationalism: The Anatomy of an Uneasy Relationship,' in *PNEUMA: The Journal of the Society for Pentecostal Studies* 6 (Fall 1984): 5–33 argues that any Pentecostal effort to embrace a dispensationalism that applies traditional dispensational notions regarding church ecclesiology (strict separation in the literal meaning of biblical texts relating to the church from those applicable to Israel) raises problems for 'the identity of Pentecostals—hermeneutically, sociologically, and politically' (5). Though early Pentecostals gave prominence to the doctrine of eschatology, particularly with an emphasis upon premillennialism, Sheppard agrees, their designation of the Christian church was that of a 'new congregation or church' and the 'repeated naming of Israel' as 'the church of Jehovah' implies terms of continuity common to Reformed Theology but alien to dispensationalism (12). Sheppard provides an historical survey of early Pentecostal theologians who consistently shaped their ecclesiology so as not to adopt a dispensational scheme that would run contrary to their Pentecostal claims.

[72]See discussion on 'anomie'—the result of the breakdown of social norms in chapter 4.

and compassionate God encourages them also to celebrate their experience of transformation in the present within a community of mutual love and respect. A personal identity emerges and the nonperson achieves personhood. Such personal realization could not merely envision the promise of history as something ambiguously encased in the indefinite future to be reached only 'as pie in the sky in the sweet by and by'. Eschatology, with its foreshadowing of the future, could not be absent in its permeation of the present.[73] Pentecostals, who live under the shadow of death, but now with newly found dignity and discovered personhood, do not live their lives only with an eye on heaven but their whole experience is overshadowed by the reality that the eschatological promise of the future has already began to push its way into the present. Clearly, the church is not a waiting room for heaven where the believers are huddled together waiting for the eschatological end.[74] Rather they are interested in appropriating the power of their Pentecostal experience to the fullest possible measure in the present.[75]

Pentecostal congregations, quite unlike a group with a mind only on heavenly things, are often characterized by the way they reach out to the women and children that have been doubly marginalized—first because they are from the ranks of the poor and secondly precisely because they are women and children. Literacy programmes for adults, offered so that believers can read the Bible for themselves, schools for children and adolescents, as well as rehabilitation programmes for alcoholics and drug addicts have been established. If their experience is, on the one hand, intensely

---

[73]See chapter 4, for a description of the meaning of the opposition of the order of the world and the order of the Kingdom—the latter as a model of new life Pentecostals begin to practise in the present. Chapter 6, where the concept of the Kingdom of God is identified as the unifying theme for Pentecostal praxis, will explore how the eschatological certainty of the Kingdom gives contemporary meaning to personal life often threatened by death. The Kingdom provides a pattern for community life that 'anticipates' the future quality of the Kingdom in its consummation.

[74]For a treatment of aspects of Pentecostal social concern see chapters 4 and 5 of this study.

[75]Though the theological concept of the Kingdom of God has not been articulated clearly in Latin American Pentecostal doctrines, the essence of the eschatological tension between the inbreaking of the Kingdom of God in the present reality ('the now') and the consummation of the Kingdom of God in the future ('the not yet') is implicit and certainly discernible in their practices. The concept of the Kingdom of God in the teachings of Jesus as an integral part of Pentecostal theology in Latin America will be developed in chapter six.

personal, spiritual, eternal and mystical, on the other hand, it is unquestionably corporate, practical, and committed to alleviating the pain of real life situations with much-needed compassion.[76]

The demonstration that Pentecostal eschatology is not solely otherworldly is implicitly illustrated in each of the other theological practices that have just been described. Their conversion experience not only prepares them for eternal life but also gives them dignity, worth and personhood in this life. The experience of the baptism of the Holy Spirit is sought after precisely so that the believer may receive empowerment for the present. Such empowerment is utilized in prayer not only for evangelization or healings *in the present* but also for miraculous answers to prayer in the finding of employment, physical protection, and other such physical needs as are represented in the family or in the community. Moral living is an expected characteristic in the present because one wants to be ready at any moment for an eschatological end.

The Pentecostal movements of Latin America have grown differently as well as rapidly. Springing from a variety of situations, the fertile soil of contemporary crisis and change has led to a broad range of movements, including those that reflect the different aspirations of ethnic groups, those built largely on diverse regions of social classes and those that accommodate diverse doctrinal, polity and denominational emphases. Moreover, an important feature of these movements is their capacity for growth, development and change. Considering that all of the groups tend to incorporate the features previously identified, they adjust to them in various ways and continue to adapt to internal and external circumstances and are reaching an advanced stage of development.

THE COMPATIBILITY OF LATIN AMERICAN CULTURE AND PENTECOSTALISM

Despite the various and diverse aspects of the Pentecostal movement, the tendency to adapt theological concepts to actual contexts, besides contributing importantly to the movement's survival and growth, gives the various groups a progressive and dynamic posture that at times appears incongruous with their stated doctrines. While

---

[76]Chapter four specifically treats the social concern of Pentecostals in Central America.

institutional evolution is apparent in many ways, theological contextualization is an interesting aspect of Pentecostal versatility.
Whiles many evangelical groups resisted the use of folk instruments
and musical styles, for example, Pentecostals readily accommodated
these cultural forms, along with contemporary instruments and
styles. If few Pentecostal churches have pianos, to say nothing of
pipe organs, they have readily adopted the electronic keyboard, an
instrument of secular entertainers.

Pentecostals bring specific features and tendencies to developing
cultures which help their movement to find broad acceptance in
Latin American culture. Pentecostalism provides specific outlooks,
values and opportunities for the movements' adherents, including
new opportunities for expression that are regularly denied the poor
and disadvantaged, moral support for standing up to adversity and
claiming one's rightful place in society, adjusting to new economic
conditions in which traditional values are handicaps and the development of a political culture that may increasingly prepare these
alienated elements for participation in national life. Pentecostalism
in these social and secular arenas presents a positive contribution to
the resolution of difficulties for large numbers of Latin Americans.
By developing self-esteem within the impoverished, by providing
them with hope and by arming them with skills applicable to the
larger social system, Pentecostalism, apparently, is enabling them to
take part in the achievement of the larger social struggles for a better
life and a more secure future.[77]

Pentecostal beliefs and states of consciousness translate at least at
times into concrete behaviour. Pentecostal meetings, in which
arousal and inspiration are recurrent, are specifically intended to
influence conduct, notably the realization of the group's values.
Persons with little interest in such motivation are unlikely to remain
within a congregation, while adherents who submit themselves to
constant motivational stimuli are likely to harbour deep commit-
ments to the group's personal rewards for participation in such a
demanding and intimate religious association. Sooner or later the

---

[77]See Pentecostal programmes for empowerment for their people discussed in chapter 4.
In his concluding comments Martin elaborates his basic thesis that Pentecostalism is
explained best as a process of forming 'alternative societies' (285), 'new cells,' an 'enclosed
haven,' a 'fraternity,' a 'social capsule,' (284), 'free social space,' 'local empowerment'
(280), all of which provide a staging area where adherents may prepare to take on the
world. Martin, *Tongues of Fire*, 280–285.

internalization of ideal behaviour and peer expectation will drive the active member into altruistic conduct. The emotional experience of Pentecostals elevates these motivations beyond a sense of simple obligation to impulses influenced by states of consciousness that at least on occasion for many adherents border on the ecstatic. Latin American Pentecostalism, which is sustained in large part by people of marginal social status, appears to draw from these beliefs and experiences in their spiritual sensitivity, aspiration and commitment to producing high levels of selfless, enthusiastic participation in the group's activities.

Chapter 4

Social Expressions of Central American Pentecostalism

PENTECOSTALS AND SOCIAL TRANSFORMATION

Human aspiration for betterment, a legitimate concept in the Western cultural legacy that in Europe and North America has played an important role in social cohesion and development, has often been frustrated in Latin America. Most people have been left to fashion for themselves, within the resources of their own experience, satisfactory responses to insecurity, rejection and injustice, often reverting atavistically to traditional beliefs and organizational structures. It is against this backdrop of betrayal and frustration, in a surge of irrepressible impatience and hope, that Latin American Pentecostalism—sometimes like new wine in old bottles—has appeared.

For the purpose of this study it is important to establish the distinctives between social ethics, social welfare and social action. The term 'theological ethics of social concern' provides the conceptual foundations for a holistic approach to social change and includes all programmes and activities that are instituted in order to minister to the needs of people. The term 'social welfare' will specifically refer to ministries or actions taken that help to alleviate the needs of people. The term 'social action' will specifically refer to ministries or actions taken that are designed to change or reform the basic conditions, structures, or circumstances that are causing the needs. This present chapter will focus on Pentecostal social welfare programmes. The following chapter will focus on community-based social action. Chapter six will develop a social ethic that supports the church's holistic mission, including as a component, reflection upon social engagement through political activity, one option among many expressions of social concern.

It is apparent from their actions that Pentecostals move beyond a simple message of evangelism to an active involvement in alleviating pain and suffering in the physical realm. In a society that systematically denies them access to basic human rights and marginalizes them in huge slums and shantytowns,[1] the Pentecostals, through the impetus of their spiritual experience, have been endowed with a sense of dignity and worth. Such experience, motivated by a personal relationship with the Holy Spirit, works its way out in very practical terms. Their vibrant faith gives them the courage and hope to demand a better existence for themselves. Pentecostal reality is not a passive escape from social responsibility, but on the contrary, the creation of a new existence for the popular masses of Latin America.[2]

José Míguez Bonino has described the social transformation that becomes an actuality for Christian communities when they are driven by what he terms the 'love motif'.[3] This motif can be seen in the power of love in the struggle for social transformation. The vast majority of Latin America's poor and displaced people have experienced alienation— anomie—that leaves them bereft of any meaningful social structure. Míguez Bonino describes 'anomie' as:

> A condition in which the worldview, the values, and norms that gave stability to individual and collective life break down, and people are left without shelter. Self and social identity, social relations, ethical norms are shattered.[4]

---

[1]See Central America's socio-economic tables in chapter five.

[2]It is José Míguez Bonino's opinion that it is wrong to look for statements that Pentecostals have made about their role in society. It is his position that an adequate analysis of the movement must, as a first stage, look at the social makeup of the movement. Pentecostals as yet have not articulated a carefully constructed social doctrine but rather display a social dynamic. Social doctrine has yet to be written. (José Míguez Bonino, Interview with author, Tape recording, Buenos Aires, Argentina, 17 January 1993.)

[3]Míguez Bonino, 'Love and Social Transformation,' 60–65. Though Míguez Bonino is writing this article in the context of base ecclesial communities he has indicated in conversations with the author that such a description is also appropriate for Pentecostal communities. I have relied heavily on Míguez Bonino for this section. (Interview with author, Tape recording, Buenos Aires, 17 January 1993.) Recent studies seem to demonstrate that Pentecostalism has been more effective in its social policy than the base ecclesial communities. See John Burdick, 'Rethinking the Study of Social Movements: The Case of Christian Base Communities in Urban Brazil,' in *The Making of Social Movements*, 171–184; and further that in Brazil the members of the CEBs apparently are affiliating with Pentecostal groups in large numbers. See Guillermo Cook, 'The Evangelical Groundswell in Latin America,' *Christian Century* 12 December 1990, 1175.

[4]Míguez Bonino, 'Love and Social Transformation,' 62. The concept of 'anomie' originates in Emile Durkeim, *Suicide: a study in sociology*, ed. George Simpson. John A. Spaulding & George Simpson (London: Routledge & Kegan Paul, 1952). and is developed by R.K. Merton in his book *Social Theory and Social Structure* (Glencove, IL: Free Press, 1957) in the chapter entitled 'Social Structure and Anomie' and later in Peter Berger and Thomas Luckman, *The Social Construction of Reality: a treatise in the sociology of knowledge* (London: The Penguin Press, 1967).

The antidote for such upheaval, Míguez Bonino asserts, is 'a re-socialization, an adaptation or transformation of the person'.[5] Accordingly, the radical shift in worldview becomes the social and psychological focus of proclamation and evangelism. The 'nonperson', who hears and receives the message of transformation, personally experiences the reality of an intimate relationship with God in his or her life. Converts are immediately thrust into a loving and caring community. Dignity, value, personal worth and identity are collectively celebrated. Míguez Bonino captures the essence of the experience when he writes that 'the center of this transformation is the experience of the community of mutual love and solidarity'.[6] And further, 'the Holy Spirit builds the ekklesia as members of the community come and celebrate together.' How is this salvation that culminates in a radical transformation to self-acceptance and self-love demonstrated to the 'nonperson', Míguez Bonino asks? Not just exclusively by proclamation, he responds, but rather by a message filled with content by the redeemed community—'a content that can be extrapolated and makes the word of free grace intelligible'. There are not two realities but a single event that is significant. The new believer, who receives a spiritual conversion, professes that because he or she has been accepted by God they now belong to the community of love. To be 'in Christ' means not just to have received eternal life, but also to have the privilege to be a participant in a loving and caring community. By being incorporated into such a community, the believer regains dignity and self-acceptance and therefore is made a meaningful participant in a religious movement which is able to create a historical project for society.[7] Míguez Bonino concludes that 'personal/communal process is of paramount importance when we think about the structural process of social transformation'.[8] Because conversion

---

[5]Míguez Bonino, '*Love and Social Transformation*,' 62.
[6]Ibid., 63.
[7]Míguez Bonino defines 'historical project' as a 'midway term between a utopia, a vision which makes no attempt to connect itself historically to the present, and a program, a technically developed model for the organization of society . . . [that] is defined enough to force options in terms of the basic structures of society'. See *Doing Theology in a Revolutionary Situation*, 38–39. The term 'historical project' is an elusive term and this thesis will further pursue a more precise use of the concept in both Pentecostal and liberation theology in chapter 6.
[8]Ibid., 64–65.

culminates in such radical transformation in the individual, the Pentecostal community of redeemed believers, gives a practical expression of their experience by daily exercising their faith in concrete individual and corporate terms. What they have experienced on the religious level they are anxious to demonstrate in the physical realm.

ALLEGATIONS OF PENTECOSTALS' SOCIAL NEGLECT

While it is unquestionably true that until recently Pentecostals have tended to abstain from involvement in political issues, and thus have avoided giving explicit support for a structural change in secular society, it is also true that Pentecostals have been remarkably active in creating a social structure within their own communities that clearly demonstrates their social concern. It is inadequate to think of Pentecostals as conservatives who are either unable or refuse to reflect upon the injustice of the social structures that have marginalized them. The consequence of reflection upon their experiences, their theological convictions about human fallenness and their suspicion of the corrupting influence of consolidated power have filled them with cynicism, however, and they are generally unwilling to give exclusive allegiance to any form of government, whether it be authoritative or democratic.[9] It is an

---

[9]Pentecostals have generally abstained from political action because they considered it to be, at best futile and, at worst, a dirty business. The *Reglamento local* of *las Asambleas de Dios* required every member to sign a *pacto de miembro* (membership agreement) that precluded members from participating in political parties. See *Reglamento local* (32). Pentecostals have seldom been involved in political action because they have felt that there was little hope of success. Their pragmatism, as well as their theology, limits them to certain arenas of action. If there is something they can do, rather than protesting to the government, they do it. Though Pentecostal social concern has traditionally avoided political involvement, in the last five or six years one can witness so many departures from the norm as to force the question as to why these departures are happening and how Pentecostals will understand and respond to this new fact. In recent elections Pentecostal leaders have been active in politics in virtually every Central American country as well as in the South American countries including Colombia, Peru, Chile, Argentina and Brazil. Though any substantial treatment of this phenomenon is in itself a subject for another study, this new Pentecostal political action clearly includes sociological facts related to numerical growth and possible powerful influence. It also raises profound theological questions for analysis. An entire issue of *TRANSFORMATION*, edited by René Padilla, analyzes the motivating elements behind the evangelical-Pentecostal awakening within the political sector and encourages evangelicals to develop a political theology that provides adequate guidelines for future action. *TRANSFORMATION: An International Evangelical Dialogue on Mission and Ethics* 9 (July/Sept. 1992): 1–32.

error, commonly made by observers of the movement, that Pentecostals' actions towards society signify an attitude of indifference in the sense that they are unaware of the injustices in society. Typical of such erroneous positions can be seen in the analysis of Nicaraguan Pentecostals by Abelino Martínez Rocha, a Central American sociologist and researcher.

In Martínez's polemical characterization of Nicaraguan popular Pentecostalism, he describes the difficulties of daily life for Nicaraguans in general and for the Pentecostals in particular. The horrors of war hang like a shadow over the populous, writes Martínez, In addition the economic crisis results in sickness and pain. In tandem with the effects of war, the accompanying social crisis culminates in a personal and collective tension that produces indescribable suffering.[10] How is it, he asks rhetorically, in light of so much suffering that is most evident among the popular sectors of society, that Pentecostals can demonstrate so much indifference towards the social context? This indifference he considers to be religiously sanctioned.[11] He follows with a series of questions:

> Let us then understand a case of religiously sanctioned indifference. Why does Pentecostalism legitimize the social behaviour among popular groups, even in the midst of a social crisis that imposes certain political demands that endeavours to go against such behaviour? How is this Pentecostal behaviour produced and what social significance can it have within a mode of production of popular hegemony that at the same time demands the conformity and consolidation of a revolutionary subject?[12]

Martínez responds to his questions with the explanations that Pentecostal indifference has been caused by the manner in which the Nicaraguan social crisis has been filtered through the popular Pentecostal religious conscience. In Martínez' perspective, this social consciousness can be explained, in part, because popular

---

[10] Abelino Martínez Rocha, 'Comportamientos Sociales en el Protestantismo y en el Pentecostalismo Popular Nicaragüense,' in *Protestantismos y Procesos Sociales en Centroamérica*, 202–203.
[11] Ibid., 205.
[12] Ibid. All translations from Spanish to English are done by the author unless otherwise indicated.

Pentecostals have *no theology*[13] and by a proper understanding of what Martínez refers to as the phenomenon of 'supply, demand and consumption of religious salvific benefits'.[14]

PENTECOSTALS' POLITICAL APPROACH

Martínez' allegations of Pentecostals' indifference dramatically underscore the argument of this section. Pentecostals believe politics and politicians to be rife with corruption and self-interest.[15] They are cynically confident that any effort carried out by politicians on 'their behalf' will usually turn out to be in the best interests of the politicians. Abuse of power is systemic in Latin American society. Mario Diament, an Argentine playwright, graphically describes the deep-rootedness of corruption carried out principally by those who wield power:

> Latin Americans are so immersed in corruption . . . that they have become desensitized to its numerous manifestations. The police officers

[13]Several times Martínez states that popular Pentecostals have *no theology*, Ibid., 210, 213 [emphasis is mine] which, of course, is an oxymoron. However, on several occasions when Martínez presents his evaluation of Pentecostal theology he categorically states that '*Las Asambleas de Dios* has a doctrine that is almost entirely constructed from outside of the Latin American context' (224). Based on these assertions, one can conclude that Martínez believes that it is possible to have 'a doctrine' but have 'no theology,' which is a very confusing notion. What role could doctrine play without some level of critical reflection on its meaning? Without a clear definitional distinction between 'doctrine' and 'theology' from Martínez, the suspicion arises that his pejorative analysis of Pentecostal doctrine/theology serves primarily to support his theory of deprivation.

[14]Ibid., For Martínez the trauma of the social crisis creates a demand for answers to so much suffering. The Pentecostal church, in turn, provides an offer that will temporarily satisfy the demand. The seeker or the 'client' applies the offer to their personal needs in what Martínez describes as consuming. Martínez' analysis of Pentecostalism in Nicaragua appears to be a subjective and simplistic presentation of deprivation theory.

[15]Aguilar's survey data revealed that 70 per cent of all Salvadorans viewed the existing social structure as unjust (130). Perceptions of Protestants regarding the injustice of the social system was not significantly different from the population as a whole. The findings of the survey revealed that Protestants did not see the church playing a productive role in the resolution of such conflicts. The researchers suggested that 'conflict was so endemic to the Salvadoran experience . . . that all Salvadorans found it difficult to imagine human agents who could stop it, even those purporting to serve divine ends'(132). In the survey only 24 per cent of Protestants compared to 42 per cent of Catholics felt comfortable that God willed active church involvement in the restructuring of human society. See Edwin Eloy Aguilar, '*Protestantism in El Salvador*,' 130–135. The Assemblies of God in El Salvador was established at the same time as the historic *matanza* (massacre) that claimed as many as 30,000 lives within a period of only a few days. It is understandable why Pentecostals in Central America have so little confidence in the positive effects of political activity.

who rob or the judges who take bribes are no longer outcasts of the system: they are the system.[16]

Society belongs to the rich. Attempts to bring development for the 'good of the people' by any form of business enterprise, whether by the public or private sector, will, in the minds of the Pentecostals, mean profits only for the rich and such attempts usually leave social structures worse than they were to begin with. Pentecostals' radical distrust of politics and politicians is extended to successful lawyers, military men, police, landowners, priests, politicians and business-men.[17]

While Pentecostals do make scathing critiques of the evil moral structures of society that surround them, traditionally they refuse to get involved politically.[18] Pentecostals clearly see the corruption in society. They have often been exploited by their boss or the large landowner but as a general principle it is their belief that dishonest people and their corresponding actions must be left to the judgement of the Lord. Pentecostals understand that humankind has been evil since the Fall and will continue in this condition of fallenness until Christ returns. Their theology reinforced by experience teaches pessimism. Further, Pentecostals conclude, any attempt on the part of the poor to challenge the structure will inevitably end in disaster. There is little utopian hope for society in this world among them. The work and material success of those in the world may be admired by a corrupt society but it will never merit God's favour.

---

[16]Mario Diament, 'Corrupt to the Core,' *Hemisphere* 3 (Summer 1991): 21.

[17]The 1988 survey in El Salvador further demonstrated that any conspiratorial theories that linked Protestants to conservative U.S. elements were also ill-founded. Fewer Protestants than Catholics, according to the survey, believed that the 1989 election of the conservative ARENA party was honest. They were also less likely to vote for the conservative ARENA party than their Catholic counterparts and, unlike a substantial percentage of Catholics (40 per cent) who believed that human rights abuses would decrease under ARENA, Protestants, in lesser numbers (30 per cent), were more pessimistic. The surveyors concluded that Catholics were more closely aligned to the US foreign policy than were Protestants—hardly a position supporting the assumption that Protestants were political allies of conservative politics. Aguilar, *'Protestantism in El Salvador,'* 134–135.

[18]The Pentecostal stance of non-involvement in politics has rapidly changed within the recent past. See note 9. This change in involvement has been triggered largely from the phenomenal numerical growth of Pentecostals which causes them to be viewed as an important voting bloc by politicians. This change in reception will eventually require an explicitly developed Pentecostal social doctrine in order to keep behavioural practice consistent with theological understanding.

A PENTECOSTAL SOCIAL DOCTRINE

If Pentecostals, on the one hand, have refused to align with any secular movements to encourage structural social changes, they do, on the other hand, have aspirations for change in their immediate communities. Pentecostals are perceptive of what can be done to better their own *barrio*.[19] They are willing to serve as mediators between two squabbling neighbours or initiate and organize caring compassionate responses during times of need. When Pentecostals consider themselves able to meet a local challenge and that such action can be done without compromise with sinful activity, they are apparently willing to get involved. Pentecostalism generates such a strong sense of personal responsibility for bringing meaningful change in their local and church community that it is understandable that they would not look to government agencies, which they do not trust, to improve their social conditions. Questions of social structure and change are handled on the local level. Consequently, Pentecostals, through their participation in a church community, create an alternative society enabling them to make life more tolerable but they refuse to identify this substitute society with active protest against the larger recognized injustices of society.[20] Several observers have remarked that 'Pentecostals do not have a social policy, they are a social policy'.[21]

There appears to be a dialectic between religious beliefs on the one hand and political voice and behaviour on the other. The Pentecostal gains freedom and dignity initially by having a radically personal spiritual experience. When the poor understand what God has done and what he requires of them they are free and ready to participate in their own destiny. In their perception, though often not consciously, there are two orders—the Kingdom which is to come when God will consummate all things and the present material order, filled with greed, avarice, selfishness and evil. When the Pentecostals are assertive and organize their community into a tolerable and even happy existence they are speaking and acting

---

[19]See chapter 5, and chapter 6.
[20]Rowan Ireland, *Kingdoms Come*, 222.
[21]This remark, attributed to Everett A. Wilson, is cited in Jeffrey Gros, 'Confessing the Apostolic Faith from the Perspective of the Pentecostal Churches,' *PNEUMA: The Journal of the Society for Pentecostal Studies* 9 (Spring 1987): 12.

politically in a way that is motivated by their theological convictions.[22]

In societies where one has difficulty finding identity and security, Pentecostal groups offer alternative survival mechanisms, precisely because they distribute risks and opportunities. Contrary to the traditional critique that Pentecostals do not adequately demonstrate a social conscience, typically congregations provide social welfare services to needy families, the sick, the abused and the aged. If general assistance is limited, it nevertheless provides members with some minimal social guarantees of which they would be otherwise deprived. In addition, the Pentecostal community provides adult role models and surrogate parents for children. Dealing with the routine business of the congregation and the needy occupies a considerable amount of organization, activity and the development and exercise of the members' skills. In churches where vision exists, the members often attain extraordinary levels of cooperation and reliability. Planning, projection of programmes, decision-making, allocation of resources, i.e., many roles appropriate to associational life, are part of the members' participation in a Pentecostal community.

If these roles are not altogether different from those of the local Catholic parish, the system is much less dependent on tradition. While ascription remains determinative in most Latin American social situations, in Pentecostal churches, where persons of humble social status predominate, achievement is the rule. Not only does this policy permit persons of little standing to find social opportunity, but it permits the full use of everyone's talents and energies. Five specific areas can be described and analyzed where Pentecostals

---

[22]Ireland, *Kingdoms Come*, 5. An important feature of organization is the acquisition of legal recognition in the form of *personería jurídica*. Threatened with reprisals or discrimination, the members of a legally recognized congregation may assert their legitimacy even while they remain a small minority in the community. While Pentecostals may be viewed as tools of reactionary political regimes, in fact their sometimes enthusiastic support for conservative governments is largely a matter of recognizing the state as the agency that guarantees their legitimacy and their right to an independent existence. More frequently, as has also been repeatedly observed with concern, Pentecostals appear simply to withdraw from political participation in their efforts to remain independent. In Brazil, where Pentecostals command a significant constituency, they have asserted themselves politically, not necessarily, however, as clients of specific parties. Francisco Rolim argues that Pentecostals (in Brazil) ran for political office in hopes of getting the government to concede favours and to respond to their demands. *Pentecostals in Brazil*, 146. Also see Bastian, 'Metamorphosis,' 50.

demonstrate actions of social consciousness resulting in significant social concern.

PENTECOSTAL LEADERSHIP AND SOCIAL CHANGE

While one may question whether skills and roles learned in the context of the congregation may easily apply to other areas of life, there is undoubtedly some transfer. Apart from the occasional individual who had become involved in some political or administrative function in the larger community in the past, the church community provides a social recognition that draws individuals into new opportunities.[23] The approval of the larger community, even if conceded reluctantly in the form of respect for persons with strong convictions, places the members of the Pentecostal church on a platform not generally available to unaffiliated Latin Americans. Pentecostals, it has been argued, have essentially created their own separate community, not for the purpose of remaining aloof, but in order to establish for themselves a staging area from which they might more effectively operate.

Converts to Pentecostal churches typically find themselves involved in a great deal of structured activity. Beyond the opportunity for expression, neophytes have demands imposed upon them that not only affect their time and resources, but strongly encourage the development of communication and organizational skills. Recognition of one's leadership and other contributions to the survival and growth of the congregation become circular, as all members are encouraged to invest increasingly in the 'work' (*la obra*) and assume still greater responsibility for its development. Leadership, at all levels, is encouraged by an informal apprenticeship programme. Immediately upon conversion the new believers, regardless of social class or economic standing, are given something to do. Responsibility for the cleaning of the *templo*, ushering or leading the song service along with street and personal evangelism are tasks that are assumed will be carried out by all. The apprenticeship system which begins with fulfilling the daily needs of the local congregation quickly expands, especially for those who demonstrate gifts, into teaching a Sunday School class, preaching during the

---

[23]Despite a usual reluctance to take part in many community events, churches often organize marches or other outdoor events that are designed to heighten their visibility.

week-night services, and for the most apt the opportunity arises to 'pastor' a *campo blanco* (church home Bible study).[24] Bible school training, informally given by the pastor or presented through the local Bible institute, quickly follows as an equipping complement for the new worker.

Within a relatively short time a new believer has received the opportunity to be involved in a myriad of leadership opportunities and likewise to receive training, albeit not always adequate, in order to provide the basic orientation to develop successfully as a leader. Norberto Saracco recognizes that Pentecostal leadership training produces a minister who is a natural expression of his group. Rather than being 'a prefabricated model imposed on the church because of intellectual qualifications of his privileged status,' unlike so many of his counterparts in the mainline churches, the young leader is permitted to develop within and consequently authentically represent the social and economic context of the group which he serves.[25] The most capable will, after appropriate preparation in *la obra* and with the blessing of the mentoring pastor, be allowed to pastor their own congregations and receive ordination.[26] Their right to gain access to the ministry is based upon their enthusiasm, commitment and capability to establish and develop a congregation. The emerging Pentecostal leader produced by this informal apprenticeship system is 'contextual and indigenous' with the qualifications necessary to minister on the popular level.[27] Everett Wilson describes the apprenticeship process: 'A ladder of career opportunity could take a capable member of a congregation from the position of deacon or obrero (lay pastor) to the elected position of a pastor, to that of a presbyter of several churches, to an executive position representing several dozen churches and to one of several elected national positions.'[28] A dramatic example of this style of leadership

---

[24]For a description of *campos blancos* see chapter 3, note 30.
[25]J. Norberto Saracco, 'Type of Ministry Adopted by Latin American Pentecostal Churches,' *International Review of Mission* 66 (January 1977): 66–67.
[26]Nida observes that this typical apprenticeship system utilized by Pentecostals, in addition to providing leadership training, solves two difficult problems that traditional congregations unsuccessfully confront. Firstly, Pentecostal ministers can support themselves without any outside help simply by attracting sufficient members and secondly, the precarious task of selecting who is the most capable for leadership is greatly simplified by a type of 'survival of the fittest'. See Eugene Nida, 'The Indigenous Churches,' 99.
[27]Ibid.
[28]Everett A. Wilson, 'Latin American Pentecostalism: Challenging the Stereotypes of Pentecostal Passivity,' *TRANSFORMATION: An International Evangelical Dialogue on Mission and Ethics* 11 (January/March 1994): 20.

development can be seen in the emergence of the Assemblies of God national leadership in Central America.

A PROFILE OF ASSEMBLIES OF GOD NATIONAL LEADERSHIP IN CENTRAL AMERICA

The author surveyed the national leadership of the Assemblies of God in each of the five Central American republics. There are generally at least six elected church executive officials in each country known as the *presbiterio ejecutivo* (executive presbytery) comprised of a Superintendent or President, Assistant Superintendent or Vice President, Secretary, Treasurer, and two other members. This group of 30 church leaders,[29] the entire executive leadership core of the Assemblies of God in Central America, represents almost 12,500 churches and preaching points, and nearly 750,000 adult members and adherents.[30]

Table 1: Geographical Background of Central American Leaders

Rural	25
Urban	4

The survey instrument that was administered took into account the demographic data, religious background before conversion, age of conversion, age upon entering the ministry, and education of the leaders. The results show the following basic data:

It is obvious that the geographical roots of the leadership is overwhelmingly rural.[31]

---

[29]The statistical tables represent 29 or 30 responses because the participants did not always respond to every question.

[30]See table 1, chapter 2.

[31]Until the last decade Pentecostal growth was most evident in rural areas. More recently increases in growth have been more significant in the city. However, according to research by sociologist Timothy Evans among Guatemalan Pentecostals, there appears to be little difference between percentages of rural and urban dwellers in their church affiliation. What was most evident from his surveys was that there were simply more options in the urban areas. Timothy E. Evans, 'Percentage of Non-Catholics in a Representative Sample of the Guatemalan Population' prepared for the panel, *Protestantism in Latin America: The Social and Political Implications* (Washington, D. C.: Latin American Studies Association, April 4, 1991), 11.

Table 2: Father's Occupation

Labourer:	1
Farm Worker	15
Operario	2
Comerciante	6
Asalariado	2
Técnico	3
Pastor	–
Professional	–
Other	–

It is significant that 89 per cent of the families of the leaders were decidedly part of the lower class of society and an additional 11 per cent were, at best, members of the lower middle class. The terms '*operario*,' '*comerciante*' and '*asalariado*' in Spanish generally refer to small shop owners, small shop attendees, vendors, and work-for-wages employees. Their monthly incomes are in the lower 20 per cent of all earners in society. These groups are considered to be part of the 'grass-roots' group or popular masses in Latin America. Only 11 per cent of the leaders considered their family's economic status to reach as high as '*técnico*', a working strata which would still be lower-middle class. None of the leaders emerged from the middle class or higher sectors of society.

Table 3: Religious Identification

Roman Catholic:	19
Evangelical:	9
Other:	2

Table 3 represents a breakdown of categories of the religious affiliation of the Pentecostal leader during his childhood or youth and before conversion. According to the research, 63 per cent identified their background to be Roman Catholic while 30 per cent claimed an Evangelical heritage and only 7 per cent declared that their families did not have any religious orientation.[32] Many

---

[32]Though Pentecostals overtly reject any sense of continuity with the Catholic ecclesial traditions and theological positions of their past it is inevitable that certain Catholic elements have been transferred to Pentecostalism, particularly in terms of culture. For an

Table 4: Age of Conversion

Up to 10 yrs.	5
11–15	7
16–20	15
21–25	2
26–30	1

observers have noted, and this data would appear to confirm, that it is predominately the poor[33] who are disaffiliating themselves from the Catholic church at a greater rate than any other single strata of society and they tend to be joining Pentecostal churches.

90 per cent of the leaders were converted to Pentecostalism during their childhood or adolescence. Though this data is a significant indicator for future leadership development, it coincides with overall conversion age rates among Pentecostals. The greatest number of conversions has taken place within the last twenty years and within the younger age groups.[34]

Table 5: Age Upon Entering the Ministry

15–20	15
21–25	12
26–30	2

Over one-half of the leadership entered the ministry during their teenage years while 91 per cent had initiated their ministry before the age of 25. Only two leaders, who still entered the ministry rather young (26–30), were able to rise to the highest level of leadership available within the Assemblies of God in their country because of what is considered to be a late start. These figures reflect the fact that becoming a pastor is a vocation most easily attainable, with a few exceptions, generally during adolescence. The apprenticeship system appears to reinforce this pattern.

(*footnote 32 continued*)
interesting discussion of the continuity of Catholic thought in Protestant/Pentecostal concepts see José Míguez Bonino's statements in note 61.
[33]See table 2.
[34]Timothy Evans, '*Protestantism in Latin America,*' 12.

The highest percentage of members of their respective *presbiterio ejecutivo* (39 per cent) can be found in the age category 30–35 with

Table 6: Present Age of Leader

30–35	11
36–40	5
41–45	6
46–50	3
51–55	2
56–60	2
61–65	–
66–70	1

an aggregate of 86 per cent of the leaders under the age of 50. Only one *presbítero* was over 65. The average age for the entire *presbítero ejecutivo* was 41 years. The eight leaders who were 46 years of age or older had already served in their present positions for an average of 20 years, indicating that they had reached the level of *presbiterio ejecutivo* in their late 20s or early 30s.

Table 7: Education Level of the Leadership

Primary	30[35]
Secondary	27[36]
Bible Institute	27[37]
ISUM	6[38]
Technical School	3
University	9
Other	2

---

[35]Kindergarten to sixth grade.

[36]Grades seven to eleven.

[37]Typically, Bible institute programmes in Central America are offered at the rate of one semester (four months) a year over a six year programme, thus offering the student a diploma after successful completion of the six semesters. The logic for training spread over such a long period of time is that the pastor is able simultaneously to manage the pastoral responsibilities of his flock while he pursues his studies. The entire thrust of the ministerial education in the Assemblies of God in Central America is training while in ministry and in keeping with the concept of the apprenticeship programme and not in training for ministry, as is practised by most non-Pentecostal evangelical and Protestant groups.

[38]*Instituto de superación ministerial* (ISUM) is a post-Bible Institute programme comprised of four one-month seminars that include four classes each. These seminars are offered on a regional basis once a year.

All of the CELAD leadership had completed primary school, 90 per cent of the *presbíteros* had graduated from both secondary and Bible institute. Of the total leadership, 20 per cent had completed ISUM, a post-graduate course roughly equivalent to a BA, while 50 per cent have had other advanced education, including approximately 30 per cent who studied at the University level.

CONCLUSIONS REGARDING THE LEADERSHIP PROFILE

At least three conclusions about Pentecostal leadership can be drawn from this data. The first thing to note is that the members of the *presbiterio ejecutivo*, similar to their constituency, are a natural expression of their context and support the assertion that these Central American leaders are products of an indigenous background forming an integral part of the popular groups of Latin American society. Second, upon conversion during their adolescence, 65 per cent from a Roman Catholic background, these leaders almost immediately entered the ministry. It is apparent that they were given ample opportunity to progress through the informal apprenticeship system available to many new believers and thus to develop quickly their pastoral and leadership gifts in their rise to assume the top level of leadership in *las Asambleas de Dios*. Relatively young, in comparison to their counterparts in the more traditional or mainline churches, with an average age of only 41, the *presbíteros* have taken a place in their respective republics not only as religious leaders but as persons who wield significant political power in the national arena as well.[39] Third, the *ejecutivos* that comprise the Assemblies of God leadership in Central America have not only demonstrated the practical skills to fulfil their positions successfully, but they have, with just a single exception, completed secondary school, received the equivalent of three years of full-time Bible institute study and 50 per cent have studied the full-time equivalent of six years or more in post-secondary education. It seems important to note that most assumptions and presuppositions concerning the lack of formal educational preparation for these levels must be taken cautiously.

---

[39]Reports made by national executives to CELAD, Panama, December 6–10, 1992.

WOMEN IN LEADERSHIP ROLES

The role of women is also apparent in the leadership development apprenticeship system. Pentecostals believe that the Holy Spirit speaks directly to all people regardless of class, race, educational level, age or gender. All believers are empowered and expected to dedicate themselves equally to carrying out the task of proclamation as well as to care for the daily responsibilities of the church and community. The women, who in a marginalized society may not be offered opportunity to develop any of their gifts, are thrust not only into the responsibilities of overt evangelization but are also offered opportunities for leadership.[40] Though men still occupy the majority of the 'higher leadership' roles such as *presbiteros*, the women are admitted to the leadership ranks at almost every other level, including that of pastor. The *Asambleas de Dios* in Nicaragua in 1992 had forty women pastors of local churches (10 per cent of the congregations).[41] Though still a small minority of those assuming pastoral or evangelistic roles, their involvement at this level is a dynamic example of their upward mobility that, given their low economic and social status, they would have hardly enjoyed in secular programmes. The majority of the Bible institutes, both regionally and nationally, have women on the faculty teaching courses that are related not only to traditionally women's ministries, such as Christian education in Sunday schools and Bible clubs, but also to instruction in biblical subjects.[42] Consequently, in Pentecostal educational programmes in Central America, women play an integral role in the training and formation of pastors.[43] Administratively, women deaconesses comprise at least 40 per cent of the local congregation's legislative *cuerpo oficial* (deacon and

---

[40]Barbara Cavaness, 'God Calling: Women in Assemblies of God Missions,' *PNEUMA: The Journal of the Society for Pentecostal Studies* 16 (Spring 1994): 49–62.

[41]Archivos de la Conferencia Nacional de las Asambleas de Dios de Nicaragua: Managua, Nicaragua.

[42]Approximately 30 per cent of the professors in the Bible Schools in Central America are women. Additionally virtually every local Pentecostal congregation in Central America has an organized Sunday School programme largely staffed with female teachers. It is not uncommon for young girls to begin teaching their younger counterparts even before they reach adolescence.

[43]The majority of students studying in Bible institutes are already pastoring a church.

deaconess board).[44] In addition, national women's organizations such as *Ministerios del Concilio Femenil* (Women's Ministries) and *Misioneritas* (Missionettes), (programmes for women and for young girls), provide opportunities that range from pedagogical to administrative activities.[45] These women's and girl's programmes are networked not only nationally but internationally, affording young girls and women organizational status and a sense of self-worth and dignity. Admittedly, women's ministerial roles are still definitely structured to be in many senses submissive to the men's roles, but a plethora of opportunities are afforded to women.

Pentecostalism, accordingly, provides *campesinas* and poor urban women with exceptional acceptance, worth, dignity and leadership development opportunities in a society where they have historically been denied them. Upward social opportunities in participation and leadership, as evidenced in this data, would seem to indicate that Pentecostalism provides excellent social alternatives directly accessible to its membership regardless of previous social, economic or educational status.

Whether or not such opportunities exist elsewhere, the church with its community life fulfils the realization of latent personal aspirations for recognition, provides the forum for the development of leadership skills and gives the rewarding experience of exercising one's abilities. Observers have often remarked on the weakness of Pentecostal groups because of the pastor's lack of formal training and rapid rise to a position of responsibility. This alleged weakness,

---

[44]See *Reglamento local*, 26. The *Reglamento local*, written in 1932 when women had virtually no leadership involvement in secular society, specified that women must hold at least 40 per cent of the positions on the *cuerpo oficial*. Cornelia B. Flora's study in Colombia indicates that 31 per cent of Pentecostal women held church office versus only 3 per cent of Catholic women. Cornelia B. Flora, 'Pentecostal Women in Colombia: Religious Change and the Status of Working-Class Women,' *Journal of Interamerican Studies and World Affairs* 17 (November 1975): 417.

[45]According to the *Manual de Ministerios Femeniles*, *Ministerios Femeniles* (Women's Ministries) is a programme designed to help women better themselves 'physically, socially, intellectually and spiritually'. *Las Misioneritas* (Missionettes) instructs and encourages girls and young ladies in similar areas. *Manual de las Misioneritas*. Women's Ministries and Missionettes have over 3000 women's groups and 1000 girls' groups with a total aggregate participation of 60,000 and 20,000 in the respective groups in Central America. Each group requires seven elected leaders on the local church level as well as elected regional and national positions. There are a total of 4000 women and girls fulfilling leadership positions within the two organizations. Statistics taken from the archives of CELAD.

however, often appears to be the reason for the vitality of local Pentecostal groups and congregations. The doctrine of spiritual gifts (*charismata*), whatever the interpretation of practices, provides a theological justification for diffusion of leadership, a division of labour and the right to contest, at least in principle, formalized organizational authority.

REDEMPTION AND LIFT

Throughout the last two decades, Central America has been the arena for revolution, counter revolution, military repression, and massive dislocation. The lives of millions of people have been affected by inflation, drought, illness, illiteracy, and deprivation. The social reality for the majority of the popular masses leaves them on the fringes of survival.

It is not surprising that many Central Americans have turned to religion for help, given the absence of other options, and have found it to be a source of economic mobility. A Central American Pentecostal named Sonia Brenes Vargas provides a typical illustration of this dynamic of 'redemption and lift'. A woman of thirty-eight, Sonia is the mother of three children, Yorleny (18), Eveyln (17) and Jorge (5). In 1980 her husband, Cokie, an alcoholic, was unable to hold steady work because of his drinking. He frequently abandoned Sonia and her two little daughters without adequate food to eat for days at a time in their slum home. By chance, in April of 1980, Sonia, in a moment of desperation, went to a neighbouring *barrio* and rang the doorbell of a middle class home in hopes that the family would need a maid to do their cleaning and cooking. The lady who answered the door, a Pentecostal, did need someone for household responsibilities and, by chance, hired a lady with a sad story to tell. Within three months the Pentecostal *patrona* was instrumental in Sonia's conversion. Within a year, Sonia's husband, noting the dramatic change in his wife, was also converted and shared her enthusiasm for their new-found faith. According to the family, Cokie immediately and miraculously ceased his drinking and began to care diligently for his family. He established his own motorcycle repair shop. Over the years their economic situation changed substantially. They moved from their rented marginal shack to a home of their own. Their two daughters attended and graduated from both primary and secondary school and are presently in career training programmes. Sonia was able to have another son, Jorge, because the family's financial situation no longer required her to work outside the home. Her husband, Cokie, is a deacon in the Pentecostal church in the *barrio* where they live. By becoming Pentecostals this family claims not only to have found peace and happiness in their home, but their conversion and resultant changed life style directly impacted their economic life. Consequently, new and previously unreachable opportunities were provided for themselves and especially for their three children.

Also notable was the informal training opportunities that Cokie received because of his responsibilities with the local Pentecostal congregation. It would seem apparent that the acceptance by the Pentecostal community as well as the personal dignity and leadership skills he developed because of his involvement in church life would be transferable to the establishment and on-going success of his own business.[46] Most significant are the increased opportunities, such as adequate food, clothing, shelter and education, afforded the children of Pentecostal believers.[47] Certainly individual illustrations could lead to generalizations. However, when similar stories are a regular aspect of the testimonials heard by the author in hundreds of services it could be deduced that they are representative.

Sheldon Annis, likewise, finds legitimate demonstration that there are certain economical benefits to being a believer which he encapsulates succinctly in the phrase 'The Holy Trek: *Del suelo al cielo.*'[48] In a series of case studies among converted families on the 'spiritual-economic pathway' from the *suelo al cielo* he demonstrates how these typically landless Protestants maximized their incomes in comparison with their Catholic counterparts.[49] Annis clearly states that the reasons for conversions among the Guatemalan Indians were far more complex than simply a desire to realize personal economic gain. The believer's transition from the old religion to the new involved a complete transformation from their

---

[46]David Martin, 'The Fall of Rome: Today's Catholic Predicament,' in *Religion* 24 (April 1994): 100.
[47]Chapter five will treat exclusively the opportunities for social change that are afforded to children of all faiths in the *Programa integral de educacion de las Asambleas de Dios* (PIEDAD).
[48]Sheldon Annis, *God and Production in a Guatemalan Town*, 81.
[49]Ibid., 81–105.

past and an acceptance of Christ as personal Saviour. This break with the past, Annis notes, usually resulted in great personal cost to the new convert.[50] Annis's studies suggest that Protestantism, particularly the Pentecostal version, however, is a compelling agent of social transformation because it offers a means of development in a rapidly changing and often hostile environment.[51]

The Brenes family is not atypical of tens of thousands of poor people who comprise the Pentecostal church in Central America. In looking at the emergence of Pentecostalism as related to its economic and social impact upon its adherents' lives, it appears that Pentecostalism provided numerous opportunities that produced the effect of economic and social advantage. Conversion accompanied by rejection of old vices and habits had the apparent result of reliable effort in work habits, culminating in promotion and advance in the workplace. Resources were directed to the welfare of the family rather than to vices, i.e., personal consumption. According to some sympathetic accounts, the impact of conversion is significant, as an assessment of religious change in El Salvador demonstrates.

> Evangelicals [Pentecostals] are having a powerful impact on Salvadoran culture, family life, and politics, all of which have been heavily influenced by the country's matriarchal family structure, extreme poverty, and dominant Catholic faith. . . . Many evangelical leaders teach that God is masculine. Alcohol is strictly shunned, while monogamy, male headship, and paternal responsibility are held up as essential Christian virtues. . . Many men have turned their lives over to Christ, and they are no longer irresponsible drunkards and adulterers. They've become very hard-working. The change in these men is so dramatic that even nonevangelicals are beginning to adopt this family structure.[52]

---

[50]Ibid., 78–81. Examples of the personal cost required of new converts see page 74 and notes 24 and 25 in chapter 3.

[51]Annis' research is notably disinterested. It was his original intention to research the anthropological impact that tourism had upon the Guatemalan community. Unable to proceed as he had planned because of the earthquake of 1976, Annis decided to test empirically the impact of Protestantism in a Guatemalan setting. Annis notes in his introduction that he is a non-practising, agnostic Jew without any predispositional theories that he brings to this particular study, See Annis, *God and Production*, xii; 11–12.

[52]Jan Harris Long, 'No Longer a Silent Majority,' *Christianity Today*, 5 April 1993, 72.

UNDERSTANDING THE CONSEQUENCES OF CONVERSION

Though transformation accompanied by rejection of vices and the development of reliable work habits may result in upward mobility, such economic success is not the motivating factor for the Pentecostal's activity. Unlike the Weberian model[53] that argued that Protestant groups generate the type of work ethic and entreprenuership that promotes capitalism, even though this economic function was a latent one and not a manifest function of Protestant faith, Pentecostals bring ethical and moral fervency to the workplace simply because they are inspired by their salvation experience to be responsible and productive. However, Pentecostals seem to share the fundamental motivation with the early Puritans of Protestant tradition that work is done responsibly and to the letter, not to achieve recognition and promotion but because one pleases God by one's actions. Work is of worth only if it is done according to God's laws.[54] Pentecostals do their assignments to the best of their ability even if those around them, including their bosses, do not. It is not a work ethic that labours in order to accomplish, but rather a work ethic that God desires and is found pleasing to him.[55] The Pentecostal makes very little distinction between leisure and work times and spiritual activity. Ideally their time, even while working, is dedicated to God's glory. Throughout the day they sing hymns, pray silently and reflect upon the spiritual impact of their activities.

Undoubtedly, there are many occasions where a Pentecostal's avoidance of vices and reliability in the workplace results in upward mobility, and this economic rise is an important though secondary

[53]Max Weber's, *The Protestant Work Ethic and the Spirit of Capitalism* (New York: Charles Scribner's Sons, 1958). It should be noted that Weber is writing in the context of a rising middle class and an expanding economy. Unquestionably, Latin Americans are generally poor and the economies are stagnant, thus presenting critical distinctions in the application of Weber's overall thesis for Latin America.

[54]I. E. Maldonado, 'Building Fundamentalism from the Family in Latin America,' in *Fundamentalism and Society*, eds. Martin E. Marty and R. Scott Appleby (Chicago, IL: University of Chicago Press, 1993), 222–223.

[55]There is an entire chapter that outlines a discussion between Rowan Ireland, an American social scientist, and 'Severino,' an Assemblies of God believer in Brazil that exceptionally captures the interplay between religious conviction and the social and political voice often displayed by Pentecostals. See Ireland, *Kingdoms Come*, 37–76.

consequence of Pentecostal behaviour.[56] However, for the vast majority of Pentecostals, the existing social structures will deny them any significant opportunities, no matter how righteous, diligent and frugal they may be. Lalive d'Epinay, in support of this contention, argued that for most Pentecostals saving money that might previously have been used on alcohol, smoking, gambling did not accumulate as 'sins transformed into savings,' but rather as a 'more balanced' form of spending.[57] Recent studies conducted among 1,065 families in El Salvador reported that Protestant families have less education than the general populus and are almost invariably part of the very lowest economic sectors of society. Their life is a constant struggle for daily survival, and consequently, they are unable to generate savings, investments or implement entrepreneurial activity.[58]

While many Pentecostals have experienced some social mobility, and while the groups have increasingly attracted elements from the middle class, Pentecostals still consist overwhelmingly of persons at the bottom of the social scale, more often, studies indicate, from the ranks of the self-employed, on the one hand, and the deeply alienated within the system but certainly not demoralized, on the other.[59] Apparently these sectors are less likely than the demoralized poor to accept their disadvantages and most likely to assert their own interests.[60] Pentecostals have been likened, in fact, to the religious counterpart of the informal economy, achieving on their own and for themselves, what they have been unable to achieve through the normal structures of society.

MUTUAL HELP PROGRAMMES AND WELFARE PRACTICES

Although the legitimacy of the 'redemption and lift' concept is helpful in interpreting the rise of social consciousness among Pentecostals, this chapter argues that certain proactive alternatives designed to mete out welfare assistance and confront directly the

---

[56]It should be noted that Pentecostals do not avoid vices and assume responsibility so that they can become prosperous, but rather they do so as a consequence of conversion.
[57]Lalive d'Epinay, *Haven of the Masses*, 151. See the tables of statistics relating to social and educational conditions, especially among children, in chapter 5.
[58]Aguilar, *'Protestantism in El Salvador,'* 121–125.
[59]Eugene Nida, *'Indigenous Churches,'* 100.
[60]See chapter 6.

real problems of society must also be addressed by Pentecostals in their pursuit of a viable social policy.

David Stoll correctly notes that Pentecostalism in Central America, because of its background of marginalization and extreme poverty, has been mostly passive regarding active involvement in secular, social and political activities.[61] Pentecostalism, as should be expected from an economically poor movement, lacks the sophisticated structural views needed for societal and political change. Their 'mute and strangled voices' have been largely unheard or ignored in society.[62] However, as this chapter has already noted, Pentecostalism offers to its followers a sense of personal dignity and worth as well as communal structures of mutual support. This

---

[61]Stoll, '*A Protestant Reformation in Latin America?*', 45–46. Míguez Bonino argues that Protestantism was initiated as a 'protest' movement and has often been significantly involved in social concern programmes in many parts of the world. There is nothing inherent within Protestant theology to preclude social action. It is Míguez Bonino's contention that Protestant passivity in Latin America has been a direct legacy of the missionaries' North Atlantic political orientation rather than from Protestant theology. See José Míguez Bonino, 'Historia y misión,' in *Protestantismo y liberalismo en América Latina*, eds. Carmelo Alvarez, José Míguez Bonino, and Roberto Craig (San José, Costa Rica: Departamento Ecuménico de Investigaciones [DEI], 1993), 15–36. Undeniably so, but it must be remembered that almost all Pentecostals, at least 75 per cent, were formerly Catholic who also bring with them a legacy of Catholic social teachings, particularly with respect to a 'doctrine of providence,' that many Pentecostals still hold, albeit subconsciously. It would appear that the legacy that Latin American Protestants/Pentecostals received from their Catholic heritage would play an even stronger role than the influence of Protestant missionaries in their resistance to active social involvement. These Catholic notions may be summarized as first, that God is in control of the universe and everyone's destiny and thus every person is born into a preordained place and fate; second, conformity to this preordained status is rewarded by salvation; third, since the Church provides the holy place where God may be found and the priests are the guardians of God's laws access to God is held in the hands of the priests and is dependent upon one's obedience to God's laws. It is important to underscore a statement by Míguez Bonino, *Doing Theology in a Revolutionary Situation*, 7 that forcefully makes this point:

> There is no doubt that the Christian faith, co-opted into the total Spanish national-religious project, played the role of legitimizing and sacralizing the social and economic structure implanted in [Latin] America. It served as an ideology to cover and justify existing conditions. God in his Heaven, the king of Spain on his throne, the landlord in his residence: this was 'the order of things,' God's eternal and sacred order. Class structure and land ownership (and the forms of consciousness corresponding to them) are thus created into the world of sacred representation.

It would appear that a natural consequence of a Catholic legacy inbred for so many centuries in the fabric of religious and social society would be deeply instilled in the ethos of Latin culture and would not be brought to the surface for Pentecostals unless it was directly addressed.

[62]Martin, *Tongues of Fire*, 108.

section and the one that follows are concerned with an analysis of a sampling of both the formal and informal mutual-help pro-grammes that are an integral part of the 'substitute society' of Latin American Pentecostal church life.

PENTECOSTAL WELFARE PRACTICES

The emergence of Pentecostal churches during a period of massive migration and abandonment of many traditional forms of social guarantees like those of the extended family, kinship and the rural community, where help was extended to persons and families suffering extraordinary loss or dependency, indicates the Pentecostals' assumption of social obligations. The congregation, made up of members whose contributions to the work of the church qualifies them for special consideration in times of emerg-ency, at the same time produces a reservoir of personal and financial resources adequate to meet the members' catastrophic needs.

Beyond emergency care, most churches maintain some ongoing assistance for families who are perennially in need. In some cases the assistance goes well beyond informal help by programming the aid through a committee with fixed criteria and policies.[63] Com-missaries, help in finding employment, reciprocity in providing services (commercial as well as in kind) and special appeals for the assistance of the needy, including scholarship programmes, are generally part of this approach to social needs. It would not be improbable that up to 10 per cent of the members and their families receive regular assistance (widows, elderly and the unemployed) and up to 20 per cent occasional help, always, understandably, with strong demands on moral conduct in keeping with the group's religious beliefs and values.[64]

No small part of the assistance given these groups could be

---

[63]Generally aid is occasional if a head-of-family is able bodied. For a family with children, whether single-parent or with a non–Pentecostal father, small amounts of extended aid may be given.

[64]Due to obvious logistical limitations it was not feasible to sample randomly the entire Central American Pentecostal population regarding their involvement in social concern programmes and social welfare activities. Therefore, the author chose a limited area in the northern Costa Rican province of Guanacaste (47 churches) and several urban lower class barrios in San José (25 churches). Additionally a research survey of Pentecostal commu-nities in Nicaragua (400 churches) and El Salvador (500 churches) was utilized. The author's main concern was to locate areas that included a representative mix of Pentecostal groups of urban and rural dwellers in the traditionally poorer socio-economic strata from which Pentecostals emerge.

considered 'socialization,' assistance in eliminating the problems that create dependency. Typically, Pentecostals have disavowed styles of life in those they are helping that disable and restrict personal growth, family stability and vision for improvement.

While the stark realities of survival life are representative for a large proportion of Latin Americans who are deprived of social guarantees, the help provided by Pentecostals in these circumstances is certainly meaningful. Mutual assistance for abandoned children and women, the unemployed and the marginally employed, single-parent families and the destitute, while not adequate, is significant.

STRUCTURED SOCIAL PROGRAMMES

Additionally, Pentecostal pastors, churches and national conferences have been involved in organized and systematic programmes that, though limited in scope, demonstrate intentional social concern and present potential for social change. The author has chosen one programme from each of four countries in Central America to describe the structural focus of the social concern.[65]

HOGAR C.U.N.A. IN SAN JOSÉ, COSTA RICA

El Hogar C.U.N.A. (*Cristianos Unidos por el Niño Agredido*) is a children's home designed to serve the specific needs of children who have been abused sexually, physically or emotionally. Operating under the auspices of the *Centro Evangelístico de las Asambleas de Dios*, the home provides care for fifteen to twenty children referred to them by the *Hospital Nacional de Niños* or the *Patronato* (Child Welfare Agency) of the Costa Rican government. The Hogar C.U.N.A. offers professional psychological and social attention as well as health and medical care. Food, housing, education, and love provide the basis for a programme characterized by compassion demonstrated by the members of the congregation. If the parent of the abused child cannot be rehabilitated, as a first resort, every attempt is then made to place the child in the home of adoptive parents. The objective of this caring community of Pentecostal believers, through their offerings and volunteer help, is

---

[65]The *Asambleas de Dios* in each Central American country has many social concern efforts extending from kindergartens for children, feeding programmes and drug rehabilitation outreaches. Many of these programmes merit considerable attention by other scholars at a later date. Space limits the author to describe a single programme selected geographically.

to provide a service that will integrally touch the life of the children that are entrusted to their care.[66] The annual operating budget of the Hogar C.U.N.A. is in excess of $50,000.[67]

INSTITUTO DE DESARROLLO SOCIAL DE LAS ASAMBLEAS DE DIOS IN NICARAGUA

In 1987 the *Conferencia Evangélica Pentecostés de las Asambleas de Nicaragua* formed the *Instituto de Desarrollo Social de las Asambleas de Dios* (IDSAD), a legally organized social agency established to serve the critical social needs of the many impoverished urban and rural communities. IDSAD's main and ambitious purposes, as set out in their constitution, were to develop social-economic projects in both the rural sectors in the areas of agriculture and cattle farming, as well as in the urban sectors with small businesses and industries. IDSAD also wished to include comprehensive educational and health programmes, ecological preservation, and the construction of lower-class housing.[68] Whether or not IDSAD would be able successfully to establish and develop all of the projects that had been outlined was questionable. There was little doubt, however, about their serious commitment to social concern projects.[69] IDSAD's 1989 annual report to the *presbiterio ejecutivo de las Asambleas de Dios* gives an account of the social agency's accomplishments. The report indicated that IDSAD had helped 32 communities plant corn and rice, aided in the construction of 96 homes, provided monthly retirement benefits for 13 pastors and had given food, clothes, and shoes to 26,500 families. The total investment in these projects was listed as $2,000,0000.[70] *Las Asambleas de Dios* in Nicaragua, in receiving the report, stated that 'in

---

[66]Information on the Hogar C.U.N.A. has been taken from the constitution and statutes of the *Asociación de Bienestar Social del Centro Evangelístico* and the brochure *HOGAR CUNA por qué existimos?*.

[67]Partial funding is provided by the *Patronato* and *Programa integral de educación de las Asambleas de Dios*, but the majority of the donations are given by the members of the local congregation. Copies of the financial reports are in the possession of the author.

[68]*Estatutos del Instituto de Desarrollo Social de las Asambleas de Dios* (IDSAD) (Managua, Nicaragua 1990). For a discussion of the relationship between *las Asambleas de Dios* and CEPAD, see Appendix II:CEPAD, pages 236–237.

[69]See the earlier discussion in this chapter regarding indifference.

[70]The majority of the funds for these projects were provided by European agencies, including a joint effort between Norway's NORAD and the Norwegian Pentecostal Foreign Mission (*Pinsevennenes Ytre Misjon PYM*), England's TEAR fund and from German pastor Waldemar Sardackzuc's Christian Aid—Nehemiah organization. Monies were also received from World Relief and PIEDAD as well as from several smaller donations. The report indicates that 20 per cent of the funds came from national donors.

spite of our limitations [with respect to the overwhelming social needs of the nation] we were actively present in order to give testimony of our faith and our social responsibility.'[71]

CENTRO EVANGELÍSTICO EN SAN SALVADOR

The *Conferencia Nacional de las Asambleas de Dios* and the *Centro Evangelístico* in San Salvador, El Salvador, provide an ideal example of a cooperative effort in institutional social development between the *presbiterio ejecutivo* and a local church. *La Conferencia* is the largest non-Roman Catholic grouping in the country and the *Centro Evangelístico* is a congregation of approximately 3000 members.[72] For more than 30 years the church has exhibited an intentional strategy in the area of social concern. It has established a large school system in the poorest communities of San Salvador that currently is comprised of 32 campuses and has an enrolment of 24,000 students. It has also initiated a university, health clinics and a variety of self-help programmes for its membership.[73] After the 1987 earthquake that devastated San Salvador, the national *Conferencia*

---

[71]*Estatutos del Instituto de Desarrollo Social de las Asambleas de Dios*, 1. The demonstrable social concern of *las Asambleas de Dios* in Nicaragua is a contradiction of Abelino Martínez' allegation of social indifference and of the CEPAD REPORT. However, it needs to be acknowledged that Martinez's allegation and the CEPAD REPORT measure social concern, not by social welfare, but by political commitment. See Appendix II.

[72]Some journalistic descriptions of Latin American Pentecostalism have demonstrated a superficial, uninformed, or biased methodology. Typical of this style of journalism is the following non-scholarly critique filled with misrepresentation, misstatements, exaggerations and complete inaccuracies. Sara Diamond's, *Spiritual Warfare: The Politics of the Christian Right* (London: Pluto Press, 1989) illustrates the above negative characteristics when she describes the work of the *Centro Evangelístico*.

> Christian Right activists provide ideological support for the powers of the Salvadoran military and oligarchy to plunder and kill. Assemblies of God minister John Bueno, whose Centro Evangelístico sponsors a network of grade schools attended by 30,000 Salvadoran children, for example, provides New Testaments to government officials, giving them a theological justification for their exercise in authority.

Diamond is correct in her claims that some members of the Christian Right in the United States have provided ideological support for certain political projects. However, she indiscriminately applies her presuppositions without substantiating evidence. First, John Bueno gave the Bibles to José Napoleon Duarte, the democratically elected left-of-centre President of El Salvador, not to the military. Second, Editorial Vida, a Miami-based publishing company, provided Bibles for *all* the government leaders in *each* country in Latin America regardless of their political persuasion. It is a leap in logic to assume that presenting a Bible to government officials constitutes a legitimation of their political actions. Diamond has never interviewed John Bueno and would have no way of knowing his political persuasions.

[73]PIEDAD (*Programa integral de educación de las Asambleas de Dios*) originated in this local congregation. The programme of PIEDAD will be treated in chapter 5.

and the *Centro Evangelístico* joined ranks to construct a new communal development for several dozen families that had been displaced because of the earthquake. Together they purchased *la finca Bonanza* (the Bonanza farm), ten kilometers from the capital city and constructed 32 houses, water wells, a day school with an enrolment of 218 children and a church. They also initiated a small chicken raising industry that could help the new community become self-sufficient.[74] The community is now formally known as the *Colonia de la finca Bonanza.*

Abelino Martínez Rocha, perhaps with an unintended compliment, describes the social role of the El Salvadoran Pentecostals in the midst of civil war and social crisis. To paraphrase Rocha, while the war waged on and the bullets sailed, the Pentecostals did not seem to notice. They preferred to train their people for evangelism and social action as their form of answer to the national crisis.[75] Several years after the conclusion of the civil war the social action of the Pentecostals continues.

Social Programmes in Guatemala

Third, in Guatemala the Pentecostal churches are carrying out a significant amount of social work. In addition to their collaboration with over 40 schools established in lower-income communities, they have initiated several programmes that give social assistance to a myriad of needs. These programmes include ministerial helps such as *el fondo de jubilación* (Jubilee Fund) that benefits retiring ministers as well as those that are incapacitated, *el fondo de Jakubec* (Jakubec Fund) that helps to cover funeral expenses for ministers as well as a fund that assists in the immediate hospital and medical expenses of any minister who is involved in an accident. There is also a *fondo para emergencia nacional* (National Emergency Fund) that channels monies to victims in case of natural disaster and a *fondo pro-viudas* (Widow's Fund) to aid, in particular but not exclusively, pastors' wives who have been widowed.[76] Similar programmes have been established by the Assemblies of God in each of their respective countries.

---

[74]Information gathered from personal observation of the project as well as interviews with the administrator of the Colonia, Joaquín García on Feb. 25, 1994.
[75]Abelino Martínez Rocha, in 'Los Protestantismos en la Crisis Salvadoreña,' 126–127.
[76]1992 Annual report of the Assemblies of God of Guatemala.

The Jubilee Fund, Jakubec Fund, National Emergency Fund and the Widow's Fund from Guatemala are representative of social programmes that hundreds of Pentecostal churches have established throughout Central America. Further, during times of national emergencies, such as earthquakes or hurricanes, the national churches have joined together and have been at the vanguard of social relief efforts. In all of the Central American republics the Assemblies of God have been selected by governmental authorities as an effective channel by which to direct national and international aid for immediate needs such as emergency food and clothing to the general public.[77] Further, in El Salvador and Nicaragua, Pentecostals have been integrally involved in the construction of low-cost housing for those left without homes because of national disasters.[78] These programmes clearly demonstrate that many Pentecostals are not without a social conscience, nor have they become escapist.

While it is true that Pentecostals have demonstrated social services instead of political engagement, it should also be recognized that until recently it was inconceivable that secular, social and political involvement by Pentecostals would result in a positive restructuring of the social system because of their minority position, as well as their deep-rooted and well-founded suspicion of the legitimacy of the existing social process.[79] Pentecostals are often

---

[77] In the aftermath of the devastating earthquakes in both El Salvador and Costa Rica, *las Asambleas de Dios* was designated as official centres through which international and local government aid could be funnelled to needy people in the effected areas.

[78] Since the tragic earthquakes that struck Nicaragua in 1972 and Guatemala in 1976, costing thousands of lives, the Assemblies of God in each of the Central American republics has established a permanent emergency committee that is prepared effectively to mobilize in a minimal amount of time. Governments have recognized their organizational skills and have channeled large amounts of aid for the general public through their agency during national crises.

[79] See note 9. Pentecostals, despite their traditional non-involvement political stance, are already deeply involved in politics. Attempts have been made by evangelical groups, largely comprised of Pentecostals, to form their own political parties in all of the Central American republics. In March 1994, the national superintendents of *las Asambleas de Dios* from Central America met in Costa Rica to discuss the role of the Pentecostal church in the political arena. Alfonso de los Reyes, president of CONELA and Superintendent of *las Asambleas de Dios* in Mexico, presented a paper at CELAD in Panama City, Panama (December 1–4 1993) entitled 'Unificando Criterios sobre la posición de las Asambleas de Dios en la sociedad'. De los Reyes outlined four criteria that required the participation of the *Asambleas de Dios* in society. Included in these criteria was the 'concientización' of the Pentecostal church regarding its political responsibilities. He included in his report the Table of Contents of the *Expositor* (the weekly Sunday School guide written and published by the *Asambleas de Dios* of Mexico) specifically prepared for church education

criticized for their lack of interest or at least their reticence to attack the causes of the needs. Gaxiola-Gaxiola is right when he assesses that it would be unfair to demand that Pentecostals bring about social changes that no other church, including the 'activists and theologians of liberation' have been able to do.[80] However, Pentecostals have been actively involved in the process of social concern. Increasingly, it is clear that the groups' intentions are not narrowly limited. While Pentecostals have often been considered largely irrelevant to the life of Latin America, they provide serious institutional alternatives for many people who, with limited options, gladly welcome this resource.

WOMEN AND SOCIAL CONCERN

Pentecostals have also dealt with the disabilities that tend to face all women in Latin American culture.[81] Beyond some leadership roles, including that of pastor, discussed earlier in the chapter, they invariably control the selection of the (usually male) pastor through their majority vote and indirectly control all congregational polities through their offerings. Some observers have tended to see the Pentecostal churches as essentially a protest mounted by women, in what could be considered a response to social class or ethnic disqualification. Martin notes that 'women are among the "voiceless" given a new tongue in the circle of Pentecostal communication'.[82] Women, in particular, in Latin American society suffer from a lack of self-worth and self-acceptance. The conversion experience, for such people, means an acceptance of self and a sense of dignity. In addition,

---

(*footnote 79 continued*)

and social change. The table of Contents outlined 26 general objectives to be used for the process of *concientización*. Listed among these objectives were (1) The Conservation of the Environment, (2) Political participation, (3) Labour relationships, (4) Foreigners, widows, orphans and the poor, (5) Inalienable rights, (6) Women's, children's and healthcare rights, (7) The Procreation of justice, and (8) Citizen's rights and responsibilities. El Expositor, *La Responsibilidad Social de las Iglesias* (Mexico, DF: Editorial Cristiana Continental de las Asambleas de Dios, 1992).

[80]Manuel Gaxiola-Gaxiola, 'The Pentecostal Ministry,'*International Review of Mission* 66 (January 1977): 58.

[81]Cornelia Butler Flora, 'Pentecostal Women in Colombia: Religious Change and the Status of Working-Class Women,' *Journal of Interamerican Studies* 17 (November 1975): 412–413.

[82]Martin, *Tongues of Fire*, 180.

conversion may increase a woman's authority in the home.[83] By receiving the Holy Spirit and following the commands of the Bible, contends Burdick, a woman paradoxically, instead of being dependent upon the desires of her husband, senses a divine confidence and authority to speak to him when his behaviour is contrary to God's laws.[84] Instead of the continual fighting that characterized the marriage before conversion, the woman seeks to encourage her husband's conversion through her own behaviour in a manner that may be authoritative but not confrontational. 'Before I was converted, my husband would not listen to me about his drinking,' a new believer told me, 'I have stopped shouting at him and he has not been drinking nearly as much. As time has gone by he has even been defending my decision to be a Pentecostal to other family members. He encourages our daughter to participate with me—something he would have completely opposed earlier. Although he will not make a decision to convert, he has become a much better husband since my conversion.'[85] For many Pentecostal women, their decision to convert has resulted in a sense of authority that has permitted them to gain control of their domestic affairs. The double moral standard prevalent in Latin American society that justifies the male's immoral behaviour, where ideally the male should be faithful to his spouse but realistically immoral actions are tolerated, is challenged by the converted wife. These moral deviations by the husband are no longer seen as the inevitable foibles of *machismo* but rather as actions that are contrary to God's laws.[86] Though still submissive to their husbands, their

---

[83]John Burdick, 'Rethinking the Study of Social Movements: The Case of Christian Base Communities in Urban Brazil,' 177.

[84]Ibid.

[85]Cecilia Rodríguez, conversations with author, over a period of months in 1985, shortly after her conversion.

[86]The concept of *Machismo* (male dominance) when taken to its extreme is defined by James Vigil as an attitude that 'encourages indiscriminate sexual conquest of females, with the aim of lowering their status; escape from reality through alcohol or drug use; and fighting and even killing each other for even minor reasons'. See James Diego Vigil, *From Indians to Chicanos: A Sociocultural History* (London: C. V. Mosby Co., 1980), 229. The literature on *machismo* is immense. For still one of the most readable descriptions see Eugene Nida, *Understanding Latin Americans*, 56–79. For probably the most thorough treatment of the subject see Elizabeth Brusco, 'The Household Basis of Evangelical religions and the reformation of machismo in Colombia' (Ph. D. diss., University of New York, 1986).

experience of conversion has filled them with a sense of equality.[87] Cornelia Butler Flora compares the aspects of religious change and the status of women between Catholic and Pentecostals. Even though the Pentecostal woman's decision to convert to Pentecostalism may be considered a 'deviant act which symbolically separates the believer from many of the most treasured cultural institutions,' Pentecostal women realize a sense of self-worth and equality that makes the decision worthwhile.[88]

ASSESSING PENTECOSTAL SOCIAL CONCERN

Pentecostals are no less inclined, if not always astute, in addressing other problems, such as acquiring greater political voice for disadvantaged popular groups by a display of organizational strength.[89] Often appearing pragmatic, these groups have used a variety of means to advance their cause, generally, however, without abandoning their principal reason-for-being and without unduly compromising themselves. Their political independence, as well as their tentativeness and a wide variety of mechanisms for bringing about change, permits a variety of approaches and strategies.

Everett Wilson succinctly summarizes Pentecostal social perspectives:

> Despite the stereotypes, Pentecostals are not passive and otherworldly. They are in the movement because they have found solutions to practical problems. They themselves are primary victims of social oppression, dehumanizing economic policies, and corrupt politics. Their rejection of political initiatives for revolution is based on their

---

[87]Burdick, *Christian Base Communities*, 178.

[88]Cornelia Butler Flora, 'Pentecostal Women in Colombia: Religious Change and the Status of Working-Class Women,' 412–413.

[89]Garma Navarro C., 'Liderazgo Protestante en una lucha campesina en México,' *América Indígena* 44 (1984): 127–141. The often-criticized tendency of Pentecostal groups to fragment serves as an extremely effective means of applying a variety of different approaches to difficult problems. This 'speciation,' as in the biological analogy, ensures that some groups will survive even as others fail, resulting in the perpetuation of the movement. See Gerlach, *Religious Movements in Contemporary America*, 1974. Moreover, the growth of Pentecostal groups in Latin America has led to the conclusion that the differences between Pentecostals and other evangelicals have been somewhat reduced as non-Pentecostals have increasingly become 'pentecostalized'. While pragmatism and adaptability may gravely weaken Pentecostal distinctives, flexibility must be recognized as a characteristic which, on balance, is most often a strength.

perception of options, not indifference. Their policies may be expected to reflect their marginal social status, their rejection of short-term solutions, and their cynicism of political messiahs and temporal ideologies.[90]

The internal structure of Latin American Pentecostal groups, articulated in the previous chapter, appears to explain the groups' dynamic development. Moving from a large 'pool' of potential adherents, many of whom bring with them considerable personal resources of vision, personal abilities and material resources, Pentecostals have formed themselves into voluntary associations that produce the following strategic features of a social organization. They enjoy the immediate benefits of a surrogate extended family or community, including acceptance and a proprietary interest in a legally constituted, property-owning collectivity. Moreover, the congregation enhances the further development of the initiates by encouraging and validating an intense subjective experience and morally reinforcing their values, beliefs and conduct. In a society where status and networks could be largely ascribed, the adherent is presented with the opportunity for personal growth, peer recognition and extended influence, as well as the acquisition of skills that have broad application outside the church community.

While various other voluntary associations and networks could theoretically provide similar benefits of organization, the Pentecostals' motivation, perspective of worldview, discipline and moral restraints contribute indispensably to the survival and growth of their churches. Recurrent cycles of recruitment, constituent formation and institutional development, over a period of time, produce dynamic, effective popular institutions appropriate for orienting and mentoring contemporary Latin American groups in transition.[91] The organizational effectiveness of these groups, however, appears to lie in large part in their religious propensities. Without the intense, morally vindicated efforts of the adherents,

---

[90]Everett A. Wilson, 'Latin American Pentecostals: Their Potential for Ecumenical Dialogue,' *PNEUMA: The Journal of the Society for Pentecostal Studies* 8 (Fall 1986): 87. In spite of the truthfulness of Wilson's statement that Pentecostals have a certain 'cynicism of political messiahs,' critics can point to some Protestants (including Pentecostals) enamoured with some military dictators such as Agosto Pinochet in Chile as well as 'democratically' elected leaders like Alberto Fujimori in Peru and José Efraín Ríos Montt and Serrano Elías in Guatemala.

[91]The mentoring process is described earlier in this chapter.

congregations would lack much of the incentive, personal discipline and sacrificial effort that are necessary for institutional success.[92] It would seem apparent from the explicit statements of Pentecostal leadership that the movement is ready and prepared institutionally to address in a systematic fashion the structural evils in Latin American society. This willingness on the part of the leadership to confront social injustice was convincing in the keynote message of Miguel García, superintendent of *las Asambleas de Dios*, in the Dominican Republic to the conference of CELAD in 1992. He challenged the leadership to an active role in social service.

> The Assemblies of God is the largest Pentecostal movement in Latin America . . . What will the Assemblies of God do to help the poor, the children in the streets, the elderly? . . . What will we do with prostitution? What will the church do with the plague of AIDS? What will we do about abortion? What will the church do about the manipulation of the resources of the State in the hands of two or three? . . . What is the role of the church in confronting these realities . . . Society demands that the church [Pentecostal] actively participate in the social context. . . . This is the type of gospel that the Word teaches us to preach.[93]

The existence of the formal and informal social programmes described in this chapter and the insistence of leaders like Miguel García should make it plain that Pentecostals are not suggesting a short-circuiting of reality in the realm of social concern. The Latin American context, rife with social injustice, provides the horizon which commits Pentecostals to a concerted effort at transforming the 'the nature of things'. Pentecostals, in addition to their social welfare activities, must also, however, provide viable alternatives that will affect significant change in the social structures.

---

[92]Ireland feels that because Pentecostal *creyentes* have a tendency to be hermetic, even if they form alternative societies, 'their experiments in new ways of naming and addressing the problems of life at the grass roots stay locked within the group because they lack the horizontal linkage to poor neighbors of other faiths and the vertical linkage to individuals and organizations with more direct access to the means of cultural production. . . . Furthermore, contends Ireland, as these groups continue to grow they are likely to be incorporated into 'centralized, authoritarian state projects.' See Ireland, *Kingdoms Come*, 222.

[93]Miguel García, 'Un Reto para Servir' (A Challenge for Service) an address to the *presbiterios ejecutivos* of the fourteen countries that comprise the area of CELAD. García's message was printed in the official bulletin of CELAD, *Boletin de CELAD* (February 1993): 3–4.

Chapter 5

Latin America Childcare: A Case Study in Pentecostal Praxis

THE FOCUS OF PENTECOSTAL SOCIAL CONCERN

Having generally classified Pentecostal groups as theologically conservative, pietistic, premillennial, 'other-worldly' and quietist, earlier observers have assumed that Pentecostals also show little social concern and have few if any social programmes. However, investigation of Pentecostal movements has called such assumptions in question.[1] Increasingly, Pentecostalism is now viewed as an initiative expressed in religious form by aspiring but disadvantaged social individuals and groups. David Martin has recast previous images of Pentecostal groups such as Lalive d'Epinay's 'Haven of the Masses' to see them as movements of the poor, rather than movements for the poor.[2] Similarly, Sheldon Annis, in his 1987 study entitled *God and Production in a Guatemalan Town*, reported the Guatemalan version of 'rags to riches,' '*del suelo al cielo*,' (from the earth to the sky) in recognition of the impact of evangelical/Pentecostal values on Mayan Indians.[3] In addition scholars recognize that these movements, rather than being a product of foreign influence, are autochthonous and largely spontaneous. In contrast to the social withdrawal attributed to them, the case studies by Annis and Martin bear out the tendency of Pentecostals to address broadly the needs of their communities.

If, indeed, Pentecostal intentions and concerns have been misunderstood, what have been the theological bases and inspiration that incite social concern on behalf of their own church community as well as the larger local community? We shall argue in this chapter that this aspect of Latin American Pentecostalism has resulted from a gradually growing and deepening awareness

---

[1] See Rowan Ireland, *Kingdoms Come*, (1991); John Burdick, *The Making of Social Movements in Latin America*, (1992) and *Rethinking Protestantism in Latin America*, (1993).
[2] Martin, *Tongues of Fire*, 108.
[3] Annis, *God and production*, 86, 87. For a discussion of Annis' phrase 'del suelo al cielo' see chapter 4.

that was implicit in the movement's concern for the entire individual, including physical and material needs. Thus, out of a rather vague and charitable concern toward persons who needed evangelization, it will be proposed, grows a sense of their God-given right to provision for their basic needs. This chapter will explore the social effect when members of a Pentecostal community are encouraged to appropriate covenants of divine grace. The analysis will seek to discover whether biblical promises are easily extended beyond subjective peace and a sense of righteousness to considerations of other concerns, already made explicit, such as divine healing and divine intervention in one's personal life. If physical healing and guarantees of provision for their material needs become planks in their system of belief, other provisions may then follow as the comprehension grows that structural factors have caused the injustices. This analysis will attempt to discover if a Pentecostal understanding of the above leads to a realization of the need for an intentionally designed programme of social action. If there is a relationship between divine intervention in the Pentecostal's experience and the social process, there inevitably follows an association of theological reflection with socio-economic analyses and options. Pentecostals, of which Latin America Childcare (LACC) is representative if not necessarily typical, have endeavoured to implement a strategy designed to bring structural change over the long term, by institutionally developing their social programmes. Pentecostals envision alternative institutions that form part of the infrastructure of society and thus become ongoing, transforming agents in society. If they influence their local communities by offering alternative courses of action, Pentecostals are in a position to offer previously unreachable hopes and opportunities for marginal sectors.

A readily available device for assessing Pentecostal social concern is the group's attention to the plight of children who are the most vulnerable social elements among them, who often live in extreme poverty. For them, the most immediate problems of food, housing and security are followed closely by the need for some means of extricating themselves from the vicious cycle of misery. As they grow up they struggle with inadequate healthcare and education, as well as a lack of the moral support that comes from a sense of belonging to a supportive community. Without such a community, even the few ameliorative measures available cannot combat the demoralizing effect of their social conditions. On the other hand, with sense of community and where there is health and educational opportunities the effects of poor material conditions may be overcome, or at least mitigated to a degree. Specifically LACC is part of an extended long-range commitment to build a proposed alternative system of education that could help children break out of the cycle of poverty. LACC desires not only to provide relief for those children who are the victims of poverty but to change the conditions that perpetuate a life of poverty for children. This they hope to do by establishing a new educational system within the infrastructure of the region which will determine an alternative future for children in the slum areas.

This chapter describes the early history and international extension of Latin America ChildCare, analyzes their most significant internal philosophical, theological and strategic documents, and demonstrates the influence that LACC has had upon the Latin American context in general and upon specific individuals in particular. The chapter will also pose certain critical questions. While the ideological and the strategical context and commitment of the author to this historical project cannot simply be jettisoned, disguised or disregarded, the task of critical analysis must be made of the distinctive content, quality and results of LACC. The disadvantages of writing from an 'insider perspective' are obvious. An assessment of LACC by the author, who is also the director, poses the obvious problems of objectivity and self-interest. One so intimately involved in a project must constantly be aware of the danger of subjectivity and consequently make a conscious effort to engage in an adequately-constructed critical exercise. At the same time, the writer's intimate awareness of the development of the programme and his familiarity with the personnel, philosophies and objectives of LACC give him access and insights unavailable to other researchers. Within these acknowledged limits, the following section attempts to analyze critically the evolution.

THE STATUS OF LATIN AMERICAN CHILDREN

The Latin American continent is typical of the difficulties confronting most developing countries. Of a population of 440 million, nearly one-half live in poverty, of whom a disproportionate number are women and children.[4] UNICEF reports indicate that 42 per cent of the population, 181 million, live below the poverty level. Of this impoverished population, 78 million are children below the age of eighteen years. Since 42 per cent are found in the category of the poorer population, the report concludes, 'in practical terms the majority of the poor are children'.[5] Decades of armed conflicts and political and social violence have had a devastating effect on the children in the numbers dead, disappeared, orphaned, injured and displaced. UNICEF estimates that as a result of the Central American conflicts alone, 3 million people, the most of them children, have suffered unacceptable consequences.[6]

Of Central America's 26.5 million people, 57 per cent or 15.1 million are children and 45 per cent—more than one-half of them children—live below the poverty level (table 1).[7] The suffering which accompanies poverty is easily documented, with 40 per cent of the population without running water and 42 per cent without access to healthcare. Among the worst illustrations of this misery is the case of the Guatemalans where an appalling 66 per cent of the population are without adequate medical attention. Malnutrition among children 5 years of age and younger is suffered by 30 per cent of the children of Honduras and El Salvador and 70 per cent of the children from Guatemala.[8] Because of the lack of running water and basic health services, children contract intestinal infections that often result in premature death (table 2).[9]

---

[4] *Los Niños De Las Americas: Supervivencia, Protección y Desarrollo Integral De La Niñez, En El Decenio de 1990* (UNICEF: Santa Fe de Bogotá, 1992), 7. The definition of poverty is a much disputed issue. Poverty is defined in this book as the economic level at which a person lives when one does not have sufficient income to provide for a minimum diet, adequate housing, and similar basic essentials such as access to running water, healthcare and education.

[5] Ibid., 7.

[6] Ibid., 9. During the decade of the 1980s, the civil wars claimed the lives of 160,000 Central Americans, the vast majority of whom were civilians. In El Salvador where 75,000 people were killed, an additional 500,000 have been displaced from their homes, the majority of whom were children. UNICEF, 16. A new tragedy has become reality for most of the slum-dwelling children accustomed to violence and poverty—the introduction of narcotics. The results of narcotic consumption, especially among children, severely increase the effect of already devastating circumstances.

[7] More than half of the children live in poverty largely because of the devastating effects of the civil wars.

[8] Ibid., 31.

[9] UNICEF reports that the vast majority of children die from avoidable causes (25).

Adequate education of Latin America's children is essential in order to break the cycle of poverty and deprivation. One third of all children in Central America are denied access to public education. Of the remaining two-thirds who begin primary school, only 36 per cent finish the sixth grade (table 3).[10] Correspondingly, the poorest families register the highest birth and death rates, the highest levels of malnutrition and the highest rates of school failure. It is the poor and particularly the children of the poor, who suffer the consequences of unavailable healthcare, unemployment and underemployment and the severest disintegration of family life.[11]

The preceding UNICEF report indicates that in Latin America 'there is no question that the most important political, economic and social priority is to liberate the poor that comprise one-half of the population. . . and this priority, in the first place, must begin with those who are most vulnerable, the children.'[12]

> Neither economic growth nor democracy can be consolidated while the one-half of the population that is poor is permanently excluded from productive activity. . . because of a lack of training and opportunities to integrate [the poor] into social life. It is not only an injustice, it is also a great waste, especially in the case of the poor population that is mostly young. There is no question [that society] is producing an underutilization and a waste of the quality of the national human resources.[13]

It is the conclusion of the UNICEF study that '[the children's]

---

[10]UNICEF studies reveal that even when children have the opportunity to attend *primaria* there are serious deficiencies in the quality of education received, particularly in the poorer sectors. In comparison with the other social classes, three times as many children in the poor sectors in Guatemala and twice as many in Honduras, for example, do not finish the primary grades (37). Every country has its own educational system so it is difficult to evaluate the quality of education the children are receiving. UNICEF defines *primaria* as 'the minimum training required (reading, writing and maths) to carry out daily personal work(39). Generally this educational process should take six years. However, UNICEF's studies indicate that 40 per cent of students repeat first grade and an average of 30 per cent repeat additional grades. The average age of a child who achieves the equivalency of sixth grade (the completion of *primaria*) in Latin America is 14 years. Moreover, UNICEF believes this data to be underestimated (36).

[11]Brant L. Meyers. 'State of the World's Children: Critical Challenge to Christian Mission,' *International Bulletin of Missionary Research* 18 (July 1994): 98–102.

[12]UNICEF, 11.

[13]Ibid., 9

destiny will be decided in the near future. They can be the first *generation of change* in the transition to the new world of the XXI century or they can become the last *lost generation* of the XX century.'[14] It is the widespread conviction of sociologists and political analysts, reflected in the UNICEF report, that the condition of children; their care, education and ethical training is essential for any kind of structural change that will include democratic participation and a stable future.[15] The focus of LACC is the children who make up 50% of Latin America's population, half of whom are poor, often undernourished and without basic health services.[16] Of these impoverished children, fully one third have no access to educational services of any kind.[17] LACC has been designed intentionally to provide an institutional alternative.

LATIN AMERICA CHILDCARE (PIEDAD)

This chapter will examine the *Programa Integral de Educación de las Asambleas de Dios* (PIEDAD), a social programme directed primarily toward the child inhabitants of the slum areas of rural and urban Latin America. This case study will be analyzed to understand how one Pentecostal group, *Las Asambleas de Dios*, in the course of applying its theological beliefs initiated and developed a programme of social action. Known in Latin America as the *Programa integral de educación de las Asambleas de Dios (PIEDAD)*, the programme is known outside the region as Latin America ChildCare (LACC).[18] LACC focuses on grass-roots community with an intentional emphasis to undertake actions that will directly address and reform circumstances and basic social structures that result in injustice. LACC is the largest evangelical institutional programme of social action in

---

[14]Ibid.
[15]Ibid.
[16]See table 1.
[17]See table 3.
[18]The acronym *PIEDAD* signifies love for one another or mercy, the latter representing that virtue that causes one to have compassion for those whom one does not even know. The English name Latin America ChildCare (LACC) will be used throughout this chapter to maintain consistency. LACC is understood explicitly as a social action programme specifically designed to bring about significant change in the social structure. See the discussion in chapter 4, for a definition of the distinctives between the terms *social welfare* and *social action* and how they are used in this study.

Latin America and, according to available educational directories, is also the largest unified network of evangelical educational institutions found anywhere.[19] In 1993 LACC had 198 primary *colegios*[20], 63 secondary *colegios* for a total of 261 projects in 18 countries (table 4), not including special projects.[21] Collectively, these schools provide education for 67,487 children.[22] The majority of both school projects and the numbers of children attending school are found in the five Central American republics (table 5).[23]

In spite of its size, LACC has received little recognition, within

---

[19]Information supplied by the Association of Christian Schools International (ASCI), Whittier, California, July 9, 1993. ASCI is independently associated to LACC. Though the Assemblies of God school institutions are not affiliated legislatively internationally or nationally, they are all part of a fraternal relationship and voluntarily affiliate and function under the larger umbrella of LACC.

[20]The nomenclature for schools and for schooling levels differs from country to country. This study will use the term *colegio* for most types of schools unless otherwise stipulated. We will understand primary education (*el primer ciclo*) to cover the first seven years of schooling (preparatory and grades 1–6), secondary education to be divided into middle education (*el segundo ciclo*) generally grades 7–8, and high school education (*el tercer ciclo*) covering grades 9–11 and in certain countries an additional twelfth year.

[21]Special projects include an accredited university in El Salvador offering nineteen academic disciplines with an enrolment of over 1,000 students. Vocational schools in several countries teach adolescents practical skills such as carpentry, electrical work, and small appliance repair. Also included in special projects is the Costa Rican home for abused children (HOGAR CUNA). For a description of the *Hogar Cuna* see the previous chapter. Additionally, there are adult literacy school programmes in most countries. In 1994 *ENLACE* (Entidad Natural Latinoamericana de Cooperación Estratégica), a sister organization to LACC, was established with the express purpose of promoting socioeconomic development. In addition to the educational opportunities provided by LACC in low-income communities in Latin America, ENLACE assists in the development of projects that are integrated, self-sustaining and participatory. ENLACE focuses on achieving long-term development by promoting projects that facilitate organization, solidarity and participation within targeted communities. ENLACE projects range from short-term relief and aid and mid-term development strategies to long-term institutional programmes. ENLACE has developed microenterprises such as a bakery, shoe factory and a fruit-tree farm by working with local grass-roots organizations. Additionally, ENLACE has trained community members to introduce more efficient aquaculture technology in the improvement of fish production and provided research at the request of the Salvadoran Secretary of Environment regarding the consumption of trees used for fuel and the contamination resulting from domestic and industrial waste.

[22]There are scores of *colegios* sponsored by local churches of *las Asambleas de Dios* in different Latin American countries that operate independently of LACC.

[23]Because the *colegios* were established in El Salvador and then first extended to the neighbouring Central American nations and later to the Caribbean and South America, LACC has seen most of its development take place in Central America. For dates that LACC was established in each country, see table 4.

or outside its own denominational circles.[24] Given the revision of the traditional portrayals of Pentecostal movements in Latin America as an escapist 'haven of the masses,' an emotional refuge for frustrated marginal groups, LACC is an overt expression of social action that should not be ignored in any serious research on the emergence of these movements. In a recent historical analysis of LACC, Pentecostal historian Everett A. Wilson, in calling for awareness of LACC, asks, 'If a social program like PIEDAD [LACC] is, indeed, implicit in the proselytism and teachings of Latin American Pentecostals, why has this feature of the movement remained for so long unrecognized? And what are the implications of such programs for these groups and their impact on their respective societies?' His study provides a useful historical review of 'how Latin American Pentecostals, at their own initiative . . . have improvised an educational alternative to meet the needs of their communities and those of their socially marginal neighbors'.[25]

LATIN AMERICA CHILDCARE IN EL SALVADOR[26]

Latin American ChildCare (LACC) began in 1963, when John Bueno, the American-born and Chilean-reared pastor of the Centro Evangelistico, San Salvador, El Salvador, confronted the demoralizing poverty and hopelessness of children in the *barrio* that surrounded his church.[27] Though the resources of his local congregation were limited, he felt that it was imperative to make some attempt, however modest, to help these children escape from their prisons of poverty. The first school, called the Liceo Cristiano, began on February 4, 1963, with 152 children meeting in three of the church's Sunday School classrooms.[28]

---

[24]In a review of the literature on Latin American Pentecostalism the author has found only one passing ambiguous reference to the existence of LACC and it was inaccurately cited. See Sara Diamond, *Spiritual Welfare*, 171.

[25]Everett A. Wilson, 'Latin American Pentecostalism: Challenging the Stereotypes of Pentecostal Passivity,' 23.

[26]The organization of the El Salvadoran schools into the entity of LATIN AMERICA CHILDCARE did not take place until 1977. The author, along with John Bueno, were the co-founders.

[27]John Bueno, a North American, was the son of missionary parents in Chile. He was educated in Spanish schools in Santiago, went to the United States for his theological training at eighteen years of age (1956), and went to El Salvador at the age of twenty-three (1961).

[28]Information gathered from a personal document sent to the author from Joaquín García who is the administrator of LACC in El Salvador.

While the initial efforts at starting a school were tentative, the project was nonetheless at least modestly successful from the beginning.[29] Enrolment increased substantially each year and new programmes, including a high school and night school, were added as the children advanced through the grade levels to complete the elementary programme. School policies were often pragmatic, making use of a variety of imaginative approaches and improvising as necessary. Later, facilities were constructed exclusively for educational use, and, correspondingly, the instructional programme was strengthened with the recruitment of teachers with better formal qualifications, including, initially, a limited number of non-evangelical personnel.[30] Examinations given under the supervision of the Ministry of Education confirmed that the students were receiving a competitive education and were in most cases continuing their studies at the University of El Salvador, the Evangelical University, the Christian University, the Jesuit-operated 'José Simeon Cañas' University and various technical schools.[31]

During these early years, the *Liceo*,[32] as well as *colegios* in several of the other Central American republics, depended entirely on their own resources, except for occasional, relatively small donations for classroom supplies and furnishings. Although they later succeeded in acquiring foreign funds to expand their programmes to other marginal *barrios*, they never relinquished control over their own institutions.[33]

---

[29]Everett Wilson provides a historical review of the early origins of LACC in El Salvador. See 'Latin American Pentecostalism: Challenging the Stereotypes of Pentecostal Passivity,' 19–24.

[30]Increasingly, qualified evangelical teachers became available, in part, apparently, because non-evangelicals became converted after beginning their association with the schools. Several prominent LACC national leaders, including Joaquín García, are among this group. Joaquín García, current Director of the entire LACC programme in El Salvador, and a member of LACC's international board, has been an influential leader in the philosophical and contextual formations of LACC. For an example of his writings see *Documents of PIEDAD* (1984–1994) (San Salvador: PIEDAD). The *Documents of PIEDAD* are available in the central office of LACC in each Latin American country where the programme exists. Presently virtually all teachers are evangelicals from a variety of evangelical denominations.

[31]Joaquín García stated that an 'estimated 75 per cent of the students graduated from LACC schools go on to one or another of the universities, while the remaining go directly to some employment'. (Taped interview, 16 May 1993.)

[32]In El Salvador the term *liceo* is used for schools instead of *colegio*.

[33]The annual budgets for LACC schools exceeds $15 million. 77 per cent or $11.5 million is generated from local country sources including minimal tuition fees, institutional and personal donors, church support as well as public government funding. For a discussion of the basis and process for the funding of LACC projects see Wilson, 'Latin American Pentecostalism: Challenging the Stereotypes of Pentecostal Passivity,' 22.

Liceo Cristiano's first building constructed purposely for educational use, was a three-storey structure. Interestingly, at its inauguration, the congregation was credited with having funded the entire project, despite the fact that few of the 1000 church members at the time owned their own homes and scarcely any owned an automobile.

Educating children whose home environments were insecure and deprived soon necessitated compensatory programmes in counselling, nutrition and preventative medicine. In response to this need, the *Liceo* formed parent organizations and solicited the donated services of sympathetic professionals in these fields. The Pentecostal community, showing pride in having broken through difficult economic and social barriers to provide educational opportunity for their children, generously contributed to special appeals from their sparse incomes and savings, on occasion in the form of rings, watches and other gifts in kind.

During the process of its development, the Liceo suffered disadvantages in comparison with the Roman Catholic institutions operating in the country. Despite constitutional provision for the free practice of religion, evangelical institutions were treated discriminately as commercial entities for tax purposes.[34] Only gradually, through petition and legislation, were exemptions from various taxes obtained.[35] In time, the Liceo was freed from municipal and corporation taxes on properties used exclusively for religious services or those set apart as open 'green belts' and recreational areas.[36] The school continued to pay taxes on its educational buildings. No significant assistance or encouragement was received from the national government until the 1980s. At that time, during El Salvador's civil war, offers of government assistance were received and forthrightly rejected for fear of political compromise.[37]

---

[34]In a number of Central American countries such as El Salvador, Nicaragua and Costa Rica, only the Roman Catholic Church is exempted from taxes and duties. Evangelical churches are treated by governments in a similar way to commercial businesses.

[35]In few of the Latin American countries do evangelical organizations receive the same governmental benefits as their Roman Catholic counterparts.

[36]In many cases governments impose more requirements on the LACC schools than on their own public school systems. However, this practice is rapidly changing. Schools in El Salvador, Belize and Chile receive a significant number of salaries from the Department of Education specifically designated for teachers. Costa Rican LACC projects have been the recipients of monthly subsidies for feeding programmes as well as other similar welfare help.

[37]The Liceo's relations with the national government have remained tentative, through concern for identifying the church with partisan politics and controversial policies. An ambivalence of political sympathies and issues continues to preclude concerted political

From the outset the Liceo has remained innovative in its efforts to serve its community. Having begun kindergarten and *bachillerato* programmes almost immediately, the Liceo introduced a vocational programme in an outlying area in 1978, and a secondary night programme at the central campus in the same year. Taking advantage of newly passed legislation that permitted private institutions to offer career preparation, formerly restricted to select institutions, the Liceo in 1983 obtained a charter as a university to develop, primarily, professional programmes in education. Eventually over 50 per cent of the institution's more than 500 teachers would receive their professional degrees at the *Universidad Cristiana de El Salvador.*[38] In effect, the developing system continued its pragmatic policy of providing for its own personnel needs whenever possible, in this case, by preparing its own teachers and administrators.

EARLY EXPANSION OF LACC IN EL SALVADOR

The Liceo's first satellite campus was constructed in 1973 in *El Granjero. El Granjero* is a slum settled by refugees trying to escape from the insecurity of the countryside as tensions between the insurgents and the government erupted in armed violence. This annex began with 300 students, followed in 1976 by a second campus in *Candelaria.* Though *Candelaria* was a more settled *barrio* it had a reputation for prostitution and bars. The result of an evangelistic campaign, the growing congregation founded a school with 103 students. A third school was built in *Soyapango*, a suburb of San Salvador, in 1977.[39] A report of the Liceo's assets compiled

---

(*footnote 37 continued*)
action. Such a policy of neutrality has been interpreted by critics as support for the *status quo*. Pentecostals' non-involvement in political structures has been observed since the beginning of the movement. See chapter four note 9. Recognizing that structural change in society could result not only from political involvement the Liceos in El Salvador established schools in several anti-government strongholds. Active *guerrilleros* and those sympathetic to the FMLN matriculated their children in these Liceos. During the decade of the 1980s when the civil war in El Salvador claimed the lives of 80,000 people, the Liceos were understood as 'neutral ground' by both sides and were largely unaffected by the war. Interview with Joaquín García, April 19, 1992.

[38]In 1994 the *Universidad Cristiana de El Salvador* had an enrolment of 1,000 students. Nineteen separate career programmes were offered, including social sciences, economics, education and theology. (Interview with the University's rector, Dr. Adrian Fernando Archila, February 28, 1994 in San Salvador, El Salvador.

[39]José Alfredo Guerrero, 'Origin, Desarrollo Y Filosofía de los Liceos Cristianos,' *SIEELA* (San Salvador, El Salvador: Documents of PIEDAD, 1984): 1–3.

in 1978 indicated that $185,000 had been invested in land and improvements for the main campus and the three annex schools. The total enrolment of the four campuses of the Liceo Cristiano of 1687 students in 1973 had expanded to 2671 four years later.

The Liceo's expansion to annexes in the marginal areas in the 1970s reemphasized its social mission. Reflecting on the course of the school's evolution, Joaquín García, the system's director, articulated the view held generally by the Pentecostal school system in its efforts to effect genuine social change:

> God has given us the enormous and delicate mission of transforming— or at least improving—our society by putting under our care children and young people that study in our schools. They represent the future of our nation, and if we win them for Christ, also winning their families, we will have a better society in the future.[40]

By 1992 the Liceo Cristiano in El Salvador, then integrated into LACC, had 34 primary and 30 secondary schools that provided education for 23,350 children. Of these, 18,000 received some form of assistance, including tuition scholarships, uniforms and meals, and medical and dental care.[41] The vision to help children in the slum communities that had commenced with the formation of the school system of the *Liceo Cristiano* of El Salvador took on a new dimension in November of 1977 with the establishment of LACC, an international programme that became known as Latin America ChildCare (LACC) in English and *Programa integral de educación de las Asambleas de Dios* (PIEDAD) in Spanish.

---

[40]Joaquín García, 'Nuestra responsibilidad como servidores de una institución educativa cristiana,' *SIEELA* (San José, Costa Rica: Documents of PIEDAD, 1985), 11. Translation by Everett Wilson and cited in 'Latin American Pentecostalism: Challenging Stereotypes of Pentecostal Passivity,' 22.

[41]Of the 18,000 children receiving assistance, 6,660 were sponsored by individuals in North America and the remaining 11,340 received help through national resources within the country of El Salvador. Beyond providing instruction and basic health programmes for students, LACC in exceptional cases provides other assistance, including shoes, corrective lenses, uniforms and school supplies. All of the national programmes provide feeding for children from needy homes, either breakfast or the noon meal, as well as instruction in hygiene and periodic prophylaxes for parasites. Through arrangements with national medical programmes and volunteer private physicians and dentists, and the use of mobile health units, regular examination of students occurs in most systems. El Salvador has carried the programme the furthest with the establishment of a permanent clinic offering medical and dental services for students and their families. *La Nación*, the leading daily newspaper in San José, Costa Rica, reported that PIEDAD had provided for Costa Rican children in 1993, 760,000 meals and 11,100 uniforms, shoes or eyeglasses. Amalia Palacio, 'Superación en la Pobreza,' *La Nación*, (7 de Setiembre 1994), 1B.

LATIN AMERICA CHILDCARE INTERNATIONAL

LACC began with a three-fold purpose. First, there was the desire to share with other countries the concern for marginalized children and to encourage the already existing vision, particularly within the neighbouring republics of Central America. Second, LACC wished to provide philosophical and theological guidelines that would help to maintain the integral primary focus of evangelism and overt social concern.[42] The means created to provide this intellectual basis for the programme was the *Seminario de Instituciones Educativas Evangélicas de Latinoamerica* (SIEELA). These week-long conferences were held annually from 1984 to 1991, and were conducted biennially thereafter in several different Latin American countries.[43] Third, LACC presented a channel by which interested donors in the United States and Canada, and later Europe, could provide economic help for children who would not normally have opportunity to attend school.[44] By 1982 LACC began to expand in an organized fashion to the other Central American republics.

The operation of LACC schools in Nicaragua is in some ways typical of those found elsewhere, despite substantial differences that result from the severe problems of economic devastation and profound ideological tensions during and since the assumption of power by the Sandinista government. These schools are for the most part in deeply distressed areas. In most cases they are sponsored by a local congregation, usually with a pastor who has a vision for assisting the families of the congregation and for reaching the surrounding community. Most of the country's 56 projects are tiny installations of several classrooms adjoining a church building and operated by national teachers who are typically paid about the equivalent of $100 per month. In all LACC schools, administrators comply with the requirements of the respective Ministry of

---

[42]See Latin America ChildCare Mission Statement drafted in Tegucigalpa, Honduras in February of 1992 (*Documents of PIEDAD*).

[43]See discussion concerning the role of SIEELA in the overall programme of LACC presented later in this chapter.

[44]LACC seeks sponsors that will provide a monthly financial commitment. The sponsorships provide preventative medical and dental care, a daily nutritious meal, and a good quality education. When a school is established, children are enrolled, whether or not they have a sponsor.

Education in regard to curricula and policies.[45] Given the dismal condition of most *barrios* where LACC schools are located, even the minimal facilities provided are generally much better than would be found without LACC assistance. An article in the daily newspaper, *Barricada*, graphically demonstrates the overwhelming needs of the children. From recent studies, the newspaper reported an estimated 500,000 Nicaraguan children who work in the streets, demonstrating the need for LACC activism on behalf of these children. Sociologist Bertha Rosa Guerra, a consultant for UNICEF, reflects that 'in all practical terms the children [of Nicaragua] are without a future. They try to survive in the present by any means possible.'[46]

As is the case with LACC elsewhere in Latin America, most of the schools are located in slum areas where students and staff personnel are subjected to demoralizing conditions of poverty. The littered streets in many cases are simply dirt roads that become barely passable during the rainy season. In some cases water is not drinkable or is frequently cut off. The social environment in some neighbourhoods has led to harassment by gang members. Against all of these handicaps, the sense of pride and hope produced by having their children in school has resulted in strong support for the local LACC programme by parents and other members of the community.

Latin America ChildCare and its educational programmes were extended to Belize (1978), to Costa Rica (1982), Guatemala and Honduras (1983), Panama (1984), and Nicaragua (1985).[47] By 1992 the programme operated in the South American republics of Colombia, Ecuador, Bolivia, Peru, Chile, Argentina, Paraguay and Uruguay, and in the Caribbean countries of Haiti, Jamaica, and the

---

[45]LACC has developed its own philosophy of education that is infused into all the curriculum. See the section *Latin America ChildCare's Educational and Philosophical Principles* presented later in this chapter.

[46]Cited in 'Medio millón de niños: Generación sin futuro,' *Barricada* (Managua, Nicaragua), 28 November 1993, 12.

[47]Although some schools of the *Concilio Nacional de las Asambleas de Guatemala* have affiliated with LACC since 1983, the programme dates back to 1967 when missionary Quentin Shortes founded the Colegio Evangélico Nazaret in the departamental capital of Esquintla, and to 1973, with the founding of the *Liceo Cristiano Betesda* by pastor Armando Sazo and his wife Ernestina. Likewise, in the Dominican Republic as well as in other countries, schools affiliated with *Las Asambleas de Dios* have chosen to function in cooperation with LACC as an umbrella organization that serves to provide training and operational and/or capital funding.

Dominican Republic. With the growth of these national programmes increasing attention was given to the development of
appropriate policies for achieving the desired goals (table 5).

It is the intention of Latin America ChildCare, in each of the
countries where they are working, to provide training and funding,
as well as to encourage local Assemblies of God congregations to
take the initiative in providing educational and social services to
poor families. Such programmes often fall outside the capacity of
the typically small congregation, but where the national and local
denominational leadership demonstrate both vision and administrative competence by previous initiatives, they are considered for
LACC assistance in the form of either sponsorships or capital
funding. Additionally, the school project must be constructed
adjacent to the local church (*templo*) and must function as an integral
part of the services the local church renders to its own and the
surrounding communities. Funding is generally available for only
the most marginalized areas. A preliminary report describing conditions in a recent project in the *barrio* of Los Guido, in San José,
Costa Rica, is representative of the areas and social conditions
where LACC chooses to establish a school.

> [The proposed site] is a marginal community that forms part of the
> circle of slums (*anillo de miseria*) that surrounds the capital [of San José].
> There are about 4,500 families with low incomes, characterized as
> unemployed and underemployed. There is a disproportionate number
> of single-parent families, mostly mothers with small children and
> children supported by grandparents. There are high rates of drug
> addiction, alcoholism, prostitution and vagrancy.[48]

With the emergence of many similar programmes and frequent
petitions for additional schools, the leaders of the stronger national
programmes, including Joaquín García in El Salvador, Rodolfo
Sáenz, Johnnie Esquivel and Gerardo Barrantes in Costa Rica,
Mario Canaca in Honduras and Francia Hernández in the Dominican Republic, along with scores of other educators and
denominational executives, have attempted to coordinate and
improve the individual efforts undertaken at the national level

---

[48]Internal memorandum describing the Los Guido project from Maria Sibaja, secretary
to Johnnie Esquivel, Director of the Costa Rica Escuelas Cristianas, the national affiliate
of LACC.

with the formation of the *Seminario de las Instituciones Educativas Evangélicas de Latino América*. The involvement and commitment of a variety of different national leaders have assured that LACC is deeply contextual and grass-roots in nature. These are a series of ongoing seminars and consultations that are designed to address philosophical, theological and practical approaches to common areas of concern.

THE SEMINARIOS DE LAS INSTITUCIONES EDUCATIVAS EVANGELICAS DE LATINOAMERICA (SIEELA)[49]

SIEELA has played a central role in the development of new directions for LACC in Latin America. In general, SIEELA has focused on the philosophical and strategic guidelines for extending education through professional staff development and soliciting funding through provision of subscribed scholarships. Discussions at the conferences have emphasized holistic development, recognizing the multifaceted nature of the child, including the intellectual, the physical, the social, the emotional, the civic, the artistic and the professional, as well as the spiritual. The conferences have also provided opportunity for the participants, both formally and informally, to engage in critical evaluation.

In keeping with the groups' theology, social emphases are considered foundational to the transformation of the individual through an experiential transformation or conversion. Thus, while the norms set for individuals are in some respects radically different from those of traditional society, the process focuses on reaching the child in his or her socio-economic context. The philosophy of these programmes, worked out in each SIEELA conference, indicates the thoroughgoing structural changes the members aspire to effect.[50]

SIEELA came into existence in 1984 when the leaders of several national school systems met in San Salvador, El Salvador, to draw up some guidelines for these philosophical, theological and strategic

---

[49]Seminars of Latin American Evangelical Educational Institutions.

[50]Mario Canaca, 'La actividad académica y los servicios estudiantiles en los centros educativos cristianos "Asambleas de Dios" en Honduras.' *SIEELA* (Tegucigalpa, Honduras: Documents of PIEDAD, 1985).

goals. In attendance were 54 participants representing 11 countries and consisting of 45 national directors, administrators and teachers, along with nine North American missionaries. The documents in that first conference set the tone for the goals of LACC developed thereafter.[51]

The conferences, consultations and small group meetings of the SIEELA meetings played a significant role in the formation of LACC throughout the continent, emphasizing particularly the desirability of consensus in theological and strategic considerations. The participants wanted to frame their task of evangelization and social concern within the reality of oppression in the continent.

A second SIEELA meeting was held in 1985, again in San Salvador. Two theological documents dealt with the Old and New Testament bases for biblical justice. Murray Dempster, a Pentecostal social ethicist, contended that the social ethical basis for justice on the part of Pentecostals is firmly rooted in the Old Testament moral tradition. It is the Old Testament, argued Dempster, that presents social justice as God's desire for society and further, God implores his people actively to pursue it. He identified particularly the theocentric character of ethical thinking, the concept of the *Imago Dei*, the notion of covenant in forming community, the prophetic traditions concerning social concern, and the Jubilee teachings as the relevant Old Testament ethical principles by which social concern can be instigated, nurtured and guided within the context of any society.[52]

The document on biblical justice in the New Testament focused upon a rereading of Luke 4:18–19 from within the context of the reality of poverty in Latin America in general and of Latin American children in particular. Concern for the marginalized is directly tied to the ministry of Jesus. Luke, emphasizing that Jesus' mission and message centred around his proclamation of the Kingdom of God, claimed that Jesus started his public ministry with his declaration in Luke 4:18–19. The participants in the SIEELA meeting agreed that concern for the marginalized is established in the ministry of Jesus. A quotation from Dietrich Bonhoeffer, *Letters from Prison*,

---

[51]See *Documents of PIEDAD* (San Salvador, El Salvador: 1984).

[52]Murray W. Dempster, 'Old Testament Foundations for Social Concern', *SIEELA* (San Salvador, El Salvador: Documents of PIEDAD, 1985). For development of these Old Testament ethical principles see chapter 6.

emphasized the need for justice among men.[53] Whether everyone identified as a Pentecostal would employ the same language or even understand Bonhoeffer's intention is doubtful. Nevertheless, for substantial elements within the movement, especially in Latin America but also in North America, the message of the Kingdom imposes moral demands for promoting social concern. These values, in turn, lead to the question of how they can be applied. LACC has tapped such sentiments in continually growing proportions, indicating that a reservoir of biblically inspired concern for advancing the Kingdom exists.[54]

The fourth SIEELA conference in Honduras revolved around the theme of '*Alcanzando nuestra generación actual*' (Reaching Our Present Generation). The speakers at the seminar, attended by 89 participants from nine countries, presented papers that dealt with philosophical and theological concerns and stressed the urgent need for structural changes in the realm of education as well as in society as a whole. A significant paper offered by Lic. Joaquín García entitled *La mística de PIEDAD* (The mystique of PIEDAD), was soon thereafter included in the respective school handbooks of several countries. García identified the two fundamentals that he viewed as indispensable to the programme. First, the responsibility of a LACC school is to the community, especially to the parents and to the child. If these persons are equipped with a sense of dignity there is greater opportunity for creativity, character, productive work habits, and constant desire for self-improvement. Second, it is not sufficient merely to equip a child for the present, but the task of the educator is to assist every child to have a spiritual and personal conversion. The spiritual experience, combined with an adequate social empowerment of the child, is the task of LACC and the essence of the programme.[55]

In García's thinking, the establishment and ongoing work of the type of schools that LACC desires depends upon a careful selection

---

[53]'In order to be Christians today,' Bonhoeffer asserted, 'there must be two ingredients: prayer and justice between men. All Christian thought must begin with prayer and action, which should lead to a new comprehension of biblical language. There will be a language of justice and truth that proclaims the peace of God for men and the coming of the Kingdom.' Dietrich Bonhoeffer, *Letters and Papers from Prison*, rev. ed. (New York, NY: SCM Press, 1971).

[54]Douglas Petersen, 'New Testament Foundations for Social Concern,' *SIEELA* (San Salvador, El Salvador: Documents of PIEDAD, 1985).

[55]Joaquín García, 'La Mística de PIEDAD,' *SIEELA* (San Pedro Sula, Honduras: Documents of PIEDAD, 1987).

of the most competent personnel, followed by a thoughtful and consistent orientation of those chosen. García contended that LACC will be successful only when every teacher, administrator and director shares the same commitment to philosophy as the leadership.

Mario Canaca, a professor at the University of Honduras and the national director of LACC in that republic, followed with a critical paper on Latin American educational issues entitled 'In Search of Academic Excellence'. Canaca contended that opporunities for formal education provide the basis for the hope of functioning successfully within society. In this way it is possible to anticipate a more humane future and to participate in the construction of a society that does not oppress its marginalized sectors. The attainment of academic development at all levels in general, but at higher grades in particular, called for practices that could create new thought-patterns and teaching methods that could take advantage of the great store of international knowledge. Academic excellence, he argued, must not just be composed of 'hard forms' of knowledge, but there was an urgent need for it to include the capacity to speak critically about politics, economics, sociology, education and other disciplines that are much more complex.[56]

Professor Canaca listed a series of considerations that traditionally serve as obstacles in the achievement of academic adequacy within the Iberoamerican context. Among these problems is, first, the dilemma of unequal opportunities that prejudiciously and systematically exclude the poorest social sectors, both in rural and urban areas, from access to even primary education. Second, a significant number of teachers have not been adequately prepared to educate competently the children and young people in their classes. The typical emphasis in Latin American educational teaching training programmes has placed a higher priority on a stagnant methodology that encourages the rote memorization of information rather than

---

[56]Latin America educators have traditionally adhered to the acceptance of objective structures and conditions. For a description of this position see William K. Cummings, *Low-Cost Primary Education: Implementing an Innovation in Six Nations* (Ottawa, ONT: International Development Research Centre, 1986); Dole A. Anderson, *Management Education in Developing Countries: The Brazilian Experience*, Latin American Monograph Series, Michigan State University, (Boulder, CO: Westview Press, 1987) and Sylvain Lourié, *Education and Development: Strategies and Decisions in Central America* (Paris: United Nations Educational, Scientific, and Cultural Organization, 1989).

on a creative process that equips the child to respond to his or her contextual needs. Third, existent programmes of education do not adequately lead to the integral formation of the individual nor provide an appropriate orientation for successful participation in daily secular life. Fourth, is the use of teaching methods that do not allow the teacher to utilize new and important technological resources.[57] Fifth, is the inadequacy of current educative administrative structures to facilitate pedagogical research necessary to meet the demands of current educational systems.

In a response to these obstacles, Canaca proposed the adoption of new policies within the structure of LACC that would enable the schools to meet the aspirations of the Latin American people. These new policies needed to include primarily a modern method of teaching that would encourage intellectual and creative development and at the same time provide the student with the competencies necessary to take advantage of modern, technological and educational resources. Additionally, policies needed to be adopted within LACC that would guarantee adequate preparation, stability and legitimate administrative and economic rights to the teacher.

Canaca proposed the creation of an organization that could provide pedagogical workshops for administrators, directors and teachers within LACC. He called for a preferential concern for the most marginalized people within society, and suggested that the development of these people must include an education that takes seriously cultural identity and foments civic, moral and spiritual values. This educational process would provide for the integral individual and social development of the pupil, preparing him or her to exercise responsible judgements freely. Canaca concluded

---

[57]In an open letter to the Costa Rican presidential candidates, the leading educators of that republic declared that the reason that Latin American education was so notably mediocre was the rigid thinking that resulted from the over-emphasis on the correct use of 'methodology' in teaching. According to the educators, the inflexibility of methodology held creative learning hostage. Such rigidity, concerned more with the methodology than with content and creativity had led to an unacceptable 'pedagogical vicious circle.' The Costa Rican educators argued that while pedagogical processes were more concerned with the methodology or the 'how' of teaching rather than the 'why and what' of teaching, better administration, more legislation, or higher budgets, though important factors, would not halt the severe deterioration of educational instruction nor improve the results. The educators urged the future President to institute a fundamental conceptual change in the Universities that would provide a radically reformed pedagogy in the training of preparing new teachers. 'Pedagogismo y educación mediocre,' *La Nación*, (6 de febrero 1994), 14A.

his presentation with the following challenge to the schools working under the umbrella of LACC.

> I propose that in addition to the cognitive, psychomotive, and affective development [of the student] that we fulfil our responsibility to 'Forge New Spirits,' [the motto of the Liceo Cristiano] and that can only be done if we follow the footsteps and the example of our Lord Jesus Christ: 'And Jesus grew in wisdom and in stature, and in favour with God and men' (Lk 2:52).[58]

Mario Canaca's presentation became an important influence in the pedagogical development of LACC personnel. An organization for teacher training was subsequently formed that provides more than fifty different seminars to deal with cognitive as well as philosophical and theological issues.[59] A methodology of teaching was instituted in LACC that employed a more radical educational approach which afforded teachers the opportunity to utilize creative practices and thus, challenge old methodologies and traditional structuralist orthodoxy. This approach included emphasis on greater contextualization and flexibility in keeping with the social origins and the worldview of the students.[60]

Building upon the documents from the previous conferences, the participants of the 1992 SIEELA conference in Tegucigalpa, Honduras, forged a mission statement that could serve as a basis for future reflection and action. The first paragraph of the statement portrays the nature and commitment of the LACC participants:

> The focus of LACC has always been to the poor—to those who have no one to plead their cause. This focus has always been on people and our programme's desire is to show compassion tangibly to the least of these. Human dignity and the respect for life demonstrated through the actions of LACC is the enfleshment of the eternal concerns of Christ's kingdom. . . . Investment in children from the marginal classes of Latin America allows the possibility of a future generation emerging who will no longer be victims of tragedy but recreators of

---

[58]Lic. Mario Antonio Canaca Jiménez, 'En Busca de la Excelencia Académica,' *SIEELA* (San Pedro Sula, Honduras: Documents of PIEDAD, 1987): 25–30.
[59]Annual seminars are held in each country with approximately ten issues treated on each occasion.
[60]LACC educational philosophy will be treated later on in this chapter.

societal structures that will impact the future of their respective nations.[61]

It is notable that SIEELA originated as working consultations among teachers and administrators who understood both the challenges and opportunities of schools in the slums and who, as well, had a vision for improvements based on their Christian faith. The evolution of their thought by means of various international meetings prevented their lapsing into either traditional modes of interpretation and instruction or into the dogmatism that tends to afflict persons with high-minded, intense convictions on how to resolve social problems.

The sociological, pedagogical and theoretical issues raised in the SIEELA meetings reflected a desire to encourage local initiative, without which the particular problems of a given school was unlikely to be met.[62] Resolving the bigger problems was largely a matter of decentralization, devising locally attainable objectives with minimal resources and a great deal of improvization, attention and intelligence. The survival of the schools with high levels of morale gave indication that the approach was effective. The reports of student progress, though incomplete, are an indication that the strategy may be working.[63]

The SIEELA conferences provided the fora where LACC could offer a more concrete perspective for approaching social problems. It was within this framework, forged by frank discussion and common goals, that LACC's theoretical, theological and philosophical orientation toward social concern took form in the concrete historical context of the Latin American slums.[64] As such,

---

[61]'LACC Mission Statement,' *SIEELA* (Tegucigalpa, Honduras: Documents of PIEDAD, 1993).

[62]Annually, each country conducts local '*SIEELAS*' utilizing the materials that the leadership has brought from the international meetings with all their country's LACC personnel.

[63]Evaluations of the LACC programmes in each country demonstrate similar philosophical approaches. However, methodology varies according to the context of not only the local country but the local community as well.

[64]A cadre of educators, administrators and pastors have been instrumental in the dynamic formation of LACC's philosophical, theological, pedagogical and strategical fundamentals. Juan Bueno (El Salvador) and Rodolfo Sáenz (Costa Rica) have done much to form the philosophical and theological principles that guide LACC's pastoral action. Lic. Joaquín García (El Salvador), Lic. Mario Canaca (Honduras) and Lic. Francia Hernández (Dominican Republic) have made major contributions in the areas of educational formation. The strategical and administrative development has been most significantly impacted by

it is a necessary reflection and valuable exercise for participants in LACC to understand clearly that the work of LACC cannot be a merely accidental response, a peripheral activity or a mere emotional reaction. LACC deliberately attempts to meet in a systematic and intelligent way a challenge that the gospel has presented in the encounter with social reality. The following philosophical and educational principles developed as a result of active participation in the social context, commonly held and practised by the educators of LACC,[65] provide a framework by which critical evaluation can be made of the effectiveness of LACC.[66]

THE PHILOSOPHY OF LATIN AMERICA CHILDCARE

The policies developed by the SIEELA conferences for the administration of LACC schools disclose the roles that LACC envisions for itself. Sufficient time has now elapsed for us to begin to evaluate their effectiveness. The remainder of this chapter attempts to formulate a methodology for assessing whether in some measure the schools within the system do indeed provide an alternative education with corresponding prospects for eventually producing structural changes in these national societies.

Three initial points emerge in evaluation of the system now in place. First, all teachers, directors, administrators and pastors working in LACC are Latin Americans. Two thousand national educators were employed in LACC schools in 1992. That is, LACC is committed to a contextualization of the educational experience, making it a movement of the people.[67] Organizational structures and philosophies have been developed by national professionals in

---

(*footnote 64 continued*)
Johnnie Esquivel Tenorio, Mayela Flores and Gerardo Barrantes (Costa Rica). Numerous others have contributed to a plethora of areas such as health and medical care. See *Documents of PIEDAD* and locally published national constitutional and administrative statements of each country.

[65] The author is indebted to the educators of Latin America ChildCare for their input into this section. Of particular value is a paper written by Mario Canaca, 'Filosofia del programa PIEDAD frente a la educación publica,' *SIEELA* (Tegucigalpa, Honduras: Documents of PIEDAD, 1993).

[66] The construction of a theological framework to provide basis for the social policy of Pentecostals, including those involved in LACC, will be presented in chapter 6.

[67] For a discussion of the national autonomous nature of Latin American Pentecostals see chapter 2.

the countries where the schools are located to ensure that they correspond to the immediate sociocultural milieu. Moreover, they operate as autonomous entities, either under the umbrella of a local church board, or under the larger umbrella of the national Assemblies of God educational department. Autonomy of projects requires confidence on the part of the executive national leadership. Naturally, some projects will require assistance and orientation, but LACC as a national or international entity cannot supersede local initiative. As a demonstration of this self-reliance, the finances of LACC schools are in the hands of local administration. Moreover, no more is demanded than the usually required audits periodically submitted to national educational commissions to demonstrate the school's sound administration.

Since LACC schools are encouraged to operate at their own initiative and follow their own individual practices, they do not form a homogenous system and an overarching administrative oversight is difficult if not impossible. The weaknesses of such an approach is offset by the benefits of retaining grass-roots involvement necessary for the schools to affect the communities where they are located. Without local church, community and pastoral commitment to the project, LACC believes, the programme would soon become dependent and paralyzed. As John Yoder has observed, social transformation is most effective when the 'primary social structure through which the gospel works to change the structures is that of the Christian community'.[68] Where an identification of the school with the church and local community does exist, however, many of the goals of the programme can be achieved even with the problems of diversity, personnel and other restraints that tend to limit educational effectiveness.

Second, the pedagogical practices employed by the teachers in Latin America ChildCare are not governed by any single educational tradition, provided the school is successful in its pass/fail rate. LACC educators have the freedom to appropriate and adopt distinctive educational models to their own culture and context. The schools are in most cases required to follow a prescribed official curriculum, which it is necessary and desirable to apply creatively in keeping with the social realities found in each

---

[68]John Howard Yoder, *The Politics of Jesus* (Grand Rapids, MI: Wm. B. Eerdmans Publishing Co., 1972), 157.

situation.[69] In most countries LACC has made a commitment to rely as much as possible on teachers selected for their personal qualifications and ability to nurture students, rather than strictly by professional qualifications. Thus, LACC schools are generally deeply involved in teacher preparation throughout their period of service. Through years of experience LACC has demonstrated that it is better to encourage originality, creativity and even risk-taking in pedagogical practices among young and inexperienced teachers than it is to redirect the thinking and approaches of teachers already committed to another educational philosophy.

It follows from the stated objectives of LACC that the teacher is the most important feature of the system, exceeding in importance methodology, resources and funding.[70] Especially in working with disadvantaged children, the teacher's attitude and example are critical. Certain questions must necessarily be asked constantly. Why is the child not performing well? Is the child sick, hungry or physically or emotionally abused? Is the child disturbed by his or her background in a broken or dysfunctional home? The teacher must be aware of a myriad of circumstances that affect the child and, in a pastoral manner, take steps to address the disruptive, inhibiting problems he or she confronts.[71] The commitment of the teacher in a typical LACC school is apparent. Unfortunately, the majority of the teachers are not paid the equivalent salary that they could earn by working in a public school because of lack of funds. In spite of this obvious drawback, the work of the teachers is exemplary.

Only teachers that have deliberately been trained will employ

---

[69]For an excellent summary of past, current and future trends in Latin American education and social change see Rolland G. Paulston's review of fourteen recent texts dealing with distinctive educational perspectives. 'Ways of Seeing Education and Social Change in Latin America: A Phenomenographic Perspective', *Latin American Research Review* 27, (1992): 177–1202.

[70]Jere R. Behrman, professor of economics at the University of Pennsylvania, demonstrates that the amount of per capita investment in education in each Latin American country, though an important element for quality education, is not directly translatable into better quality education. He contends that although increased schooling investment is warranted, other factors, specifically the quality of the teacher, may produce higher returns. See Jere R. Behrman, 'Schooling in Latin America: What Are the Patterns And What Is The Impact?,' *Journal Of Interamerican Studies* 27, (Winter 1985–86): 21–35.

[71]Descriptive, analytical and theological elements that provide an effective basis for effective action will be demonstrated in a Pentecostal adaptation of the hermeneutical circle in chapter 6.

LACC's commitment that the pedagogical language employed by the educator should not be neutral. Language should convey basic concepts that provide foundational support for LACC's educational and theological philosophy. Paulo Freire, a Catholic educator in Brazil, pioneered the use of conceptual tools in literacy training to empower the poor to understand better their social and personal reality.[72] Latin American educators, such as Freire, who have encouraged a radical-interpretative approach to education, emphasize the urgency of overthrowing the restrictions that traditional social structures place upon the marginalized sectors.[73] Meaningful structural change requires that those who have been dominated experience a genuine liberation in their circumstances in order to become agents of change. Freire formed a philosophy of education and practical methodology designed to serve as a liberating force for the poor to transform their society in the still developing countries. Freire's *Pedagogy of the Oppressed* was born out of his work with the desperately poor masses of northeast Brazil. From his daily work with the poverty-stricken peoples of Brazil, he recognized that illiteracy was a key factor that determined the fate of the poor. Friere contended, however, that the poor needed more than the opportunity to read and write in order to make a significant break with the *status quo*. The key concept in *Pedagogy of the Oppressed* is the conscientization of the poor through literacy training. By conscientization, Freire means the use of literacy training to raise the consciousness of the poor to challenge their own sense of fatalism and resignation to the *status quo* and to stimulate them to take charge of their own destiny. To accomplish this task, Freire developed a core vocabulary which meant something to the concrete life situations of the poor and which could provide them with the capacity to contribute to a dialogue about their condition with the teacher who served only as a facilitator and catalyst. Language thus became the pedagogical tool for the oppressed to reflect on their own social and economic situation. When they have gained an un-

---

[72]Paulo Freire, *The Pedagogy of the Oppressed* (New York, NY: Seabury Press, 1970).

[73]The radical interpretive approach to education can be understood as 'a frame of reference that is committed to a view of society which emphasizes the importance of overthrowing or transcending the limitations of existing social relations'. Gibson Burrell and Morgan Gareth, *Sociological Paradigms and Organizational Analysis* (Portsmouth, NH: Heinemann, 1979), 32.

derstanding as to why they are poor, argues Freire, they will be in a position to begin to take control over their own future. 'Deutero-learning,' or the on-going capacity of learning to learn, finds its intellectual roots in the theory of Paulo Freire.[74] It could be argued that the radical-interpretative ideas of educators like Freire are really the ideas of the 'view from above' and are not really representative of the ideas of the marginalized. Not only does Friere employ a top-down control but this type of educational process is greatly influenced by the political inclinations of the teacher. It is often the 'intellectual' who decides what the poor *should* think of themselves and then becomes angered when the people do not respond. It is also true that 'what the poor really think of themselves' is also what the dominating sectors—for example, through education and the mass media—make them think.

Freire's radical perspective typically sees education as a revolutionary tool that can be employed to free the poor from their dominated position and bring about revolutionary social change. Similarly, liberation theologian Gustavo Gutiérrez argues that the poor, once understanding the reasons for their poverty, must be organized themselves in order to bring change to structures that are patently unjust.[75] José Míguez Bonino reflects the framework of these two theologians in an apt summary of Gutiérrez's reflections:

> He said (in summary) I discovered three things. I discovered that *poverty was a destructive thing*, something to be fought against and destroyed, not merely something which was the object of charity. Secondly, I discovered that *poverty was not accidental*. The fact that these people are poor and not rich is not just a matter of chance, but the result of a structure. Thirdly, I discovered that *poor people were a social class*. When I discovered that poverty was something to be fought against, that

---

[74]The ideas of Freire on adult non-formal education, though originally presented in the 1960s, have not significantly changed in his more recent works. See Paulo Freire and Antonio Faundez, *Learning to Question: A Pedagogy of Liberation* (New York, NY: Continuum, 1989) and Myles Horton and Paulo Freire, *We Make The Road By Walking: Conversations on Education and Social Change* (Philadelphia, PA: Temple University Press, 1990).

[75]Gustavo Gutiérrez, *A Theology of Liberation*, rev. ed. trans. Sister Caridad Inda and John Eagleson (Maryknoll, NY: Orbis Books, 1988).

poverty was structural, that poor people were a class [and could organize], it became crystal clear that in order to serve the poor, one had to move into political action.[76]

The educators of Latin America ChildCare would not disagree with the educational philosophy of Paulo Freire regarding the principle of consciousness-raising as an aspect of education. Nor would they disagree with the social analysis of Gustavo Gutiérrez. However, contrary to the pastoral action theory of Freire and Gutiérrez, who would contend for primarily a political option directed to the macro-perspective of social structures[77] to enable radical change, LACC would prefer to approach similar educational and social inequities from the micro-perspective of an alternative option based upon Christocentric schools in general, and upon impacting the individual personal life of the marginalized child in particular. Rejection of radical political methods is based less on deference, tradition and moral restraint than on investment of one's time and energy that will bring lasting benefits. Most political action undertaken by the masses in Latin America has been unsuccessful. This is not only because the protagonists use children and the desperately poor or the romantic or the pathologically angry, but also because the process of hating or destroying in turn destroys the individual engaged in, allegedly, redeeming society. The focus of LACC is on realizing the blighted child's potential. After the child has been nourished on positive sentiments he or she will select appropriate methods for dealing with injustice. Christianity makes responsibility very personal. So does LACC.

Consequently, the language of the primers utilized in the primary grades of the schools of LACC is filled with a rich description of the concepts of love, hope, and, most importantly empowerment undergirded by the basic premise that all people are created in God's image. Additionally, LACC has developed a Christian Education curriculum for each grade level from grades one through six that

---

[76]José Míguez Bonino, 'Statement by José Míguez Bonino,' in *Theology in the Americas* (Detroit II Conference Papers), eds. Sergio Torres and John Eagleson (Maryknoll, NY: Orbis Books, 1976), 278.

[77]Observers of Pentecostalism have consistently criticized the movement for its lack of 'political involvement' beyond its own context and within civil society. However, the definition of social concern to include only political, state and civil categories cannot capture other equally important areas of social concern such as a sense of personal dignity and value, the role of women, and personal morality.

focuses on six major topics—spiritual life, Bible and theology, the role of the church, Christian service and Christian ethics. This educational process borrows an underlying premise of Freire's thought that language should not be neutral but seek to provide a positive alternative known in LACC as the 'pedagogy of hope'.[78]

Contrary to the radical interpretive actions of Freire,[79] LACC endeavours to liberate the marginalized child by focusing individually upon the concept that because all people are created in God's own image they have intrinsic and unique value and worth.[80] In general, LACC is committed to this type of adequate and creative training of its personnel. It is apparent that the success in influencing the social structures in a meaningful way will have much to do with not only the competence of the teacher but with his or her thorough understanding of LACC's methodology for teaching.

Third, LACC emphasizes the importance of the children themselves. In the selection of new projects, priority is given to the residents of areas where the most need exists.[81] It is recognized that these needs are material as well as educational and must be preceded by instilling in the child a sense of human dignity and self-worth. Children usually enter the programme with low self-esteem and a sense of social inferiority. They often accept the stereotype (to the degree that they are reflective or sensitive) that they cannot be successful and that they are destined to continue to be part of the

---

[78]Cheryl Bridges Johns, in her doctoral dissertation, relates the constructs of Freire's pedagogical process to the context of Pentecostalism. She argues that Pentecostalism, an authentic movement of social transformation, provides an excellent context for a catechesis which presents a unique environment for a true pedagogy of the oppressed. Her dissertation has been published, *Pentecostal Formation: A Pedagogy Among the Oppressed* (Sheffield: Sheffield Academic Press, 1993).

[79]It would appear that Pentecostals have 'tuned in' to how marginalized people really live and act and think while frequently base communities and liberation theology have failed. The question and challenge is whether the transformation of life in the Pentecostal experience is or is not also a 'renewal of the mind' (Romans 8:1ff) which is able to break the spell of the 'schemata of the world'—introjected by all the influences—and create a 'mind' which conforms to God's good and perfect will. The theological formulation in chapter six endeavours to provide structure to this process.

[80]The concept of *Imago Dei*, that human life is created in God's image and can thus be distinguished from all other aspects of God's creation, will be described as the theological foundation for ethical principles and actions in the following chapter,

[81]John Bueno, '*Reflexiones sobre el Origen y Filosofía del Programa Integral de Educación de las Asambleas de Dios, PIEDAD*' [Reflections concerning the origin and philosophy of LACC] *SIEELA* (San Salvador, El Salvador: Documents of PIEDAD, 1984).

marginal sectors.[82] An illustration of this lack of vision for self-improvement, is the conversation the author had with a seven-year-old student named Wendy in an LACC school in El Salvador.

'Do you have a mommy and daddy?'
'Just a daddy.'
'Where is your mommy?'
'I don't know.'
'Whom do you live with?'
'I live with my daddy and my little brother.'
'What does your daddy do?'
'He sells lottery tickets and cigarettes.'
'What do you want to do when you grow up?'
'I want to sell lottery tickets like my daddy.'

Wendy had few dreams or significant hopes for the future and little concept that she had been created in God's image. This child lived with her father and little brother in a one-room shack in an urban slum in San Salvador. Her father was blind. Everyday she took her little brother across the city on the bus to attend an Assemblies of God school that had granted them a *beca* (scholarship). The goal of LACC is to impart to this child, and as many as possible like her, a sense of self-dignity, worth and a chance to dream.

LACC believes that the best hope for a child to comprehend and demonstrate self-dignity and worth will be through a personal relationship with God. The priority of the salvation experience should be taught to every child. Certainly, the basic responsibility of Christians is to address the needs of people wherever they may be found. The compassion of Christian responsibility leaves no other choice. However, the fundamental necessity of humanity is a relationship with Jesus Christ, and the intention of LACC is that every boy and girl, man or woman who has association with the programme will be introduced to such a relationship. At the same time, teachers are careful to allow students the freedom to make their own choices without any pressure or consequences.[83]

---

[82]The Catholic Church, prior to Vatican II, reinforced this view and marginalized people often fatalistically accepted it. See chapter four, note 59 and for a critique of the church's role in society see the analyzes by Gustavo Gutiérrez and Juan Luis Segundo in the following chapter.

[83]Children are not required or coerced to be of a certain religious orientation in order to attend and receive all the benefits of an LACC school.

ASSESSING THE SOCIAL IMPACT OF LATIN AMERICA CHILDCARE

While LACC is committed to the premise that its style of radical education will result in individual and social change, the educators in the programme recognize that significant social change is a long-term process.

Since no external comprehensive assessment by personnel not related to LACC has been done, the leadership has resorted to available criteria and data to evaluate the schools' effectiveness.[84] The programmes begun in El Salvador and Costa Rica, with the most years of operation, best demonstrate the long-term influence of the programme. One indication of the effectiveness is drawn from the central school in San Salvador, where in 1976 most of the 1500 students were supported by foreign sponsors. At present, however, the profile of this school is quite different. The student body of 1994 was completely self-supporting, with funds from the school also maintaining a school of 300 children in a neighbouring slum through monthly donations from the students and their families. The central school also provides scholarships to hundreds of children and is paying the university tuition fees for students that have graduated from high school but were unable to cover costs of advanced studies. Probably a combination of improved economic conditions for hundreds of families within the local church community and the enrolment of children who had the capacity to pay a monthly tuition fee were significant factors. More importantly, however, was the process of social conscientization that evolved as part of the educational process.

Thousands of El Salvador's young people have become agents of social change by practising active solidarity and participation in concrete terms. While LACC regularly reports many examples of children for whom strategically available educational opportunity has been significant, the experience of the Cabellero family from

---

[84]It would be desirable to conduct a comprehensive survey of several thousand children who have graduated from the programme in order to measure the influence their educational formation from LACC has had upon their current situations. However, because LACC projects are located in the poorest slums of Latin America resulting in 1) a transient population and 2) the fact that most young people as soon as they graduate find work and leave the slum community, it is almost impossible to track them with the limited financial resources available to LACC.

El Salvador bordered on the dramatic. Seventeen years after the recently widowed and destitute Lucy Cabellero arrived at the Liceo in 1968 asking for help to educate her seven children, aged 6 to 15, the school could point to the eldest, Tobias, who was then an electrical engineer, the next two sons who were both high school teachers, the next two daughters who were commercial secretaries, the sixth child, Raquel, who was completing her professional training as a psychologist, and the youngest, Pablo, was studying accounting, all with the *bachillerato* from the Liceo Cristiano. If the theme of the school was a frankly idealistic aspiration, 'Forging new spirits,' the Cabelleros provide a concrete example of its achievement. Many similar cases have been registered, as indigent families are enabled to overcome demoralization and gain the skills and inspiration to address the demands of a competitive life. Cecilia Maríz, in studying Pentecostals in Brazil, concludes with Bryan Roberts and other students of the movement that 'Pentecostalism helps people to believe that they can overcome their difficulties. Because of this, it seems to be more useful for those in crisis than for those "on their feet",' according to Maríz.[85] Similarly, John Burdick summarizes recent scholarship by arguing that 'the self-valorization brought about by Pentecostal conversion often paves the way for a strong sense of natural rights and citizenship'.[86] Although there remains uncertainty about the social mobility of Pentecostal converts, there seems to be little question on the part of current scholars that Pentecostalism functions in various communities in Latin America just as the LACC programme is designed to act, by first dealing with self-esteem and dignity.

The LACC programme leads children into a new life by means of altering their perspectives and attitudes. Many LACC children for the first time see the world from a different perspective. They are encouraged to respect their own abilities and opinions, are socialized to feel comfortable in a society with a broader selection of career options and are equipped with the skills to compete in a competitive job market. Given these advantages in the context of a moralistic, theologically reinforced and highly motivational pro-

---

[85]Cecilia Loreto Maríz, *Coping With Poverty: Pentecostals and Christian Base Communities in Brazil* (Philadelphia, PA: Temple University Press, 1994), 42.

[86]John Burdick, 'Struggling Against the Devil: Pentecostalism and Social Movements in Urban Brazil,' in *Rethinking Protestantism in Latin America*, eds. Virginia Garrard Burnett and David Stoll (Philadelphia, PA: Temple University Press, 1993), 20.

gramme where their teachers and other role models are committed to social service, there is good reason to believe that students will develop similar social concerns, leading as adults to appropriate conduct to effect social change. Ultimately, LACC sees the rescue of children from dismal, hopeless poverty as only the first phase of their transformation. Eventually, they must acquire a sense of responsibility for changing the conditions that perpetuate poverty and powerlessness.

The students in LACC schools located in marginal communities, in addition to receiving affirmation, consistently outperform students in neighbouring public schools. In 1993 *las escuelas cristianas* in Costa Rica had a 98.5 per cent passing rate of their sixth grade classes on the required governmental exams while the neighbouring public schools registered less than a 50 per cent pass rate.[87] LACC also has been successful in slowing down the school drop-out rate in comparison with national averages. UNICEF reports that in countries such as Guatemala only one in ten children successfully complete sixth grade, while in countries with the most favourable economic levels, such as Costa Rica, Venezuela and Chile the proportion of children who finish the sixth grade reaches only 50 per cent.[88] Over the past six years LACC has followed the educational progress of 16,000 children enrolled in LACC schools in eighteen Latin American countries—three out of four students complete *primaria*, an amazing contrast with the average governmental statistics.[89]

Despite the scarce attention given to LACC by persons and agencies concerned with Latin American social development, the work of the Pentecostal colegios has been recognized in a few instances.[90] Initial contacts were made by the Spanish-language *Readers' Digest (Selecciones)* regarding the possibility of a story describing its work. In 1985 and again in 1986, a Costa Rican public

---

[87] *Reporte Anual de las escuelas cristianas de las Asambleas de Dios*, March 1994. LACC schools are also evaluated on a regular basis throughout each school year by public government educational supervisors. These evaluations are generally received in a written form. It is not unusual for the LACC schools to be commended by these government officials as superior in comparison with public schools in similar communities.

[88] *UNICEF*, 39.

[89] *PIEDAD Annual Reports* (San José, Costa Rica).

[90] A critical study of Latin America ChildCare and its impact upon community life is currently being done in the doctoral dissertation of Ron Bueno at the American University in Washington, D.C.

relations group, *Relacionistas Internacionales Costarricenses y Extranjeros*
(CIRCE) honoured the Costa Rican *Escuelas Cristianas de las
Asambleas de Dios* with an award 'in consideration of their labour
on behalf of human and public relations to advance the image of
democracy in Costa Rica'. On the first occasion, CIRCE granted
the award also to the Nobel Peace Prize recipient Oscar Arias and
other prominent Central Americans associated with humanitarian
projects. The presentation to LACC was made by José 'Pepe'
Figueres, the patriarch of Costa Rican democracy. Specifically, the
award was given to LACC not just for its educational programme
in the slum community of *Los Cuadros*, but also because LACC,
through the organization of its local school, had been instrumental
in influencing the government to supply running water, electricity
and passable roads so that buses could provide public transport.[91]
On September 7, 1994 in a front page feature story in the Sunday
section of Costa Rica's leading daily newspaper *La Nación* the
reporter not only emphasized the LACC's provision of medical
assistance, daily feeding programmes, gifts of uniforms and eyeglasses as well as education to over 4,000 children in the marginal
slum areas but also documented that the existence of the LACC
schools over time brought significant and real changes to the entire
community, including running water and better housing.[92]

Admittedly these examples can be individually interpreted
subjectively, but when taken together they do describe a particular
direction and commitment that LACC has taken. They are
certainly concrete enough to frame a general critique of the
activities of LACC on behalf of children in Latin America. The
examples document that the goals set by the programme are both
necessary and noble. Obviously, the trophies LACC seeks are the
changes in the lives of otherwise severely restricted children, both
as an end in itself and as the basis for making modifications in
the society and the culture of the Latin American poor accessible
to LACC.

Specifically, LACC has emerged as part of an effort to break the
cycle of poverty that traps poor families. By providing an alternative
education, the programme at once offers relief for children by
providing them with schooling, structure in their often chaotic

---

[91] See award *PRESENCIA* (November 1989).
[92] Amalia Palacio, 'Superación en la Pobreza,' 1B.

lives, improved nutrition and most importantly, concern for their complete social, physical, intellectual and moral development.

Demonstration that fundamental Pentecostal beliefs have produced social concern leads necessarily to the movement's continuing theological support for such programmes. If in its early stages these groups developed schools as a means to change lives on the way to effecting social change, what theological foundations will sustain these groups? While Pentecostals have been too intent on their work to give much reflection to why they are doing it, increasingly they will need to demonstrate that they have an adequate theological articulation to provide continuing support for their social programmes. This working out of Pentecostal principles will be taken up in the following chapter.

Table 1: Social Conditions in Central America

Country	Inflation	Unemployment	Under-employment	Poverty index	Per capita income	Population without access to healthcare	Population without access to portable water
Costa Rica	27%	4.6%	much	24%★★ 1990	1900.00 1991	20%★ 1985–90	8%★ 1989–90
Honduras	26% 1991	15% 1989	30–40% 1989	75%★★ 1990	1050.00 1991	34% 1985–90	27%★ 1988–90
Nicaragua	776% 1991	13% 1991	50% 1991	62%† 1980	425.00 1991	17%★ 1985–90	46%★ 1988–90
El Salvador		8%★★ 1988–89		68%★† 1980	680.00 1984–85	44%★ 1985–90	52%★ 1988–90
Guatemala	40% 1991	6.7% 1989	30–40% 1989	71%† 1980	1260.00 1991	66%★★ 1985–90	39%★ 1988–90

All statistics are from 1992 unless otherwise noted

All statistics are from *World Factbook* with the following exceptions:

★ Statistics are from UNICEF

★★ Statistics are from 1992 edition of the *Statistical Yearbook for Latin America and the Caribbean*

† Statistics are from Richard Garfield, Glen Williams, *Healthcare in Nicaragua: Primary Care in Changing Regimes* (Oxford: Oxford University Press, 1992)

Table 2: Social Conditions in Central America

Country	Population	Birthrate	Deathrate	Infant mortality	Mortality under 5 yrs. of age	Literacy	Life expectancy
Costa Rica	3,187,085	27/1000	4/1000	12/1000	22/1000★ 1990	93%★★	75–m 79–f
Honduras	5,092,776	37/1000	7/1000	54/1000	84/1000★ 1990	73% 1990	65–m 68–f
Nicaragua	3,378,150	37/1000	7/1000	57/1000	78/1000★ 1990	87% (1985)★★ 57%(1971)★★	60–m 66–f
El Salvador	5,574,279	33/1000	5/1000	26/1000	87/1000★ 1990	73%(1990) (76%–m, 70%–f)	68–m 75–m
Guatemala	9,784,275 2.4% growth rate	34/1000	8/1000	56/1000	94/1000 1990	55%(1990) (63%–m, 47%–f)	61–m 66–f

All statistics are from 1992 unless otherwise noted
All statistics are from *World Factbook* with the following exceptions:
★ Statistics are from UNICEF
★★ Statistics are from 1992 edition of the *Statistical Yearbook for Latin America and the Caribbean*

Table 3: Public Education in Latin America

Country	Children without access to education	Children completed primaria	Public spending on education (percentage of PNB)	Public spending on military (percentage of PNB)
Guatemala	36%	36%	1.80%	2.60% in 1987
El Salvador	30%	30%	2.00%	3.50%
Honduras	12%	43%	4.90%	8.40%
Nicaragua	26%	35%	3.90%	28.30%
Costa Rica	13%	76%	4.40%	0.40%

All statistics are from UNICEF

Table 4: Latin America ChildCare General Statistics 1993

Country	Primary Schools	Secondary Schools	Total	Student Enrolment
Mexico	2		2	300
Guatemala	11	7	18	4,600
El Salvador	34	30	64	23,350
Honduras	11	1	12	3,000
Nicaragua	52	4	56	6,500
Costa Rica	9	3	12	4,700
Panama	4	1	5	1,400
Belize	5		5	765
Haiti	6		6	1,200
Jamaica	2			500
Dominican Republic	18	5	23	10,032
Colombia	3		3	(est.) 1,000
Peru	10		10	(est.) 1,000
Ecuador	4	2	6	4,740
Paraguay	7	1	8	2,100
Chile	8	8		(est.) 1,000
Argentina	10	1	11	(est.) 1,000
Uruguay	2		2	300
Totals:				
18 Countries	198	63	261	67,487

Table 5: Latin America ChildCare: Central America

Country	Primary Schools	Secondary Schools	Total	Student Enrollment
Guatemala	11	7	18	4,600
El Salvador	34	30	64	23,350
Honduras	11	1	12	3,000
Nicaragua	52	4	56	6,500
Costa Rica	9	3	12	4,700
Totals:				
	117	45	162	42,150

Chapter 6
Toward A Social Doctrine for Latin American Pentecostals

THE FORMULATION OF A PENTECOSTAL SOCIAL DOCTRINE

The previous chapters have demonstrated that Latin American Pentecostals, indigenous and autonomous in nature,[1] practise a social ethic as part of their faith.[2] However, despite considerable informal, mutual assistance and some structured programmes intended to meet the material and social needs of specific groups like children, single-parent heads of families and prison inmates, little effort has been devoted to the formulation of a Pentecostal social doctrine. José Míguez Bonino perceptibly notes that as a first stage one must look at the social dynamic of the Pentecostal movement to discover their intentions; an explicit social doctrine follows at a second stage.[3]

Having acquired greater resources and recognition, Latin American Pentecostals must now recognize that their social action must be undergirded by a comprehensive and coherent theological statement that critically interacts with what they are presently doing. The articulation of a consistent theological basis for their social action is needed to explain adherents' ethical and moral

---

[1]See chapter 2 'The Formation of Popular, National, Autonomous Churches in Latin America.'

[2]See chapter 4 'Social Expressions of Central American Pentecostalism', and chapter 5 'Latin America ChildCare: A Case Study in Pentecostal Praxis'.

[3]José Míguez Bonino, interview by author, Buenos Aires, Argentina, 28 November 1993. It is Míguez Bonino's opinion that the development of a coherent social doctrine by Latin American Pentecostals takes time. He suggests that a grass-roots movement growing as quickly as are the Pentecostals is not likely to take the time or even have the necessary advanced educational training at such an early stage of its development. And elsewhere, though in a different context but certainly applicable to this situation, Míguez Bonino affirms that the articulation of a theological stance 'comes at the rear guard, as a reflection, as a help to rethink and deepen a commitment already undertaken as an act of obedience'. José Míguez Bonino, 'For Life and Against Death: A Theology That Takes Sides,' in *Theologians in Transitions: The Christian Century 'How my mind has changed' series*, ed. James M. Wall (New York, NY: Crossroads, 1991), 172.

concerns both to themselves and to the society of which they are a part.[4]

This chapter will focus on the theological ethics of social concern that provides the conceptual foundations for a holistic approach to social change that includes 'redemption and lift,' programmes of social welfare and community-based programmes of social transformation.

In this chapter I will use a hermeneutical circle in order to articulate a Pentecostal social ethic. The basis for Pentecostal social thinking and action springs from a transforming experience, an empowerment derived from an intense, transcendent sense of the divine presence. Armed with this personal knowledge of God's self-revelatory nature and sensitive to the personal and social demands of the Old Testament prophetic teachings, the Pentecostal finds that ethic amplified and made explicit in the New Testament portrayal of Jesus and the teachings on the Kingdom of God. The demands of this reign, characterized by justice, mercy, love and peace, were transferred to the Christian community at the coming of the Spirit at Pentecost, as described in Acts, and served as the ethical foundation of the primitive Christian church. The actualization of this empowering on a large scale in the experience of contemporary Latin American Pentecostals provides a laboratory to examine the actual operation of the New Testament ethic and permits the formulation of a uniquely Pentecostal social ethic.[5]

---

[4]See the following works for excellent descriptions of the church and contemporary ethical issues. This chapter has been informed by each of these books. Larry Rasmussen and Bruce Birch, *Bible and Ethics in the Christian Life* (Minneapolis, MN: Augsberg , 1976); William K. Frankena, *Ethics*, 2d ed. (Englewood Cliffs, NJ: Prentice Hall, 1973); James M. Gustafason, *Christian Ethics and the Community* (Philadelphia, PA: Pilgrim Press, 1971); Stephen Mott, *Biblical Ethics and Social Change*, 1982; Allan Verhey, *The Great Reversal: Ethics and the New Testament* (Grand Rapids, MI: Wm. B. Eerdmans Publishing Co., 1984); R. E. O. White, *Biblical Ethics* (Atlanta, GA: John Knox Press, 1979); José Míguez Bonino, *Toward a Christian Political Ethics* (Philadelphia, PA: Fortress Press, 1983); David Cook, *The Moral Maze: A way of exploring Christian ethics* (London: SPCK, 1983) and Bruce C. Birch, *Let Justice Roll Down: The Old Testament, Ethics, and Christian Life* (Louisville, KY: John Knox Press, 1991).

[5]See chapter 3, for an explanation of the aspects that constitute an evangelical/Pentecostal doctrine.

THE HERMENEUTICAL CIRCLE AND PENTECOSTAL SOCIAL PRAXIS

That Pentecostals adopt a dynamic hermeneutic methodology that interacts with the concrete historical reality of Latin America on the one hand, and the biblical text on the other is foundational to respond adequately in an integral manner to the spiritual and physical needs of the people of Latin America.[6]

The motivation for such a contextual hermeneutic is generated by following the thought-provoking trail that certain Latin American liberation theologians have travelled in their critique of academically-bound religion in order to liberate theology to act within the context of a real world scarred by injustice and sin.[7] In particular, the landmark contribution of Juan Luis Segundo's hermeneutical circle will be presented. Segundo's 'preliminary definition' of his hermeneutical circle is a process of

> the continuing change in our interpretation of the Bible which is dictated by the continuing changes in our present-day reality, both individual and societal.[8]

Segundo's hermeneutical circle becomes operational only when two preconditions exist. The first precondition is that a question arises from within one's experience that is so profound that it causes

---

[6]The use of the hermeneutical circle for Pentecostal praxis in an embryonic form was first developed for a paper 'Análisis, Reflexión y Teología,' which the author read at the SIEELA conference of Latin America ChildCare, March 30–April 4, 1987 in Tegucigalpa, Honduras. A revision of the paper, substantially rewritten was published as 'The Kingdom of God and the Hermeneutical Circle: Pentecostal Praxis in the Third World,' in *Called and Empowered: A Pentecostal Perspective*, 44–58. This chapter seeks to build upon and further develop this theme of 'Pentecostal Praxis'.

[7]Literature on the subject of liberation theology is now immense. For some of the foundational works see Gustavo Gutiérrez, *A Theology of Liberation: History, Politics and Salvation*, 1988; José Míguez Bonino, *Doing Theology in a Revolutionary Situation* (Philadelphia, PA: Fortress Press, 1975); Juan Luis Segundo, *The Liberation of Theology* (Maryknoll, NY: Orbis Books, 1976); Jon Sobrino, *Christology at the Crossroads: A Latin American Approach*, trans. John Drury (Maryknoll, NY: Orbis Books, 1978); Leonardo Boff, *Jesus Christ liberator: a critical Christology for our time*, trans. by Patrick Hughes (Maryknoll, NY: Orbis Books, 1978); Fernando. A. Belo, *A Materialist Reading of the Gospel of Mark*, trans. Matthew J. O'Connell (Maryknoll, NY: Orbis Books, 1981); Enrique Dussel, *A History of the Church in Latin America: Colonialism to Liberation*, trans. and revised by Alan Neeley (Grand Rapids, MI: Wm. B. Eerdmans Publishing Co., 1981) and Marc H. Ellis and Otto Maduro, eds., *Expanding the View: Gustavo Gutiérrez and the Future of Liberation Theology* (Maryknoll, NY: Orbis Books, 1990).

[8]Juan Luis Segundo, *The Liberation of Theology*, 8.

ordinary explanations to be called into question. The second precondition is that our question cannot be adequately answered by our customary interpretation of Scripture, causing the reader to look deeper and more broadly into exegesis of the Bible for a serviceable answer to address the experience. Thus, the profound question from the encounter with the context triggers a more profound understanding of the Bible.

Segundo delineates this theological reflection on historical actions on behalf of the poor in a four-step process:

> Firstly there is our way of experiencing reality, which leads us to ideological suspicion. Secondly there is the application of our ideological suspicion to the whole ideological superstructure in general and to theology in particular. Thirdly there comes a new way of experiencing theological reality that leads us to exegetical suspicion, that is, to the suspicion that the prevailing interpretation of the Bible has not taken important pieces of data into account. Fourthly we have our new hermeneutic, that is, our new way of interpreting the fountainhead of our faith (i.e. Scripture) with the new elements at our disposal.[9]

Juan Luis Segundo's 'ideological suspicion'[10] of the injustices within the social structures corresponds in general to much of the groundwork laid by Gustavo Gutiérrez. Gutiérrez was the first to challenge the inertia of the Catholic Church with his presentation at the 1968 Council of Latin American Bishops (CELAM) in Medellín, Colombia.[11] Gutiérrez, in the presence of Pope Paul VI, called for the church to move from a concept of development to one of liberation.[12] Gutiérrez contended that the church had at one

---

[9]Ibid., 9.

[10]Segundo defines his use of the term 'ideology' to describe a rather neutral way to refer to the 'view of the world', and the understanding of reality without making a judgement as to whether the ideology is correct or wrong. He specifically defines ideology as a term 'for all systems of means, be they natural or artificial, that are used to attain some end or goal. . . . ideology is the system aggregate of all that we wish for in a *hypothetical* rather than an absolute way. In other words, it is every system of means.' Juan Luis Segundo, *Jesus Of Nazareth Yesterday and Today: Faith and Ideology*, vol. 1 (Maryknoll, NY: Orbis Books, 1984).

[11]Vatican II made the evangelization of the poor their principal focus. In a self-critical analysis of her history Vatican II consciously entered into reflection upon the world of the poor. The actions of Vatican II, made clearer at Medellín in 1968, have had numerous consequences upon the church in Latin America.

[12]This paper later appeared in fully developed form in Gutiérrez' now famous *A Theology of Liberation*. In the 25th anniversary revised edition of *A Theology of Liberation* (Maryknoll,

time abrogated its earthly responsibility and desperately needed to recapture a new understanding of its role in the world. He argued that historically in Latin America, the church had merely fulfilled a 'religious' category, thereby having little impact upon the real lives of the people. He called for the church to become a visible signpost of the Kingdom of God in the world by demonstrating its struggle for justice for the poor and liberation for the oppressed.[13]

Gutiérrez argued that because abject poverty in Latin America was a destructive force and because this poverty emerged from the results of the social structure, the role of the church became crystal clear. He proposed a mandate for political involvement in order for the church to give expression as God's agent of liberation on behalf of the poor and the oppressed. Without political action directed against a social system which perpetuated the class reality of Latin America there would be no liberation for the poor and the oppressed. Such action would be, in effect, a signpost of the Kingdom of God, a legitimate representative of the claims of the Kingdom.[14] Political action could be taken only if theological reflection began from 'the view from below,' from 'the underside,'… the marginalized person, or from the poor. Like Gutiérrez, Juan Luis Segundo submitted that through the generations the

---

(*footnote 12 continued*)
NY: Orbis Books, 1988) Gutiérrez, in a long Preface, clarifies several important issues raised in the original edition including, what he considered to be, an over-reliance of liberation theology upon the use of the social sciences and the inadequacy of the 'theory of dependence' to explain the internal dynamics of Latin American countries. For a recent overview of Gutiérrez' writings, see Robert McAfee Brown, *Gustavo Gutiérrez: An Introduction to Liberation Theology* (Maryknoll, NY: Orbis Books, 1990).

[13]Gutiérrez, *A Theology of Liberation*, 148.

[14]Ibid., 121–140. Gutiérrez identifies the perspectives of liberation theology which will revitalize the church to stand in solidarity with the poor in protest against the systems of oppression. See Gutiérrez, *The Theology of Liberation*, 79–173. Gutiérrez was roundly criticized for his supposed lack of commitment to the tradition of spirituality as well as a dearth of any developed Christology. In fact, Gutiérrez himself cited spirituality, among others, as part of the unfinished task for liberation theologians in the future (120). Gutiérrez has subsequently addressed the area of spirituality with his own book, *We Drink From Our Own Wells*, trans. Matthew J. O'Connell (Maryknoll, NY: Orbis, 1984) as well as his *The truth shall make you free: confrontations*, trans. Matthew J. O'Connell (Maryknoll, NY: Orbis Books, 1990). The other area of Christology has been impressively handled in the later development of liberation theology by Jon Sobrino, *Christology at the Crossroads*, trans. John Drury (Maryknoll, NY: Orbis Books, 1978) and Leonardo Boff, *Jesus Christ liberator: a critical Christology for our time*, trans. Patrick Hughes (Maryknoll, NY: Orbis Books, 1978) and José Míguez Bonino, ed., *Faces of Jesus: Latin American Christologies*, trans. Robert A. Barr (Maryknoll, NY: Orbis Books, 1984).

church had been a captive of the ruling classes of Latin American society. That is, the structure of society, with its extreme differences of social classes, neglect of native peoples, and tolerance for corruption in public life, owed much to the complacency of the Catholic Church. The church, therefore, had become an unwitting participant in perpetuating the unjust economic system that marginalized large numbers of Latin Americans and led in turn to social abuses. Given its role in neglecting the poor in Latin America, Segundo argued, the church must acknowledge its responsibility and correct the damage it had done through its alignment with the *status quo*.[15] By unmasking the unjust ideological basis for the existing structures and by promoting a theological basis for society in accordance with the authentic values of faith, Segundo aimed to put a praxis theology to the service of social transformation.[16]

To be relevant, in Segundo's estimation, theology simply must respond to the questions that the poor are asking. The marginalized are not interested in the traditionally articulated scientific/theological ideas of theologians and priests; rather, they want to know how God could abandon them so totally in the physical realm. Unless the church is a participant in this quest, the liberationists argue, it has lost reason for its existence.

Furthermore, it is impossible to address these disturbing questions unless one adequately understands the structures of a society that permits, and even defends, this kind of poverty.[17] In order to explain

---

[15]For Segundo's critique of the 'hidden motives' of Roman Catholic priests' desire to control their flocks, see the discussion in chapter 3.

[16]Segundo, *The Liberation of Theology*, 132.

[17]Segundo candidly admits the debt that liberation theology owes to Karl Marx, particularly in the methodology it uses for analysis of present-day social reality (13). Most liberationists, including Segundo, shy away from the idea that wholesale use of the Marxist line can be connected with all aspects of liberation. Marxist categories as an instrument for social analysis, however, help them to understand the structural realities of the world better (58–61). It is their opinion that it is an undeniable fact that polarized forces in the world are in conflict. Marx merely reported what seemed to be obvious. The working class is relatively powerless in the face of decisions made by the ruling class. One's perspective or worldview is conditioned by the position one holds within the class structure. Liberationists contend that if Marx's descriptions of society are true, then his thought must not only be taken seriously but could be employed as a useful tool of analysis. Protestant theologian Míguez Bonino likewise commits himself to liberation theology's key foundational plank: historical praxis and critical reflection. Míguez Bonino's *Doing Theology in a Revolutionary Situation*, 1975 has often been celebrated as one of the clearest statements on liberation theology. In his *Christians and Marxists: The Mutual Challenge to Revolution* (London: Hodder and Stoughton, 1976), Míguez Bonino makes clear, however, that a Marxist

just how the church must change to meet this challenge and thus fulfil its responsibilities, Segundo calls the church to a kind of dynamic assessment of its beliefs and practices. He suggests that a preferential option for the poor[18] undertaken by the church can be derived from a contemporary reading of the Scriptures and a commitment to appropriate action.[19] This praxis approach facilitates recognition of biblical principles that might otherwise go ignored.[20] Segundo has

---

(*footnote 17 continued*)
analysis may be used as an analytical tool to reveal the nature of the class struggle in Latin America, Míguez Bonino would also argue that Marx's social analysis is insufficient. He would not share Marx's commitment to atheism and dialectical materialism. Míguez Bonino states his theological position firmly: 'This book is written from the point of view of a person who confesses Jesus Christ as Lord and Saviour. This is his center of gravity and everything else is seen (in intention, at least) in relation to it. The reality and power of the Triune God, the witness of the only Scriptures, the story of God's salvation are not seen as hypotheses to be proved, but as the foundation of life, action, understanding and hope.' (7). Míguez Bonino forthrightly dismisses the concept that the context ever controls the biblical text. The Bible is '*the only standard for assessing contemporary events in terms of God's action and purpose . . . .*' [italics are mine]. See José Míguez Bonino, 'A God Who Acts and Renews His Church,' in *Social Justice and the Latin Churches*, ed. Church and Society in Latin America, trans. Jorge Lara Braud (Richmond, VA: John Knox Press, 1969), 38. For an explanation of Marx's materialistic conception of history see Karl Marx, *The German Ideology*, trans. S. Ryazanskaya (Mascon: Lawrence and Wishart Ltd., 1964). For a cogent and comprehensive overview of Karl Marx and his writings see David McLellan's, *Essential Writings* (Oxford: Oxford University Press, 1988); *Marxism and religion: a description and assessment of the Marxist Critique of Christianity* (London: Macmillan, 1987) and *Ideology* (Milton Keynes: Open University Press, 1986). Also see David Lyon, *Karl Marx: an assessment of his life and thought*, 2d. ed. (Australia: Lion, 1980).

[18] The preferential option for the poor, for liberationists, requires an ongoing commitment to the struggle for social justice. See Gutiérrez, *A Theology of Liberation*, xxv–xxviii. Segundo considers a commitment to this option as the hermeneutical key to understand the gospels. Juan Luis Segundo, 'La opción por los pobres como clave herméneutica para entender el Evangelio,' *Sal Terrae* (June 1986): 473–82.

[19] For a cogent example of a contemporary reading of the Scriptures that takes into account both the socio-political aspects of the text in its original form as well as a contemporary application of that text into not only a Latin American but First World context see Christopher Rowland and Mark Corner, *Liberating Exegesis*, 1990. For an exploration of the New Testament through the lens of sociological analysis see Wayne Meeks, *The first urban Christians: the social world of the Apostle Paul* (New Haven, CT: Yale University Press, 1983); Bruce Malina, *The New Testament World: Insights from Cultural Anthropology* (Louisville, KY: John Knox Press, 1981); Abraham Malherbe, *Social Aspects of Early Christianity* (Philadelphia, PA: Fortress Press, 1983) and Richard Horsley, *Sociology of the Jesus Movement* (New York, NY; Crossroad, 1989). Such sociological approaches may be especially useful in two-third world countries because of the similarities in social dynamics.

[20] The hermeneutical or pastoral circle has, in part, evolved from the concept of praxis as it is presented in Paulo Freire, *The Pedagogy of the Oppressed*, 1970. See chapter 5 of this book. For a brief overview of the development of the processes underlying the interrelationship between text and context particularly in the thought of Rudolf Bultmann, Ernst

called for a hermeneutic that stimulates praxis consistent with the Scripture mandate. His hermenuetic, grounded in two simultaneous acts—theology and action—in dynamic relationship, which he labels 'the hermeneutical circle,' compels Christians to look at and alter reality.[21] In responding to this challenge, Pentecostalism has had a dramatic influence upon a significant sector of the population and is addressing some of the compelling claims of liberation theology regarding structural change for the marginalized.

ASSESSMENT OF THE HERMENEUTICAL CIRCLE AND PENTECOSTAL PRAXIS

Evangelical Christians have generally disavowed liberation theology, viewing it as Marxism garbed in theological language. Some Pentecostals may struggle with any appropriation of the 'hermeneutical circle' because of several perceived unacceptable implications that generally accompany this process. Such issues include the poor being the initial and often the only point of involvement with insufficient emphasis placed upon the fallen nature of humankind, and the use of social scientific analysis that, on occasion, adopts a Marxist ideology. Further it is argued that the utilization of the social sciences cannot provide an adequate framework from which a comprehensive picture of the Latin American situation can be understood.[22] The evangelical would often see liberation theology as offering a situational hermeneutic that could force an application of the context upon the Scriptures rather than receiving a theology produced by a reading of Scripture. There follows, according to critics, a pastoral action that is often methodologically political in nature. This style of pastoral action reduces theology to political ideals driving toward a 'utopian' structural change in the existing order.[23] These issues, though outside the scope of this particular

---

(*footnote 20 continued*)
Fuchs, and Gerhard Ebeling, see A. C. Thiselton, 'The New Hermeneutic,' in *New Testament Interpretation: Essays on Principles and Methods*, ed. I. Howard Marshall (Grand Rapids, MI: Wm. B. Eerdmans Publishing Co., 1977).

[21] For a current review of liberation theology see Arthur F. McGovern, *Liberation Theology and Its Critics: Toward an Assessment* (Maryknoll, NY: Orbis Books, 1989).

[22] See note 14 for a corrective statement by Gutiérrez.

[23] Gutiérrez defines the use of the term 'utopia' as it is employed by most liberation theologians including Segundo. Gutiérrez, when using the term, does not mean the possibility of creating a perfect social order but rather the creation of a vision which serves

chapter, are very important and their implications for effective social action need to be understood and critically evaluated by Pentecostals who attempt to utilize the hermeneutical circle.

Though most Pentecostals do not accept certain presuppositions of theologians such as Segundo,[24] the underlying spiritual reality of a God who acts in human history inherent in this dynamic model can and should be accepted as a legitimate point of theological reflection and basis for action on the part of Pentecostals. This hermeneutical instrument, despite the critical differences between liberation theology and Pentecostal thought, can be adapted and profitably used in a Pentecostal hermenuetic.

The purpose of the hermeneutical circle is to allow the Bible itself to speak to the ever-changing world in which action on behalf of the poor needs to take on concrete form. Further, the circle allows the Bible to stand as an authority over previous man-made interpretations of the Scripture and frees the Bible to shed fresh light on, and provide renewed motivation for engaging in, the struggle for the liberation of the oppressed. The hermeneutical circle structures within it a method whereby the Scripture is read from 'the view from below': out of solidarity with the poor. Evangelical theologian, René Padilla, makes a cogent observation on the significance of this interplay between historical praxis and

---

(footnote 23 continued)

as a basis of 'a denunciation of the existing order' as well as 'an annunciation of what is not yet, but will be; it is the forecast of a different order of things, a new society. It is the field of creative imagination which proposes the alternative values to those rejected' *Theology of Liberation*, 136. The concept of utopia, for Gutiérrez, is the process of God forming his Kingdom within human history toward the historical project of liberating the poor and the oppressed and of establishing a world of justice. However, Gutiérrez denies that utopia equals the Kingdom. He says that utopia is a 'human creation' and that the hope of the Kingdom transcends all utopias. Míguez Bonino sharply differs from Gutiérrez' conviction, however, that there is 'only one history' (see the theme 'History is One' in Theology of Liberation, 153–168). The Argentine theologian contends that 'historical events and human activity' fashioned by God in the present through humankind will be culminated only 'at the second coming of the Lord' when God consummates his Kingdom. When Christians work in an obedient response of faith in the present, according to Míguez Bonino, their efforts are a sign that the Kingdom of God has pressed into the present and thus those actions have eschatological import for the future. José Míguez Bonino, 'Historical Praxis and Christian Identity,' in *Frontiers of theology in Latin America*, ed. Rosino Gibellini (Maryknoll, NY: Orbis Books, 1979), 267–277.

[24] The influence of Marxist thought upon liberation theologians has waned over the last decade. In an anthology of essays by liberation theologians not a single one was committed to Marxist analysis as a *necessary process* [emphasis mine] in their theological formations. See Rosino Gibellini, ed., *Frontiers of Theology in Latin America*, 1979.

theological reflection rooted in Scripture. 'By taking up the question raised in the world,' Padilla writes, 'it also provides a critical function in relation to the Church: by going back to the sources of revelation, it prevents pastoral action from falling into activism.'[25]

Despite some valid evangelical criticisms of liberationists,[26] liberationists' genuine concern for the poor is one point of convergence that Pentecostals share with liberation theologians and practitioners.[27] When one encounters the social realities of poverty[28] in Latin America the notion arises that perhaps something is wrong. On occasion an experience may be sufficiently intense and unsettling to cause people to question their biases toward certain areas of human life and activity. For example, a first visit to a slum in any large Latin American city will shock a visitor into asking whether such hopeless conditions are avoidable. Hungry children often live unattended in cardboard shacks because the parents are seeking a meagre living and are unable to take care of their children's material, educational, medical, and emotional needs. How does Pentecostal experience treat the discrepancy between the reality of the context and the hearing of the gospel that instructs them to live a 'new life' in Christ? Do God's instructions deal only with 'an old life' marked by sin and vice or should the living of their 'new life' entail an awareness, whether, at this point, a conceptual awareness or mainly just an emotional-existential response, that something is terribly wrong. It is just this kind of experience that sets the process of reflection in motion and leads to questioning as to whether God's intentions for humankind are being realized. If one's reading of the

---

[25]C. René Padilla, 'Liberation Theology, Part I', *The Reformed Journal* 33 (June 1983), 22.

[26]For one of the most comprehensive and objective evaluations of liberation theology from an evangelical perspective see J. Andrew Kirk, *Liberation theology: an evangelical view from the Third World* (London: Marshall, Morgan & Scott, 1979) as well as the various chapters in Carl E. Amerding, *Evangelicals and Liberation* (Phillipsburg, NJ: Presbyterian and Reformed Publishing Co., 1979).

[27]There have been numerous definitions and evaluations of convergence and disconvergence between liberation theology and evangelicals written by evangelical theologians. For useful analyses see J. Andrew Kirk, *Liberation Theology*, 1979 and 'Christian Understanding of Liberation,' Evangelical Review of Mission 10 (April 1986): 129–136; and C. René Padilla, 'Liberation Theology: An Appraisal,' in *Freedom and Discipleship: liberation theology in an Anabaptist perspective*, ed. Daniel Schipani (Maryknoll, NY: Orbis Books, 1989).

[28]It is a presupposition of most proponents of liberation theology that insertion into the hermeneutical circle must begin 'desde los pobres,' from the side of the poor. See for example Robert McAfee Brown, *Theology in a New Key*, particularly chapter two on 'The View From Below'.

Scriptures seems to reveal little in response to this kind of desperate human need, the ideological suspicion is raised as to whether or not the Bible and its interpretation are held captive by the privileged. Quite simply, customary ways of interpreting the Bible or understanding suffering appear to have omitted some basic truths applicable to this tragic scene. Like liberationists, Pentecostals have found also a certain 'praxis of faith' related to their social and personal conditions, a way of enacting or putting to work this faith experience nurtured by a constant reading of the Bible that is at the same time examined by the 'efficacy' of what they do in their everyday life. Such a dynamic experience compels one to embark upon the second step of the hermeneutical circle.

Given their emphasis upon evangelism and social programmes and their frequent neglect of theological reflection and assessment, Pentecostals have yet to explain how the foregoing description applies to their beliefs and practices, which, however, are not devoid of social concern. For Pentecostals here is a foundational key: 'What theological questions are raised by their actual experience, as well as by their social concerns and social practices, that demand a re-reading of the biblical text and, consequently, a new articulation of that theology?' Clearly Pentecostals find little difficulty in reading their Bibles and interpreting the guidance of the Spirit in such a way that moves them to ask for a better life for themselves and for their community. They readily show concern for other people's material and spiritual needs.[29] Having demonstrated theological reflective evaluation of their individual action as it relates to personal morality and holiness,[30] Pentecostals must now move beyond this limited, though invaluable personal praxis, to reflect theologically upon, and relate to, the social structures that sustain unacceptable conditions. They must recognize the need for a more distinctive ethic where the message of the biblical text and the compulsion of the Spirit will direct them to address creative responses to the context of the evil about them. It is possible that Pentecostals can find in this hermeneutical method a way to keep their theological reflection tied to concrete human experience, to the meaning of Scripture and to pastoral action.

---

[29]For a description and analyses of Pentecostal social concern in both informal and formal programmes see chapters 4 and 5.
[30]Personal holiness as one of the significant characteristics of Pentecostals is described in chapter 3.

If descriptive analyses and analytical reflection convince Pentecostals of the unacceptability of the existing state of affairs, then they should proceed to the third step of the hermeneutical process in the movement; that of theological reflection. That is, if they believe that they do not have a theological system that adequately addresses the conditions they see about them, then it is clear that additional reflective meditation and a reinterpretation of the biblical passages that relate to these conditions should be done. They would see more lucidly their call to redress wrongdoing if they were to examine more closely passages that might inform their attitudes and behaviours. Thus, believers arrive at a willingness to read the Bible in an attitude of obedience to what it may say regarding their responsibilities for these unacceptable conditions of human suffering. Then, believers form their pastoral action in fidelity to Scripture and its mandate to redress wrongdoing and to promote justice. This social action is designed to challenge the injustices that may be inherent in the social structures and turns reflection back to the descriptive task which begins the hermeneutical circle.

LATIN AMERICA CHILDCARE AND THE HERMENEUTICAL CIRCLE

This chapter intends to build upon this theological commitment and present an understanding of God's ethical actions applied to the contemporary Latin American context. Such an approach is designed to assure a system of justice applied to the social structures that is firmly based on biblical reflection.

Latin America ChildCare, a ministry of compassion directed primarily toward the poor children in the slum areas in the cities of Latin America, can be used as a case study to demonstrate how the hermeneutical circle has been effectively utilized by a Pentecostal organization to bring about structural change. LACC demonstrates the structural validity of the widespread conviction among sociologists and political analysts that the condition of children—care, education, ethical formation—is essential for any kind of structural change that will include democratic participation and produce a stable future. LACC demonstrates an appropriation of the hermeneutical circle in the specific context of Latin America's children including articulating an appropriate response to what one determines personal and corporate biblical responsibility to be in a given situation.

When LACC embarks upon the first step of the hermeneutical circle, ideological suspicion emerges from an analysis of the general concrete historical situations in Latin America. In 1991 it was estimated that two hundred million children, almost 50 per cent of the population in Latin America, were below eighteen years of age and faced a clouded future. Their present situation in which there is a dire lack of every kind of social service as well as little opportunity for change has been well documented in a host of books and articles concerning Latin America.[31] Reading about it produces theoretical knowledge. Seeing it produces ideological suspicion.

In moving to the second step of the hermeneutical circle the ideological suspicion created by the reality of the context must undergo close critical analysis. A utilization of the social sciences proves most beneficial as LACC discover reasons why the 'actors' are in a particularly difficult economic or social situation.[32] In utilizing the hermeneutical circle at this point it is important to understand which analytical tradition is being employed. Though the social sciences are important to help understand the concrete historical context, LACC, by and large, would reject the Marxist assumption that only class stratification and class conflict provide a true understanding of the historical and cultural situation. To be sure, the class structure in Latin America has played an important role in perpetuating social injustice, but such an observation can be made without buying into a Marxist ideology.

Other factors beyond class analysis can also shed light on the Latin American situation. For example, Spanish Catholicism provided the philosophical and spiritual basis for colonialism which continues to have a residual effect on Latin American psychology and culture.

---

[31] See in particular José Míguez Bonino, *Doing Theology in a Revolutionary Situation*, 1975 for an historical explanation and UNICEF, *Los Niños de las Américas*, 1992 for a statistical survey. Also refer to the socio-economic tables in chapter 5.

[32] The vast majority of the Latin American population has been excluded from participating in a social, political, and economic system that consistently marginalizes the poor by denying their existence. These non-persons are left demoralized and without dignity; they are treated as nonentities. Critics of the Pentecostal conception of 'la realidad' conclude that the problems of the third world must be laid squarely at the door of the western industrialised nations. That is to say that Latin America's under-development results from economic, political, and military dependence. However, the validity of this 'theory of dependence,' though outside the limits of this chapter, must be weighed carefully by anyone who truly wishes to understand the Latin American situation in which Pentecostals minister.

Corruption runs rampant throughout most Latin American governments. Government bureaucracy is so cumbersome that it has proved inept in the initiation and maintenance of social programmes. Of course, all of the above are ultimately the inevitable consequence of humankind's disobedience before God. The results of sin have been costly. These factors, and others, have been carefully studied and analyzed by LACC in its attempt to provide a contextually relevant sign of the Kingdom of God in this hurting area of the world.

The inherent injustices exposed from these analyzed experiences and realities provide the bases to move to the third step of the hermeneutical circle. The previous analysis of the historical context is now viewed through the lens of God's revealed word. How does the Bible address the issues of injustice that result from sin, poverty, hunger, sickness and other forms of deprivation? Is it possible to see both the structural realities of the context as well as the biblical texts with new insights? Can the Word suggest a new interpretative insight and guidelines for action particularly aimed at this actual social context? Has hearing 'the truth' from the biblical text or the common understanding of the meaning of Scripture been coloured by Western tradition? What should the Church of Jesus Christ look like in relation to this suffering continent?

Theological reflection on the main thesis of Jesus' Kingdom teachings can help address the social concerns embodied in these questions. There is little doubt from Jesus' earthly ministry recorded in the gospels that Jesus intended people to respond to his announced arrival of the Kingdom. This kingly rule in the life of the believer overcomes evil, delivers humanity from its power, and brings individuals into the messianic blessings of God's salvation. God's reign is redemptive and just. With real needs that confront people on a daily basis the believing community, in their efforts to address those needs, should reflect theologically on the Kingdom teachings of Jesus, expecting to hear a word from the biblical text. What would Jesus have them do? What pastoral action is implied in the theological reflection about LACC's mission, its relationship to God's reign and the ethic embodied in the Kingdom? From an ethical perspective the mission of LACC is to witness to the reality of what life looks like when humans respond to God's eschatological reign. This is the point where LACC moves beyond a theoretical agenda to the very essence of theological ethics. Within this view of LACC's moral mission in society, 'ministry programs of both evangelism and social concern are needed in order for the church to bear an authentic witness to the gospel'.[33] Míguez Bonino goes to the core of the substance of the argument when he succinctly writes, 'If we can give a "reasonable account of our hope" (I Pet. 3:15), then we can also give account of our "walking" and our "conversation"—that is, our "praxis" in the world.'[34]

With a description of the concrete historical situation completed, with experiences analyzed and reflected upon theologically and ethically, LACC moves to the fourth step in the hermeneutical circle: pastoral action. Given an understanding of their specific context, and having reflected upon the biblical text, the question must confront them. What pastoral action should they take? What should the reign of God look like? Pastoral action must have spiritual direction as well as a commitment to make a significant structural change in Latin America.

The steps of the hermeneutical circle lead to a specific and concrete historical project.[35] The tragic plight of Latin American children can be redressed only by way of pastoral action. Right thinking (faith) can take them only so far; right doing (action) is now called for. LACC is institutionalized pastoral action designed to change the local context. Jesus often ministered to the immediate needs of the people. To be sure, LACC recognizes the need for short-term helps because children need to be fed on a daily basis. Medical care is always necessary; but these are only stop-gap measures given to meet immediate human need. One further step is required in the pastoral action of LACC's long-term actions that will provide real structural change in the social situations. Certainly,

---

[33]Dempster, 'Evangelism, Social Concern, and the Kingdom of God,' 24.

[34]Míguez Bonino, *Toward a Christian Political Ethics*, 80.

[35]The idea of a concrete historical project often appears in Latin American sociological and theological writings. Though an illusive term, José Míguez Bonino provides a tangible explanation. Míguez places the concept of a historical project somewhere between two prevailing extremes. On one end of the spectrum is a model for the future, an abstract concept known as 'utopia,' that does not have clear coherent structures or definite historical location. At the other extreme is a model based upon specific plans, goals, schedules, strategies, timetables and tactics. The concept of a historical project can be placed in between these two extremes. 'It is a vision of the future that is sufficiently precise in its political, social, and economic contours as to constitute a coherent goal that can be expected to be realized in history.' José Míguez Bonino, *Toward a Christian Political Ethics*, 52. In the sense of Míguez Bonino's definition the author would consider Latin America ChildCare to be a historical project.

structural change can be brought about through governmental initiated reforms. However, structural change can be brought about also by building new institutions that become part of the social infrastructure, allowing new creative options for people who were previously deprived of opportunity for social advancement. Drawing from the Old Testament ethical tradition with its various Jubilee teachings which advocated bringing about structural change through institution building, and the New Testament ethical tradition which viewed the church as an alternative society, LACC represents the creation of an expanding infrastructure within Latin America, designed to alter the existing social structure.

When this step of pastoral action is made in the heremeneutical circle, it produces a basic conviction that education is one way that effectively breaks the chain of poverty in the generational reality of Latin America. Education with a Christian base from kindergarten to the university level is needed in each country. Teaching children that they have value and dignity are basic. Equipping them with the academic skills necessary to have a real impact on society is a long-term goal. Right thinking and right doing, faith and action, combine to present a whole gospel in culturally relevant terms. While it is recognized that spiritual transformation in the form of a personal encounter with Jesus Christ is absolutely necessary, faith is not separated from social action designed to change the structural conditions of Latin America through institutionalizing new educational opportunities for the children of the economically poor and socially marginalized.

In 18 countries of Latin America the results of this pastoral action have been most rewarding. In 1993 there were 67,487 children in 261 different schools. Education ranged from pre-kindergarten to a government accredited university. Over 2,000 teachers committed to the claims of the Kingdom have been in action. LACC not only builds a new infrastructure but effects changes in the resisting *status quo* by bringing in basic amenities such as electricity, water wells or running water that impact the entire slum community. Latin America ChildCare, an historical project, is already making a difference. Of course, such pastoral action with its resulting change in the structural conditions will raise new questions and new challenges and LACC will begin their hermeneutical circle again and again.

TOWARD A MODEL OF PENTECOSTAL PRAXIS

Can the specific case of LACC serve as a hermeneutical model for Pentecostal praxis that could be employed generally by Latin American Pentecostals? If a believer is truly obedient to the Christian message, then that obedience needs to be reflected in action. Luke's version was accepted literally by early twentieth-century Pentecostals as they read that 'He called the twelve together and gave them power and authority over all the demons and to cure diseases, and he sent them out to preach the Kingdom and to heal' (Lk:9:1,2 RSV). Similarly, Pentecostals have taken literally the commission to the Seventy-two who were instructed 'When you enter a town and are welcomed, eat what is set before you. Heal the sick who are there and tell them, "The Kingdom of God is near you" ' (Lk 10:8,9). Practical application of the gospel was, after all, what compelled a generation of pioneering Pentecostals to spread their message virtually around the world, often at great personal sacrifice and in the face of deep-rooted resistance. When evangelism and church mission are often closely identified with technology and convenience Pentecostals must come to terms with God's designs to reach to the non-persons of society. If Pentecostal theology adequately conveys the gospel message of the Kingdom to the poor and the needy, the Spirit-filled person finds powerful theological motivation to move from the theoretical to the practical in realizing God's purposes.[36]

The book of Acts, from which Pentecostals draw much of their authority for their theologically distinctive understanding of Holy Spirit baptism and empowerment, provides fertile ground for theological reflection on ministry application that fits with the pastoral action of the primitive Christian church. From Luke's review of Jesus' ministry of 'doing good and healing all who were under the power of the devil' (Acts 10:38, NIV), to the resuscitation of Dorcas who was 'always doing good and helping the poor' (Acts

---

[36]For a contextual approach to the hermeneutical circle from an evangelical scholar, see C. René Padilla's article 'Hermeneutics and Culture,' in *Down to Earth: Studies in Christianity and Culture*, eds. J. R. W. Scott and R. Coote (Grand Rapids, MI: Wm. B. Eerdmans Publishing Co., 1980), 63–78. An excellent practical methodology for the interrelationship between social analysis and theological reflection in a local setting has been written by Joe Holland and Peter Henriot, S.J., *Social Analysis: Linking Faith and Justice* (Maryknoll, NY: Orbis Books, 1984).

9:36), to the provision for the widows' needs (Acts 6:1–3), to Paul's collections for the impoverished saints in Jerusalem (Acts 20:35), the early church combined evangelism and pastoral action.

In modern times, despite complaints that Pentecostals have neglected 'the here and now' for 'the sweet by and by,' the fact is that the explosive growth of Pentecostalism among destitute and vulnerable peoples has made the movement a force in addressing the contemporary situation facing millions of third world adherents. But this effectiveness in resolving the immediate spiritual, psychological, and community problems of so many believers who practise New Testament Christianity raises questions of hermeneutical methodology. Without question, Pentecostals have demonstrated their commitment to the pressing social concerns within many of their communities in general as well as within their own churches. They must now ask whether they have entirely understood the biblical mandate to address intentionally the structural issues that are the root causes for the poverty that entraps further tens of millions within the larger society.

But what is the originality of the Pentecostal experience in this context? Throughout, this work has contended that Pentecostals, generally poor, marginal and powerless people, have had a transforming experience of 'empowerment' by the Spirit as an act of God's grace. This spiritual 'empowerment' has led them to share the good news with others—from the same condition—and also to minister to their material needs. However, if Pentecostals are called upon to give an account of this experience, when they have to describe why this experience moves them to do certain things for themselves and for others, do they have an adequate 'theological answer'? Is Pentecostal theology explicit enough to undergird, deepen, or correct their 'intuitive' response? The Pentecostal experience of Spirit baptism is not self-interpreting, resulting in an adequate theological framework. In other terms, the experience of Spirit baptism and its empowerment of the believer is not fully understood in all its content and force through their current biblical understanding. The task of a Pentecostal theology is to provide an interpretative theological structure that would present 'an essential connectedness' between Spirit baptism and the practice of social justice.[37] If it is true that the

---

[37]Murray W. Dempster, 'Soundings in the Moral Significance of Glossolalia,' a paper presented at the 1983 Annual meeting of the Society for Pentecostal Studies (Cleveland, Tennessee, 4 November, 1983).

Pentecostal experience is one of 'empowerment,' then the centrality of the experience based upon the pattern in Acts 2 could serve as the point of departure for 'a social Pentecostal theology'.[38]

'THE TRANSFER OF THE SPIRIT:' EXPERIENTIALLY POWERED SOCIAL THEOLOGY

Pentecostals, to the extent that they do not adopt a distinctive theology from other evangelicals, distinguish themselves by their restorationist position that Holy Spirit baptism and the Spirit's empowering recorded in the book of Acts has been restored to the church in the twentieth-century outpouring of the Holy Spirit at Bethel Bible College in Topeka, Kansas and the Azusa Street Mission in Los Angeles, California, U.S.A. For them, the events of the Acts of the Apostles are normative, and as normative, must be continuously operational.[39] This recognition of the contemporary exercise of the Holy Spirit, evident in many areas of Pentecostal beliefs and practices, has also great implications for the group's ethics. For Latin American Pentecostals, the experience of Spirit baptism can provide a social ethic that is faithful to their own theological convictions. Because of Spirit baptism they have access to empowerment not only to believe in and experience divine healing and miracles, but also for their social actions. These Pentecostals, dismayed by the misery and social injustice with which they are surrounded, can respond in constructive ways to resist spiritual, moral and social blight. Their efforts, found concretely in places where the movement has gone, should likewise proceed, in the light of this Pentecostal social ethic, based upon theological foundations, not merely from a pragmatic reaction to suffering and injustice.

Pentecostal New Testament scholar Roger Stronstad presents just such a thesis in his ground-breaking study, *The Charismatic*

---

[38]There is recognition within Pentecostal circles that standard theological interpretation of the Bible within the Pentecostal tradition is not sufficient to understand and respond integrally to the experience of poverty. Murray Dempster, a Pentecostal theologian, has done the most comprehensive work at deepening and enlarging, from within the Pentecostal community, that correct but insufficient theological treatment of ethical issues from a biblical perspective. It is my intention to use the writings of this Pentecostal scholar who is already at work within the arena, to enlarge the hermeneutical horizon, particularly within the Latin American Pentecostal context.

[39]For an explanation of an evangelical/Pentecostal theology see chapter 3.

Theology of St. Luke. Stronstad identifies a transfer-of-the-Spirit, motif beginning with Moses' delegation of leadership to the seventy elders, and continuing with similar transfers between Moses and Joshua, Elijah and Elisha, and Saul and David. According to Stronstad, the transfer of the Spirit fulfils two purposes. First, it validates the authenticity of the new leadership and secondly, and for our purposes more importantly, the transfer of the Spirit equips and empowers the new leadership and the entire community of believers in order that God's people can effectively carry out their responsibilities.[40]

According to Stronstad:

> The Pentecost narrative is the story of the transfer of the charismatic spirit from Jesus to the disciples.... By this transfer of the Spirit, the disciples become the heirs and successors to the earthly charismatic ministry of Jesus: that is, because Jesus has poured out the charismatic Spirit upon them the disciples will continue to do and teach those things which Jesus began to do and teach.[41]

This concept of the transfer of Jesus' ministry to the disciples by the coming of the Spirit at Pentecost, moreover, leads Pentecostal ethicist Murray Dempster to discern in the Acts' narrative an organizing principle for a distinctively Pentecostal social ethic.

Dempster's argument begins with the ministry of Jesus as the One anointed by the Holy Spirit to inaugurate the Kingdom of God in human history. The Kingdom, the central theological concept used by Luke in his gospel to describe Jesus' mission and ministry, is the connective between the two sections of the Luke-Acts account. 'Those things which Jesus began to do and teach' (Acts 1:1) both summarizes his earthly ministry and sets the agenda for the ministry of the apostles subsequent to their receiving the transfer of the Spirit. A critical dimension for a Pentecostal social ethic, it could be proposed, should be based exegetically on Luke-Acts and be grounded in this generating principle: the Kingdom ethic of Jesus is made operational within the charismatic community by the empowerment of the Holy Spirit. In effect, in Dempster's model, which he terms a 'Pentecost/kingdom sequential connection,' the

---

[40]The transfer of the Spirit from Jesus to his disciples in Luke-Acts is described by Roger Stronstad in his thought-provoking book, *The Charismatic Theology of St. Luke* (Peabody, MA.: Hendrickson Publishers, 1984).

[41]Ibid., 49.

Kingdom mission and ministry of Jesus—including the Kingdom
ethic—is transferred to the charismatic community by the descent
of the Spirit at Pentecost.[42]

Dempster argues that Jesus' teachings about the Kingdom of
God positioned his proclamation in direct relation with the
eschatological hopes of the people of God in the Old Testament.
Stronstad echoes this same point when he writes that the Spirit
of the Lord, as prophesied by the prophets, will be poured out
in the age to come on a universal scale. Not just individuals will
enjoy the empowerment but rather, for the first time, the entire
community of believers in the new age will have direct access to
the charismatic experience.[43] Further, Luke emphasizes that the
inaugural sermon of Jesus' public ministry was the fulfilment of
Isaiah's servant songs (Lk 4:16–21 cf. Isa. 61:1–2) and he places
Jesus' Kingdom proclamation in relationship to the law and the
prophets (Lk. 16:16).[44] 'The reign of God,' Dempster declares,
'which Jesus claimed to inaugurate in his ministry was the
fulfilment in human history of Old Testament promise.' According to Dempster, the ethical principles evident in the teachings
of Jesus on the Kingdom of God are best understood in light of
the concept of social justice operative in the Old Testament. The
reign of God, established by Jesus, cannot be fully grasped without
interpreting his teachings against the Old Testament conception
of social justice. 'Thus,' in this sense, according to Dempster, 'the
Old Testament pursuit of social justice is part of the Jewish
religious *Sitz im Leben* in which the Kingdom claims of Jesus
should be interpreted.'[45] The ministry of Jesus places him directly
in the tradition of the law and the prophets. The pursuit of social
justice is explicit in Jesus' teaching. Jesus' proclamation of the
gospel as good news to the poor, the captive and the hungry,
demonstrates his continuity with the ethical message of the Old
Testament. The law and the prophets focused on the establishment
of justice in Israel's life. In the ministry of Jesus, one sees the
fulfilment of this prophetic message. Though the teachings and
actions of Jesus indicate that a new law has been established
through his person that breaks the bonds of injustice, 'it is at the

---

[42]Murray W. Dempster, 'Evangelism, Social Concern, and the Kingdom of God,' 23.
[43]Stronstad, *Charismatic Theology of St. Luke*, 26.
[44]Dempster, 'Pentecostal Social Concern,' 147.
[45]Ibid.

same time totally the same God, the same justice, the same demand of faithfulness to the covenant relationships.'[46]

In this theological elaboration, certain ethical strands can be established between the Acts' account of Holy Spirit baptism and social justice that may be traced backward through Jesus' Kingdom teaching in Luke and the other synoptics, and, in turn, to the Old Testament moral tradition of the law and the prophets. An analysis of the transfer of Jesus' authority for ministry to the disciples at Pentecost, given the implications in his ministry for the fulfilment of the entire Old Testament—including the demands of social justice—can provide a hermeneutical foundation for the structuring of the apostolic community as the narrative unfolds. In Dempster's terms, 'Even though the category of justice is not utilized by Luke, the Holy Spirit is presented in the Acts as the One who empowers the church to overcome within its own community the entrenched gender, economic, cultural, and religious barriers of a divided world.'[47]

This establishment of a just community governed by the Holy Spirit, Dempster argues, is used apologetically by Luke to demonstrate that the church was established by the exalted Jesus Christ (Acts. 2:33, 4:32–37, 10:24–48). Dempster points to four constitutive elements within the Lucan account where the writer highlights his portrayal of the charismatic community as an expression of justice that moves beyond social activity to just its own community. The charismatic community is structured by the Spirit's power in the following manner. In Acts 2, the gender distinctions of male and female were overcome by the empowerment of the Spirit. In Acts 4 and 5, the economic distinctions between rich and poor were overcome in the economic *koinonia* established by the power of the Spirit. In Acts 10, the cultural distinctions between Jew and Gentile were overcome within the Christian community by the coming of the Spirit. In Acts 19, according to Dempster's exegesis, the religious distinctions between the disciples of Jesus and the disciples of John the Baptist were overcome by the power of the Spirit to instigate the first Christian ecumenism.[48] 'By the time the story of the Acts

---

[46]José Míguez Bonino, 'The Biblical Roots of Justice,' *Word and World: Theology for Christian Ministry* 7 (Winter 1987): 16.
[47]Dempster, *Pentecostal Social Concern*, 148.
[48]Murray W. Dempster, 'The Church's Moral Witness: A Study of Glossolalia in Luke's Theology of Acts,' Paraclete: *A Journal of Pentecostal Studies* 23 (Winter 1989): 5.

concludes, the gospel had gone unbounded throughout the world by means of the Spirit-empowered apostolic community.'[49] The gospel had the power to institute in the practice of the believing community the Kingdom ethic of Jesus which fulfilled the Old Testament proclamation for social justice to reign.

In the outpouring of the Spirit on the entire Christian community at Pentecost, accordingly, the age-long unfolding of 'God's will for justice found an empowering dynamic.'

> Spirit baptism enabled the charismatic community to break down the middle walls of partition between men and women, rich and poor, Jew and Gentile, and even demarcations of [sectarian] backgrounds with the Christian community itself.[50]

Thus, the charismatic community described by Luke contains within its own structure the visible signs of the previously promised Kingdom age. These believers had been liberated by the Spirit from their prejudices in order to view clearly within their own fellowship the social justice proclaimed by past prophets.[51]

Given the Pentecostals' commitment to the Bible as the only authoritative rule for faith and practice, the formulation of a Pentecostal social ethic must necessarily begin with an analysis of biblical moral principles. Ultimately, the position of Pentecostals will be somewhat influenced by their distinctive beliefs, despite the many commonalties that they share with other Christians.[52] However, this Lucan emphasis on the 'transfer of the Holy Spirit' in experientially empowering a Kingdom ethic for pursuing social justice could be the backdrop upon which one views the aspects of

---

[49]Dempster, '*Pentecostal Social Concern*,' 148.

[50]Ibid.

[51]Ibid. Dempster makes the point that 'Luke's pneumatology in Acts makes essentially the same point as Paul's Christology in Galations 3:28: "There is neither Jew nor Greek, there is neither slave nor free man, there is neither male nor female; for you are all one in Jesus Christ." The theological truth Paul proclaimed on the basis of his Christology is the same theological truth Luke proclaimed on the basis of his pneumatology. However, Luke emphasized in his theology the events by which this Christological truth took form in concrete history by the creative power of the Spirit'. Dempster, '*The Church's Moral Witness*,' 7. David Cook cogently observes, that although Paul was not writing specifically about ethics, it is possible to glean from his approach to moral themes the concept that 'doctrine leads to moral life'. According to Cook, in Pauline literature 'theology and ethics go hand in hand'. Cook, *The Moral Maze*, 56–57.

[52]Murray W. Dempster, '*Pentecostal Social Concern*,' 146. For a description of an evangelical/Pentecostal doctrinal position see chapter 3.

the Kingdom of God, the covenant, the law and the message of the prophets as they are actualized and become operative in the power of the Spirit.

THE KINGDOM OF GOD AND THE OLD TESTAMENT

Even though the term Kingdom of God is not found in the Old Testament, the concept is implicit. The Old Testament writers frequently refer to God as the King, both of Israel (Ex. 15:18; Num. 23:21; Deut. 33:5; Isa. 43:15) and of all the earth (2 Kings 19:15; Isa. 6:5; Jer. 46:18; Psa. 29:10, 47:2, 93, 96:10, 97:1ff, 99:1–4, 145:11ff). The prophets certainly recognize God as King, yet they speak of a time when he shall become King and shall rule over his people (Isa. 24:23, 33:22, 52:7; Zeph. 3:15; Obad. 21; Zech. 14:9ff). George Ladd rightly contends that the concept of the kingship of God 'provides the outline for the entire Old Testament.' The Psalms provide graphic examples of the dynamic characteristic of God's rule: 'They shall speak of the glory of the Kingdom and tell of thy power....Thy everlasting Kingdom, and thy dominion endures throughout all generations' (Ps. 145:11, 13). 'The Lord has established his throne in the heavens, and his Kingdom rules over all' (Ps. 103:19). This is not just an earthly regime, a political system, or even Israel. In the Old Testament, God rules over all—both Israel and the nations. According to Isaiah, 'even the enemies of Israel are in God's hands.' God's Kingdom is his own direct personal reign that he has never relinquished.[53]

It is apparent that God was at the centre of Jewish life. God had delivered Israel from Egypt and had chosen them to be his people. On many occasions he had visited them in history. His self-revelation revealed his character in all their social, political, economical and religious practices and institutions. A basic principle was predominant in Jewish life: 'What God is in his character, and what God wills in his revelation defines what is right.'[54]

Israel's ethical actions were predicated upon their understanding of God's character. The theological word preceding and following God's action provided an ethical imperative for appropriate

---

[53]George Eldon Ladd, *Jesus and the Kingdom* (New York, NY: Harper and Row, 1964), 42.
[54]Walter J. Kaiser Jr., *Toward Old Testament Ethics* (Grand Rapids, MI: Academie Books, 1983), 3.

conduct. Israel learned that as God is, so God's people should be. As God acts, so God's people ought to act. Ethical action was to be modelled after an imitation of God's character.[55] On the basis of this unfolding revelation of God's moral character, Israel developed a corresponding ethical view by which to judge the quality of its social life grounded in moral principles, such as justice, loving kindness (*hesed*), mercy and holiness. In the prophetic tradition these basic ethical features are further developed.

The divine revelation of God's character is graphically illustrated in the moral pronouncements of the prophets to the people of Israel. Murray Dempster divides the prophetic message into three categories. Their indictments against the unjust activities of Israel, based upon God's divine perspective, are filled with a forceful moral conviction. Additionally, the prophets' message demonstrates insight into the social, economic and political practices that habitually perpetuated the social injustices. Finally, the prophetic messages encouraged Israel to take a fresh look at the true moral character of God. It was the prophets' contention that if Israel could get a new glimpse of God's character and nature and consequently repent of their unjust activities, then they would bring structural reform to the unjust conditions that were part of the fabric of their society.[56] Characteristic of God's reign in the Old Testament prophetic message is that it embodies a standard of ethical life that carried the corporate moral obligation of righteousness toward the community as a whole. The eighth-century prophets, Amos, Hosea, Isaiah and Micah were all advocates of an ethical standard of life which the God of Israel required of his people.

Amos centred his message in the concept of justice.[57] Amos, discontented with Israel's economic and social practices, rebukes those who have exploited and thus benefited from their calculated abuse of the poor. He condemns those who have sold 'the righteous for silver, and the needy for a pair of sandals' (2:6. 8:6). He rails upon the exploiters who 'trample on the heads of the poor... and deny justice to the oppressed' (2:7, 5:11, 8:4). Likewise he condemns those who 'oppress the righteous and take

---

[55]Dempster, '*Pentecostal Social Concern,*' 130.
[56]Ibid., 138.
[57]This analysis of Amos' prophetic message depends largely on the study of Dempster, '*Pentecostal Social Concern,*' 138–142, and Jack Nelson, *Hunger for Justice: The Politics of Food and Faith* (Maryknoll, NY: Orbis Books, 1980).

bribes and you deprive the poor of justice in the courts' (5:12). The exploitation extends to the merchants reducing the bushel, unjustly inflating the prices and rigging the weight scales (8:5). Not only did the merchants gain unmerited profit at the expense of the optionless poor, they connived to take unjust advantage and systematically victimize the small landowner by 'doing away with the poor of the land' (8:4). Consequently, a new class of landless poor came into existence, whom the merchants could exploit even further for greater profits.

The oppression was made possible by the alliance of larger landowners and merchants who conspired to increase their own economic benefits at the expense of the weak. The courts were complicitly involved by their perverted meting out of justice to the wealthy. The religious establishment, according to Amos, provided the theological and philosophical rationale for the entire unjust system (7:10–17). The involvement of the religious establishment in the exploitation of the poor piqued Amos's sense of fairness and with words of prophecy he issues the severe rebuke:

> I hate, I despise your religious feasts. I cannot stand your assemblies. Even though you bring me burnt offerings and grain offerings, I will not accept them. Though you bring choice fellowship offerings, I will have no regard for them. Away with the noise of your songs! I will not listen to the music of your harps. But let justice roll on like a river, righteousness like a never-failing stream (Amos 5:21–24).

Amos's admonition to both the religious leaders as well as the economic benefactors was an indictment not only against them as individuals but against the entire social structure as well. Pentecostals in Latin America should have little problem in drawing the parallels with the prophetic message of Amos which could illumine their own experiences in contemporary society. These parallels which are present in their own experiences are deepened and illuminated when they read and reflect upon the prophetic account. The prophet points to God's ethical character, his demand for justice in the use of power and the denunciation of the exploitation of the poor by the merchants and by the manipulation of the law by the priests for their personal benefit. In the same manner, Latin American Pentecostals should respond to the message from the 'core' of their religious experience. A sense of justice for Pentecostals is comprehended not so much from an exegetical reading of prophets such as Amos as it is from an identification with the social conditions described in the text. In hearing Amos' pronouncements a believer has a proclivity toward developing a personal disposition to pursue justice. In other words, the interaction between the text and the hearer/reader enables one to develop a theological meditation that moves one into action. It is this Pentecostal praxis that holds the 'truth' of the text and the 'action' of the believer together.

Pentecostals could be critiqued for reading their personal interpretations into the text as a basis for their activities. However, the possibility of misinterpretation when there is an interaction between one's world and one's faith should not preclude this practice. Christopher Rowland responds that when the reader is willing to take the challenge of the text seriously in application to one's daily context, he or she is in a better position 'to hear what the text has to say'. Rowland argues that on the one hand 'there is always the risk that we will manipulate the text for our own ends'. On the other hand, he recognizes that 'risk applies just as much to the situation of the individual reader whose thought may be consciously guided by the expert whose notes comment on the text'.[58] Pentecostals do not have a sophisticated nor philosophical approach to biblical exegesis. Rather Pentecostals read the text and form the personal conviction to undertake an action that is fundamentally fair. From the interface between Amos' prophecies and Pentecostal reflection and action comes the understanding that people within their own contemporary context whose experience parallels the marginalized in Amos' day should be recipients of compassion simply because God cares for them. This is part of a Pentecostal appropriation of the hermeneutical circle.

THE CONCEPTION OF JUSTICE THAT CORRESPONDS TO GOD'S REIGN IN OLD TESTAMENT SOCIAL ETHICS

The ethical prophetic tradition of the Old Testament embodied in the moral pronouncements of the Amos, Hosea, Isaiah and Micah provides only one aspect of understanding the conception of social justice that corresponds to God's reign. In his study of the Old Testament mandate of social justice and its relevance for Pentecostal social concern, Murray Dempster outlines the parameters of social

---

[58]Rowland, *Revelation*, 14.

concern by identifying the concept of the *Imago Dei*, the concept of the Covenant People in establishing the principles of social justice, and the teachings of Jubilee in instituting the paths to social justice.[59] These social parameters may be summarized briefly.

The Imago Dei

An undergirding principle of Old Testament social justice is the acknowledgment that all persons are created in God's own image (Gen. 1:27). Because individuals are the image-bearers of God they have a distinctive and unique value. Based upon this principle all humanity is endowed with intrinsic rights that should include a sense of dignity and the right to be treated with respect. Dempster writes that this basic notion is characteristically expressed in the 'ethic of the Old Testament [that] extends the parameters of social justice beyond the dominant contemporary philosophical conceptions of our time which typically determine justice on the basis of merit, work, need, rank or legal entitlement'. In contrast to such philosophical views,' Dempster argues 'the Old Testament teaches that persons are entitled to just treatment on the basis that they are persons created in the divine image, nothing more or nothing less.'[60]

The Old Testament is filled with the admonition that because human beings are created in God's image they all have equal value and should be treated fairly and equitably. In Genesis 9, in the priestly tradition, God is the guarantor of life and his covenant has universal coverage. Actions that demean, devalue, or otherwise diminish the dignity of any of God's created people are contrary to the nature of the character of God. In the Old Testament the parameters of justice extend to all people based solely on the reality that they are created in God's image. Old Testament justice was freely extended to all, including the displaced farmer, the widow, the orphan, the alien, the stranger, the hired servant, the debtor, the poor and the needy (Ex. 22:21–27, 23:9–11; Deut. 10:18, 15:1–2, 23:19–20, 24:14–22; Lev. 19:9–34, 25:2–7).

This doctrine of humanity for all who are created in the image of God, particularly the believer, precludes one from acting as one

---

[59]Dempster, '*Pentecostal Social Concern*,' 129–153. In addition, Dempster identified the theocentric orientation of ethical thinking in establishing the platform for social justice. I have already dealt with these aspects of the Old Testament social ethics in the previous section on 'God's Reign in the Old Testament.'

[60]Dempster, '*Pentecostal Social Concern*,' 132.

pleases. There is an inherent moral responsibility towards God to act on behalf of those in contemporary society where so many of the population share a common social concern paralleled by the marginalized in the Old Testament.

The Covenant people

The covenant, established by God with Israel, contains the fundamental unifying conviction that the law codes (The Ten Commandments in Exodus 20:3–11 and the three major law codes of Exodus 20:20–23,33; Leviticus. 17–26; and the book of Deuteronomy) must be utilized by God's people to promote social justice in the everyday activities of life.[61]

> The rules of practice identified in the three law codes fleshed out the concrete meaning of the covenant for Israel's social life as God's people. Repeatedly throughout the law codes with their concern for the socially and economically disadvantaged was the same covenant theme....The covenant required that if God demonstrated such a deep social concern in the mighty act of liberating the oppressed, then God's covenant people should also incorporate into its social life an intense concern for the alien, the poor, the hungry, the widow and the orphan.[62]

The three law codes functioned to bring about a more just treatment of those who were underprivileged or disenfranchised. If Israel was to respond adequately to God, their actions were to be characterized by their concrete obedience in demonstrating concern for the poor and the weak. Only while the people of Israel practised justice were they truly representative of God's order. Míguez Bonino, in reflecting the works of Gerhard von Rad and others, emphasizes the acceptance of present day scholarship that justice is the central characteristic of God's faithful action.[63] He explicitly contends that the most adequate departure point for theological reflection on behalf of the poor in the law codes is this motif of justice. The concrete manifestation of concern for the dispossessed was at the centre of the covenant relationship between God and Israel. Their activity of justice was

---

[61]Ibid., 135.
[62]Ibid., 137.
[63]José Míguez Bonino, *Toward a Christian Political Ethics*, 84.

not optional but rather an integral part of being God's people. Therefore, if justice is accepted as the basic priority, then the concept of justice becomes a foundational hermeneutical key.[64] The corporate dimensions of justice motivated by a practical application of the law codes operated in the creating of a more just society.

Mechanisms for Social Justice

The law codes also mandated four institutions, the Jubilee Year, the Sabbath Year, the law of tithing and the law of gleaning, that functioned as mechanisms to *structure* social justice on behalf of the needy and oppressed. The Jubilee principle guaranteed that land ownership could not be held in perpetuity. God was the absolute owner of the land and the people of Israel were the stewards. This principle provided opportunity for redistribution of properties (Ezk. 45:8–9;46:18) on an equitable basis.[65]

The Sabbatical Year was designed to establish a sense of justice in a similar way.

> The Sabbatical Year provided a mechanism to institute the path of justice for the Hebrew slave, the Hebrew debtor, the hired servant, the poor and the alien.... For the Hebrew slave, the Sabbatical ordinance brought release from mandatory servitude and a gift of livestock, grain and wine as a basis for the released slave to begin his free life (Ex. 21:2–3; 15:12–18). For the Hebrew debtor, the Sabbatical Year brought the cancellation of debts (Deut. 15:1–6). For the poor, the slave, the hired servant, and the alien, the Sabbatical Year meant that the land was rested and they could gather the food that grew of its own accord (Ex. 23:10–11; Lev. 25:2–7).[66]

The third and fourth mechanisms, the law of tithing (Lev. 19:2, 9–10) and the law of gleaning (Lev. 19:1–8), provided additional resources to be available as institutional care to meet the needs of the widow, the orphan and the alien.[67]

The ethical concept of justice contained in the moral proclamations of the prophets and in the law codes is a predominant

---

[64]Ibid., 86.
[65]Dempster, *Pentecostal Social Concern*, 143–144.
[66]Ibid., 144.
[67]Ibid., 144–145

notion in Old Testament social ethics.[68] Significantly, the Scripture records that this principle of social justice is rooted in a conception of God which arose within the Jewish community. God is a God with ethical character. God's commitment to justice is the basis for the mandate that God's people ought to institute justice, particularly expressed in a concern for the poor and marginalized.

THE KINGDOM OF GOD AND THE NEW TESTAMENT

This same connection between theology and ethics that characterizes the social doctrine found in the Old Testament is carried over into the New Testament, especially emanating from Jesus' teaching about the Kingdom of God. The Old Testament social ethic was introduced in the New Testament period immediately and abruptly in the ministry of John the Baptist.

John's message was deeply ethical in nature. The Jews were convinced that the coming of the Kingdom of God would bring judgement upon their enemies. Instead, John argues that it was with Israel, the house of God, that judgement must begin. Salvation was not guaranteed because one was of Jewish heritage. Strict adherence to the law guaranteed nothing. Repentance—acknowledgment of sin and changed conduct and baptism expressing repentance—was John's message (Mark 1:4).[69]

It was into this historical context that Jesus of Nazareth came preaching, 'The time is fulfilled, and the Kingdom of God is at hand; repent, and believe in the gospel' (Mark 1:15). Although on the surface the message of John and Jesus seem similar, this was not the case. John merely proclaimed that the Kingdom of God was coming near. Jesus preached that the Kingdom of God had already broken into history. God was already visiting his people. The hope of the prophets was being fulfilled. This remarkable claim marks a distinctive element in Jesus' teachings when Jesus applies an Old Testament quotation to himself (Isa. 61:1–2). Luke records Jesus' words,

The Spirit of the Lord is upon me, because he has anointed me to

---

[68]For a brief survey of the interpretations of the biblical meaning of 'justice' see José Míguez Bonino, 'The Biblical Roots of Justice,' 12–21.
[69]Ladd, *The Presence of the Future*, 109.

preach good news to the poor. He has sent me to proclaim release to the captives and the recovery of sight to the blind, to set at liberty those who are oppressed, to proclaim the acceptable year of the Lord (Lk. 4:18–19).

Then he amazed his audience by the assertion, 'Today this scripture has been fulfilled in your hearing' (Lk. 4:21).

John had announced that God would break into history, bringing fulfilment to the eschatological hope and the coming of the messianic age. Jesus boldly proclaimed that this promise was actually being fulfilled by God through his actions.

This message of fulfilment expresses a view of the Kingdom of God which contains both present and futuristic elements.[70] On the one hand, the messianic salvation foretold by the prophets was being fulfilled in Jesus' person and mission 'as good news to the poor.' On the other hand, there remained an eschatological consummation when the messianic salvation would be perfectly accomplished in the age to come. In the teachings of Jesus, it is clear that he proclaimed that the Kingdom of God is both a future event and a present reality.

Pentecostal theologian Gordon Fee has been at the vanguard of introducing to Pentecostals the concept of the Kingdom of God. For Fee this 'already—not yet' dialectic provides additional theological foundation for the church's mission. God brings his future reign in the present with the proclamation of 'good news to the

---

[70]The concept of the Kingdom of God in the teachings of Jesus and the role of apocalyptic concepts, particularly the relationship between the present and future aspects of the Kingdom, have been hotly debated issues. For an historical overview of this eschatological discussion see Adolf von Harnack, *What is Christianity?*, trans. W. Montgomery (New York, NY: G. P. Putman, 1901); Albert Schweitzer, *The Quest of the Historical Jesus*, trans. W. Montgomery (London: Black, 1913); William Wrede, *The Messianic Secret*, trans. J. C. G. Greig (Cambridge: Clark, 1971); Johannes Weiss, *Jesus' Proclamation of the Kingdom of God*, trans. R. H. Hiers and D. L. Holland (Philadelphia, PA: Fortress Press, 1971); C. H. Dodd, *The Parables of Jesus* (London: Nisbett, 1935) and *The Founder of Christianity* (New York, NY: Macmillan Press, 1970); A. N. Wilder, *Eschatology and Ethics in the Teachings of Jesus* (New York, NY: Harper and Row, 1950); and Oscar Cullman, *Christ and Time*, trans. Floyd Filson (Philadelphia, PA: The Westminster Press, 1950). The members of *La Fraternidad Teológica Latinoamericana* (FTL) have integrated the concepts of the Kingdom of God into an evangelical theological method and then developed the method within the context of Latin America. An important series of essays reflective of this Latin American contextual process is reflected in René Padilla, *Misión Integral: Ensayos sobre el Reino y la Iglesia* (Buenos Aires y Grand Rapids, MI: Nueva Creación y Wm. B. Eerdmans Publishing Co., 1986).

poor' everywhere.[71] David Cook notes the special place the poor
have in the Kingdom of God and this is graphically depicted in
Jesus' telling of the parables. e.g. Parable of the wedding feast (Lk.
14:1–14); the poor widow (Mark 12:41–4; Lk. 21:1–4); the rich
young ruler and the rich fool who wanted to build larger barns
(Matt. 19:16–30; Mark 10:17–31; Lk 12:13–21; 18:18–29); the
shrewd manager (Lk 16:1–13); and Dives (the rich man)and Lazarus
(Lk 16:19–31). The parables clearly demonstrate responsibility
toward the poor for those who are living under God's rule.[72] The
task of the follower of Jesus, then, is not just the business of ' "saving
souls"; it is rather, as with Jesus, the bringing of wholeness to broken
people in every kind of distress.'[73] Fee summarizes the appropriate
actions for believers who live in tension 'between the times'—between the beginning and the conclusion of the End:

> The final consummation, our glorious future, has been guaranteed for
> us by the resurrection of our Lord. But meanwhile, until that future
> has come in its fullness, we are to be the people of the future in the
> present age, who continue the proclamation of the kingdom as good
> news to the poor.[74]

Because the Kingdom of God is God's dynamic rule on earth,
it is nothing less than supernatural. Only God could do it. This
gift from God cannot be established solely through the efforts
of people. The idea that one's ethical efforts on behalf of the
Kingdom will create a new society, is, according to the English
theologian Christopher Sugden, antibiblical. The new creation
'will only come when Jesus returns'. Sugden describes the 'core'
of God's intention contained in the substance of his will fulfilled
for his creation. 'Its content is rooted in the Old Testament
expectation that God will establish his will for Creation—"Your

---

[71]Gordon Fee, 'The Kingdom of God and the Church's Global Mission,' 16. Fee argues
that the use of the term 'poor' includes the poor in the traditional sense as well as those
who 'stand impoverished in Spirit'. The New Testament exegetical scholar asserts that
when Jesus 'announced good news to the poor, his proclamation was for those who were
needy in every sense of the term' (16–17) See Joachim Jeremias, *New Testament theology:
Part I. The Proclamation of Jesus*, trans. John Bowden (London: SCM, 1971), 109–113; and
E. Bammel, 'Poor,' in *Theological Dictionary of the New Testament* (Grand Rapids, MI: Wm.
B. Eerdmans Publishing Co., 1983), 6:885–915.
[72]Cook, *Living in the Kingdom: the Ethics of Jesus*, 53–56.
[73]Fee, 'The Kingdom of God and the Church's Global Mission,' 17.
[74]Ibid., 16.

kingdom come, your will be done... "—forgiveness of sins, new relationships between people, justice for all, a renewed creation and the outpouring of God's Spirit.'[75] The underlying thrust throughout is that although evil dominates the present, and it appears as though chaos reigns supreme, there is a sense in which God, in the person of Jesus and the Kingdom, has introduced something new. The future has a bearing upon the present. The best way to comprehend that future is to recognize its ethical dimension as a visible expression of love and compassion.

THE ETHICS OF JESUS' KINGDOM TEACHING

Jesus' disciples are those who have received the word of the Kingdom (Mark 4:20) and have brought their lives under God's rule (Mark 10:15). The new ethic of God's Kingdom rule is to be lived out in the disciples' lives on a daily basis. David Cook asks rhetorically, 'How does the kingdom of God arrive in the world?' His response is direct. 'Jesus brings in the kingdom:'

> He announces that the kingdom of God is at hand; he shows the values of the kingdom by the kind of life he leads; he announces what standards are to be followed by members of the kingdom of God, and it is by living out these standards that the kingdom of God is revealed to the world and God's reign is ushered in a real and living way.[76]

Complete participation in God's righteousness can be achieved only in the future eschatological Kingdom of God. Yet in a very real sense, it can be appropriated in this present age, insofar as the reign of God is actually experienced.[77]

There is a tension between the 'already' and the 'not yet' manifestation of the Kingdom of God itself and in the attainment of the righteousness of the Kingdom. The Kingdom of God has broken into history in the person of Jesus, but it will be fully consummated only in the future age. The Kingdom has become present in history, but neither individuals nor society have been transformed and the Kingdom consummated. Ethical actions, empowered by the Spirit, argues Sugden, may serve in

---

[75]Christopher Sugden, 'A Presentation of the Concern for Kingdom Ethics,' in *Kingdom and Creation in Social Ethics*, Grove Ethical Series, no. 79 (Nottingham: Grove Books Ltd., 1990), 13.

[76]David Cook, *Living in the Kingdom*, 13.

[77]Ladd, *Presence of the Future*, 128–129.

'counteracting the moral disablement evil brings in society'.[78] However, even though 'such empowerment does not guarantee that all will be able to live out the Christian ethic.... Kingdom activity unblinds the masking activity of the evil one.... It conserves society and clarifies people's choice. This makes the invitation of the gospel relevant in every situation.'[79] By analogy, even though one cannot live a perfect life, the ethics of the Kingdom of God must and should be a practical part of everyday life. The perfect life of righteousness will emerge only in that future age when the Kingdom of God has been fully consummated. However, just as the Kingdom has broken into the present to give humanity a portion of the blessings of the Kingdom to come, so the righteousness of the Kingdom of God is attainable in the same proportions. In this manner the believer should not only demonstrate an individual and radical change of lifestyle but should also be an agent for change in society. The example, set by Jesus, to feed the hungry and minister to the suffering as an indication that the Kingdom has pressed into the present, in the words of David Cook, 'implies that we are to change radically the social, cultural, political, and economic structures of our existence'.[80] Therefore, the ethics of God's reign, like the reality of the Kingdom itself, can be seen in the tension between the 'now' of the present and the 'not yet' of the future perfection.

The ethics of Jesus' teachings stand in direct contrast to the pharisaical emphasis upon outward conformity to the law. Another distinctive feature of the ethics of the Kingdom is that they place the emphasis on the inner dispositions and intentions of life which underlie outward conduct. The law condemned adultery. Jesus condemns a lustful heart that is inclined toward adulterous action as well as the act of adultery itself. Similarly, Jesus makes clear that God requires love for one's enemies and not mere outward kindness which still may allow the person to be filled inwardly with anger, bitterness, or revenge. Consequently, persons under the reign of God will desire the greatest good even for the one who is endeavouring to do them wrong. God's rule establishes a disposition to love within a person's character. This new life is indeed the gift of

---

[78]Sugden, 'Concern for Kingdom Ethics,' 15.
[79]Ibid., 16.
[80]David Cook, *Living in the Kingdom*, 26.

God's reign.[81] The tension between the present order of the Kingdom and its final consummation is a key to understanding the ethics of love. In its fulness, the ethics of God's reign must wait for the final consummation, but in its reality, Kingdom ethics can be participated in in the here and now.

In his study of 'Evangelism, Social Concern, and the Kingdom of God,' Professor Murray Dempster provides a summation of the ethical substance of human life in the present under God's reign:

> The eschatological Kingdom has a normative moral structure reflective of God's own ethical character. Jesus taught, therefore, that where God reigns, a new redemptive society is formed in which brothers and sisters enjoy an affirmative community; strangers are incorporated into the circle of neighbor love; peace is made with enemies; injustices are rectified; the poor experience solidarity with the human family and the creation; generous sharing results in the just satisfaction of human needs in which no one suffers deprivation; and all persons are entitled to respect, are to be treated with dignity, and are deserving of justice because they share the status of God's image-bearers. Such actions and social practices that embody love, justice, and shalom constitute the normative moral structure in a social ethic reflective of God's kingly rule.[82]

But how is this ethic made operational? The ethics of the Kingdom of God require a personal moral response in concrete living history on the part of the Pentecostal believer to the dynamic acts of God. The dynamic, redemptive reign of the Kingdom of God has invaded history in a concrete way. The major premise of this theological section is the historical assertion that God has acted in the events of redemptive history concerning Israel and culminating in Jesus of Nazareth to make himself known to man. Pentecostals empowered by the Spirit accept the existential truth that God reveals not only information about himself. He reveals himself. This self-disclosure is not self-evident in historical events but requires the Word of God to

---

[81]George Eldon Ladd, 'Eschatology and Ethics,' *Baker's Dictionary of Christian Ethics*, ed. C. F. H. Henry (Grand Rapids, MI: Baker Book House, 1973), 215. José Míguez Bonino finds that the predominant theme that brings coherence to all concrete actions under the rubric of the Kingdom of God is 'best articulated around the "motif" of love'. José Míguez Bonino, 'Love and Social Transformation,' 127. The evangelical ethicist and theologian David Cook observes that love resulting in obedient action 'is a primary quality in living in the kingdom'. Cook, *Living in the Kingdom*, 36.

[82]Dempster, 'Evangelism, Social Concern, and the Kingdom of God,' 24.

make it understandable as revelation. The word both precedes and follows the event and is, in fact, part of the event itself. Such a theology regards the New Testament as both the record of what God has done in Jesus Christ and the normative interpretation of the divine event. Jesus promoted a view of morality that was responsive to God's redemptive activity in every given historical context. Jesus' ethics are dynamic, involving a personal response to God who acts for the good and the right in concrete, living history. Consequently, there is a contextualist ethic rooted in the notion that the substance of moral life is to reflect upon one's own moral action in relationship to the prior action of God.[83] This spiritually discerned hermeneutic is not uncontrolled, arbitrary or even capricious. Rather it is controlled by the text. This contextual ethic is based upon a commitment to the enduring nature and validity of the ethical principles of moral character as well as the principles of moral action. Thus it is possible to judge both traits of character and kinds of moral action by their conformity to the principles outlined in this chapter from the biblical tradition. But even here, the obligations and duties required by these principles must be worked out in a specific historical context in personal response to God's action. The nature of the biblical record does not allow the reader to comprehend it from a position of experiential neutrality. George Eldon Ladd expresses this spiritual dynamic with deep commitment:

> I can only bear witness at this point to what *Heilsgeschichte* means to me. My sense of God's love and acceptance is grounded not only in the resurrected Christ but also in the Jesus of history. . . . This is not

---

[83]The context versus principles controversy in Christian ethics was identified by James Gustafason in an article for the *Harvard Theological Review* in 1965. Gustafason characterizes and summarizes a basic division in the approach to Christian ethics over the past few decades. This basic division, according to Gustafason, was between 'principled ethics' on the one hand and 'contextualist ethics' on the other hand. Through an analysis of the appropriate literature, Gustafason demonstrated that this debate had taken place in Europe and the United States in both Catholicism and Protestantism. In short, the debate characterized the field of Christian ethics in different cultures as well as in different Christian traditions. Ethicists who were identified by Gustafason as 'principled' were committed to the use of formal, prescriptive principles by which to determine proper Christian conduct. Ethicists who were identified by Gustafason as 'contextualists' were those who advocated a more existential response to a particular situation in determining proper Christian conduct. For a thorough analysis of this debate and the main proponents for each position, see Paul L. Lehmann, *Ethics in a Christian Context* (London: SCM Press Ltd. 1963) and James M. Gustafason, *Christian Ethics in the Community* (Philadelphia: United Church Press, 1971).

faith in history; it is not faith in the kerygma; it is not faith in the Bible. It is faith in God who has revealed himself to me in the historical event of the person, works, and words of Jesus of Nazareth who continues to speak to me through the prophetic word of the Bible.[84]

Similarly to Ladd, this chapter has contended that Pentecostals must interpret their faith in constant interaction with history. Faith must be constantly applied in a continuous dialogue between one's set of beliefs and the world of one's experience. At the same time, however, the integrity of the interpretation must be rooted in a commitment to biblical criticism. Textual, literary, historical, redaction or form criticism are useful exegetical tools in the hands of the trained theologian. However, any believer through faith can go to the Scriptures with an expectation to encounter a dynamic response to his or her experience.[85]

APPROPRIATENESS OF KINGDOM TEACHING FOR PENTECOSTALISM

Pentecostals operate on the level of 'the view from below' of the popular sectors. As a consequence, if their encounter with the faith and the Spirit leads them to follow Jesus in a life of discipleship that is sensitive to problems of the marginalized of society that surround them, they are in a position to do 'what Jesus said and did'.

Jesus deliberately 1) preached God's mercy for sinners, 2) discipled followers to form a community of the faithful, and 3) conducted a ministry of service where he compassionately reached out to meet the needs of those about him. When contemporary Pentecostals predicate their lives and ministries on what Jesus said and did, they also reproduce the proclamation, the discipling and the service aspects inherent in the global mission of the church. Integrity of mission is achieved, in other words, by the incorporation of these three essential features of Jesus' mission within a broader theological matrix. Such a theological understanding of the church's ministry is crucial in order for Pentecostals to recognize that their confirmed commitment to evangelism is not complete without social concern empowered by the Holy Spirit.

---

[84]George Eldon Ladd, 'The Search for Perspective,' *Interpretation* 25 (1971): 57–58.
[85]For an interplay between a 'lay-reading' and an 'exegetical reading' see Douglas Petersen, 'The Kingdom of God and the Hermeneutical Circle,' 44–45. Also see Christopher Rowland's explanation earlier in this chapter.

Within the parameters outlined in this chapter this hermeneutical circle serves as a paradigm for ministry. The following conclusions are submitted.

(1) The first step for all participants in social service and social action ministries is a personal relationship with Jesus Christ. This radical decision to come under God's management in the Kingdom is a result of a dynamic confrontation with Jesus Christ which leads to single-minded focus on God's rule.

(2) This radical spiritual overthrow that takes place in one's life thrusts one into the world as an agent of change. Pentecostals have rightly emphasized the individual dimension of spiritual transformation and personal ethics. Pentecostals must also allow their spiritual transformation to be expressed in a creatively corporate ethic that joyfully takes action in responsible participation on behalf of the poor, the needy and the oppressed.

(3) Pentecostals who have experienced the 'empowerment' of the Holy Spirit as an act of God's grace can expect this same 'new power' to motivate and equip them not only to evangelize but in the same manner to introduce justice and righteousness as a consequence of their encounter with God.

(4) The tension of the present order of the Kingdom and its final consummation is the key to understanding the ethics of love, justice, mercy and peace. In its fulness, the ethics of God's reign must wait for the final consummation, but in its reality Kingdom ethics can be participated in here and now. Personal and collective actions taken to address 'the rights of the poor and needy' in all their socio-economic significance are not 'wasted efforts' but visible expressions that the apocalyptic Kingdom of God has pressed into the present.

(5) The actual social context is not a starting point. Rather it is the point of insertion into the ministry process as a consequence of the radical spiritual transformation Pentecostals have undergone. It is the real historical context that defines the framework within which Pentecostals need to articulate a theological social doctrine. The complexity of the situation is at the same time underscored by a basic premise. The majority of the Latin American people have been systematically marginalized and their very lives threatened. It is the responsibility of the Pentecostal community to give a Spirit-empowered witness in both a spiritual vocabulary and in concrete social terms to demonstrate God's desire to bring about justice for all humankind.

(6) The emphasis of Pentecostals in social ministry should not be exclusively on the poor but on human need in all its forms. However, because the poor have absolutely no one to plead their

cause, much of the church's effort will be inclined in their direction. For example, a father has three children whom he loves equally. One of those children may require a great deal more of his time in order to *live life* at the same level as his brothers and sisters. Love, therefore, is the great equalizer.

The Kingdom of God which will be consummated at the end of this age has already broken into the present. This supernatural reign is dynamically active among all people. Those who have submitted to the rule of the King can expect to be agents of the Kingdom for love, justice and redemption, bringing good news to the poor, sight to the blind, and freedom for the oppressed. This redeemed community in its actions to bring about social transformation will stand as a signpost declaring that the Kingdom of God has pressed into the present.

A PENTECOSTAL CONTRIBUTION TO SOCIAL THEOLOGY

It is apparent from the actions of Pentecostal groups described in chapters four and five that a social dynamic plays an integral part in Pentecostal experience. However, in spite of the church's deep involvement and active participation in ministering to the physical needs of the community with both informal actions as well as with intentional programmes, it is also apparent that formal theological work must be dedicated to the development of a social doctrine. José Míguez Bonino rightly states that as a first stage one must look at the social dynamic of the Pentecostal movement—the formation of a social doctrine comes at a second stage. This chapter, in an attempt to address this second stage, has entered the realm of theory and practice by articulating a theological basis for a contextualized social doctrine. While the ethical and theological concepts outlined as a basis for social concern in this chapter are certainly not unique to Pentecostals, a social doctrine that includes Spirit baptism as an empowering focus to do justice is the unique contribution of Pentecostal tradition.

The foundational premise of this contribution is that knowledge of faith and ethical action are rooted in God's self-revelation, centred and fulfilled in Jesus Christ and powerfully evidenced by the dynamic work and empowerment of the Holy Spirit. This fundamental epistemological commitment for Pentecostal theology provides an integral framework for praxis.

This chapter has formulated a dynamic hermeneutic that will enable Pentecostals to reflect upon the biblical text and provide them with a social ethic that will undergird, and indeed enhance, their current social practices. First, it has suggested a praxis theology appropriating and adapting the structural framework of the four steps of the hermeneutical circle. Second, it has drawn on a rich tradition of evangelical scholarship in constructing a social doctrine: i.e. that theological reflection must begin with an understanding of God's self-revelatory nature and character; that Israel's social ethical actions were to demonstrate this theocentric nature and character; that the concept of the Kingdom of God, implicit in the Old Testament and explicit in the person and teachings of Jesus in the New Testament, is the unifying theme that provides a description of what life would look like under God's redemptive reign; that the reality of the reign of the Kingdom of God is characterized by the ethics of justice, mercy, love and peace as its principle moral features.

If it is true, as is argued throughout these chapters, that the Pentecostal experience of Spirit baptism is basically one for empowerment, then the task of a Pentecostal theology is to demonstrate the centrality of the experience as a key pattern to open the way to discuss the appropriation of the above evangelical traits. In particular, the ethical dimensions of the law, covenant, prophets, and jubilee teachings focused under the rubric of the Kingdom of God as they are actualized and become operative in the power of the Spirit. The ethical response of the individual who has experienced God's grace in Spirit baptism empowers one not only to participate in evangelism and supernatural events but also to enjoy the empowerment of the Spirit in the expression of ethical concerns. Therefore, it is only when contemporary Pentecostals, empowered by the Spirit, recognize and practise a confirmed commitment to *both* evangelism and to social concern that integrity of mission is accomplished. The coming of the Spirit at Pentecost and its contemporary appropriation and application by Latin American Pentecostals through the experience of Spirit baptism integrates the ethical character of God's reign into a Pentecostal social doctrine. The aspect of the social doctrine that makes it Pentecostal is the work of Spirit baptism, which draws on a wider tradition of Christian social theology in order to fulfil its full biblical purpose.

Chapter 7
Toward The Future

A PENTECOSTAL SOCIAL PROLEGOMENA

Pentecostals throughout Central America, and elsewhere in Latin America, have already begun to demonstrate their potential for mobilizing large numbers of people, ostensibly in their efforts to extend the evangelical faith, but in the process they are also creating institutional structures capable of performing various educational, community development, social service and political functions. These national Pentecostal networks of largely autonomous local congregations stand in the vanguard—not at the margins—of the Latin American clamour for a more rewarding secure future. It should be noted that in these societies, where discrimination, neglect and indifference are too often characteristic, Pentecostalism has typically gathered strength precisely among the most disadvantaged or dissatisfied sectors such as the peasantry, the urban poor, women, Indians and ethnic minorities, young adults and the independent middle groups. Thus, Pentecostalism, quite unlike some of its stereotypical portrayals as passive, otherworldly and traditional, is deeply involved in its own kind of here-and-now social struggle. Its programme of personal regeneration at the grass roots, significant both in its degree and volume of effectiveness, has far-reaching implications for social transformation.

This book has proposed a dynamic hermeneutic, empowered by the Spirit, that will enable Pentecostals to reflect upon the biblical text and provide them with a contextualized social doctrine that undergirds, deepens, and indeed enhances, their current social practices. Still, in spite of significant progress, the author's attempt to provide a cohesive unity between Latin American Pentecostals' beliefs and practices is a modest attempt, not yet moved beyond prolegomena, and is intended only to set the stage for future constructive work in this area by others. This book is interdisciplinary in nature and is written to encourage both scholars and practitioners to enter into dialogue. It is the very nature of the dynamic of the hermeneutical circle to give further encouragement to Pentecostals to address the biblical text and to point them toward the future for additional reflection.

PENTECOSTALS AND CRITICAL REFLECTION

PENTECOSTALS AND SPIRIT BAPTISM FOR SELF–SERVING PURPOSES

The study of the teachings of the Kingdom of God can stimulate
Pentecostals to ask questions that must be answered if they are
'rightly to divide the word of truth'. The emphasis in Jesus'
Kingdom teaching provides a radical view of God's continuing
action in the world. In appropriating these New Testament emphases for their own contemporary era Pentecostals can carry the
notion of God's working with them (Mark 16:20) to a broad range
of human need. Pentecostals should not use their divine empowering and faith-building message for self-serving purposes (Jam.
4:3). There is a tendency within some Pentecostal groups to
understand the experience of Spirit baptism as demonstrated only
by physical manifestations such as glossalalia and 'words of
knowledge'. Consequently, Spirit baptism, rather than equipping
the believer for supernatural empowerment on behalf of others,
becomes an obsession in one's concern for more and more personal
and extraordinary experiences. When Pentecostals utilize their
experience with the Spirit for only personal and individual edifica-
tion and neglect the social responsibilities that should accompany
this phenomenon, they on one hand, misunderstand the reason for
their receiving the gift of the Spirit, and on the other hand, they
forfeit the opportunity to execute biblical justice and compassion
on behalf of their neighbour. Rowland is right when he criticizes
those Pentecostals who are interested in Spirit baptism only for
reasons of 'miraculous interventions and escapism offered by
tongues of ecstasy'.[1] Pentecostal doctrine and practice finds fulfilment in the formation of a community of believers who take this

---

[1]Rowland, *Radical Christianity*, 136. Dempster presents a well-reasoned discussion on the
moral 'significance' of glossolalia as a theological concept tied to the existential realities of
life that points to a theological justification for ethical norms based upon metaethical
analysis. He identifies two characteristics from the glossolalic encounter with God that
could translate from theological conviction to ethical norms. First, 'an ethics of
responsibility' should conform to God's moral framework (24). Second, and most
informative for our purposes, is that the glossolalic experience should also theologically
translate to the moral norm of 'the ethics of imagination' (25). Dempster posits that what
is most necessary in a world of hostility, suffering and injustice is the power of the
imagination. Through the empowerment of God's mighty act, Pentecostals can not only
'imagine the possibility of a better world' but can take creative steps to alter the world in
a radical manner (28). Dempster, *Moral Soundings*, 1983.

Kingdom authority from the word of God and respond by providing an integral pastoral action made possible by the gift of the Spirit.[2]

PENTECOSTALS AND PREMILLENIAL VIEWS

Pentecostalism in Latin America is in a unique location to formulate and practise an integral theology. However, Pentecostals must also come to grips with the question of 'critical analysis regarding the insufficiency of their interpretation'. Pentecostals are generally critiqued for their dispensational, and premillenial views that have, at times, precluded them from participating in social concern. Earlier, I have argued that Latin American Pentecostals are not dispensational in their theology or in their practice.[3] Míguez Bonino echoes the conviction that 'the dispensational understanding of Scripture really corresponds neither to the Pentecostal experience nor to the actual use that Pentecostals make of Scripture. . . . it is a garment that does not fit—it's much too tight.'[4] Unquestionably, however, the impending premillenial return of Jesus Christ has been a theological doctrine that has impacted negatively Pentecostal attitudes toward active involvement in issues of social concern. If Jesus Christ is soon returning, some Pentecostals have argued, the emphasis should be on evangelism and conversion rather than on social activism. East European Pentecostal theologian Peter Kuzmič observes that the above argument is a Western cultural-theological creation based upon conservative American political positions rather than upon a clear reading of Scripture.[5] Because Central American Pentecostalism is autonomous, the dichotomy held between evangelism and social concern that could have been propagated in North American missionary expansion is much less evident. For Latin American Pentecostals there are two fruitful approaches they could use to counteract social pacifism as a

---

[2]See chapter 3 for a description of the practical working out of doctrinal confession in Central American Pentecostalism.
[3]See chapter 3, note 71.
[4]José Míguez Bonino, letter to author, 11 October 1994.
[5]Peter Kuzmič, 'History and Eschatology: Evangelical Views,' in *Word and Deed: Evangelism and Social Responsibility*, ed. Bruce Nicholls (Grand Rapids, Michigan, 1985). 146. To reject a dispensational interpretation need not negate a commitment to Christian responsibility in history and society. A more thoroughgoing understanding of the apocalyptic expectation may serve as a positive stimulus for historical responsibility.

consequence of holding a premillenial eschatology as part of their doctrinal position. First, theologians as diverse as the Protestant liberationist José Míguez Bonino and Pentecostal theologians Miraslov Volf and Murray Dempster have proposed that when Christians create history that is compatible with the Kingdom of God, such projects have eschatological significance: what is valid will remain.[6] Volf contends that eschatological continuity between God's present reign and the reign to come 'guarantees that noble human efforts will not be wasted'.[7] Dempster enforces the argument when he posits that 'kingdom-signifying deeds' that are carried out by believers are 'the kinds of human effort that God preserves, sanctifies and directs teleologically toward the future age of God's redemptive reign'.[8] There is merit in this discussion for Pentecostals who feel that any type of activity besides evangelism will be just wasted effort. However, the ethical theological eschatological continuity between 'this age' and 'the age to come', though valid, is not as convincing as the basic premise that Pentecostals should not be precluded from involvement in social concern, for any reason, including a premillenial doctrine, simply because they must carry out the mandate to do 'everything Jesus said and did' regardless of the consequences. In other terms, the motivation for social action should first of all result from conversion and a transformation of life, empowered by the Spirit to demonstrate love toward all humankind.

PENTECOSTALS AND TRIUMPHALISM

At the same time if Pentecostals view their works with a spirit of triumphalism they will find difficulty in transferring their 'substitute society' into the larger forum of secular society. Pentecostals who desire to effect social change in the larger arena of society should take seriously the critique that, in spite of their obvious numbers, they have a tendency to be hermetic, even when they form alternative structures. If when Pentecostals form alternative societies their experiments in new ways of naming and addressing the problems of life at the grass-

---

[6]Ibid. and also Míguez Bonino, 'Historical Praxis and Christian Identity,' 274.

[7]Miraslov Volf, 'On Loving with Hope: Eschatology and Social Responsibility,' *TRANSFORMATION: An International Dialogue on Evangelical Social Ethics* 7 (July/September 1990): 17.

[8]Murray W. Dempster, 'Christian Social Concern in Pentecostal Perspective: Reformulating Pentecostal Eschatology,' *Journal for Pentecostal Theology* 2 (1993): 62.

roots stay locked within the group, their isolation will result in neither the horizontal linkage to poor neighbours of other faiths nor the vertical linkage to individuals and organizations with more direct access to the means of cultural production. If Pentecostal groups, no matter the magnitude of their size, are content to form their own enclaves they will forfeit the opportunity to participate in radical change or structural transformation.

PENTECOSTALS AND POLITICS

Further reflection must almost certainly address the political dimension and implications of Pentecostal activity. Pentecostalism has been consistently criticized for its lack of 'political involvement' beyond its own context and within civil society. To balance this critique, I have proposed that Pentecostals could argue legitimately that they have created their own alternative institutions that can function as instruments of human justice. Through the process of institution-building it is possible that constructive alternative instruments of social justice may actually enable the church to 'break the spell cast over the modern mind that uncritically equates social action axiomatically with political action'. Social action and political action have become almost interchangeable terms in some circles of Christian social ethics. The definition of social concern that includes only political, state and civil categories cannot capture other equally important areas of social concern. Political involvement is only one alternative among several options of social action to institute social change. Pentecostals have a clear expression of serious and committed Pentecostal views, articulating a beginning agenda for a further discussion of social concern.

However, if Latin American Pentecostals are committed to praxis as a necessary presupposition for responsible social action in helping to create a more just society, in the near future, they also will have to address the critique levelled by many observers that Pentecostals have generally abstained from political action as a legitimate question. Since their beginnings in Latin America, Pentecostals have considered politics to be, at best futile and, at worst, a dirty business. Moreover, Pentecostals have seldom been involved in political action because they have had little hope that a revolutionary change of government would necessarily bring change to the social structures. Their pragmatism has limited them to certain arenas of action where they have been tepid at best and have avoided outright conflict.

With the exception of very few cases the radicalness of the Pentecostal position of non-involvement in political action is still the norm. As has been demonstrated above, Pentecostals have opted for a different approach to social concern, such as the priority given to educational social action. Though Pentecostal social concern has traditionally avoided most types of political involvement, in the last five or six years one can witness sufficient departures from the norm as to force the question as to why these departures are happening and how Pentecostals will understand and respond to this new fact. Involvement in politics can no longer be avoided. If Pentecostals intend to live out their faith as a reality in today's world, they cannot avoid coming to grips with what Míguez Bonino articulately calls 'this "thing" that shapes individual and collective life, that both confers meaning on and denies meaning to human plans and actions, that encompasses and invades all areas of human existence, and that offers and dispenses both life and death to thousand of millions—political struggle!'[9] While programmes of social action, such as LACC, are a necessary complement to the church's ministry, Pentecostals must come to an understanding as to how their social actions fit in with the overall socio-political context. The time has come when Pentecostals' critical reflection upon the 'theoretical implications' of the intermeshing of social action with politics is indispensable. The price of simple pragmatism is too high. One may or may not agree with other critiques of appropriate actions in the name of God. But Pentecostals cannot ignore the assertion issued in Míguez Bonino's statement 'that theory is necessary, in the first place, because it is unavoidable; whether acknowledged or not, it is present'. Míguez contends that political reflection 'is necessary in order that we can make explicit to ourselves the presuppositions and assumptions of our action as well as expose and critically examine forms of action suggested to us'.[10] This last sentence holds a challenge to Pentecostals to move beyond their unwillingness to deal with political issues and constructively devise political structures able to cope with the problems and give viability to the hopes of local context.

---

[9] José Míguez Bonino, *Toward a Christian Political Ethics*, 8.
[10] Ibid., 9

THE SOURCE OF PENTECOSTAL SOCIAL ACTION

When Pentecostals model the example of an integral ministry exemplified by Jesus, though directly involved in activity filled with evangelistic fervour and compassion, they are not precluded from playing an active part in bringing about change in the socio-political reality of the region. Pentecostals can offer not only a kind of spiritual refuge, therefore, but authentic social action alternatives.

Appendix 1
Evangelical/Pentecostal Statistics

Most of the commonly cited statistical estimates of the size of the evangelical/Pentecostal community in Latin America are compiled by J.P. Johnstone. Operation World 4th edition (Kent, England: STL and WEC International. 1986): Atlas de COMIBAM (Sao Paulo, Brazil: Operation Mobilization, 1987): and Servicio Evangélico para America Latina (SEPAL, a Protestant-sponsored research organization whose data is published in World Christianity: Central America, ed. Clifton Holland (Monrovia, California: Missions Advanced Research and Communications Center, 1981). SEPAL's methodology for collecting and analyzing data uses a formula.[1] Estimates for the size of the evangelical Pentecostal community are based on formulas of self-reported communicant members multiplied by a given coefficient (ambiguous numbers 2.5 or 4.0—in the case of SEPAL—which is an inclusive figure). This study does not wish to enter into an involved critique of the methodology employed nor the resulting size of the estimated community. It is my opinion, however, that the statistics are inflated.

William Taylor and Emilio Núñez, in their research on Latin American Evangelicalism, also admit that accurate figures for the numbers of evangelicals do not exist. Their statistics, based upon the above sources as well as their own information allow for an error rate of 20 per cent above or below. All of the groups collecting data are in agreement that 75 per cent of the total number of evangelicals are Pentecostals. This work, while acknowledging the immense difficulty of collecting reliable data on the dynamic growth of Latin American evangelical/Pentecostalism, accepts that the statistics cited, even allowing for substantial error, may suggest significant trends that can be reasonably evaluated.

The statistics used here for the number of members and adherents of the Assemblies of God, however, do not include

---

[1] Stoll, *Is Latin America Turning Protestant?*, 333-334.

children of the adherents nor do they include an estimate of the size of the 'Pentecostal community' by multiplying the number of members and adherents by a given coefficient. Although such a formulation can be useful for certain purposes, it may also cloud a most important characteristic of Pentecostals-their lack of nominality. By including the estimates of the Pentecostals community in the statistics, the numbers are not only inflated but the quotient of 2 or 3 sympathizers for each member immediately adds the dimension of millions of 'nominal Pentecostals' a description, that, until now, has been a contradiction in terms among Pentecostals.

Indeed, the very concept of a 'nominal' Pentecostal distorts our comprehension of the characteristics of Pentecostal believers.

CEPAD

An evangelical agency, *Comite Evagélico Proayuda a Los Damnificados* (CEPAD) was formed in 1972 to help the victims of the earthquake which had virtually destroyed the centre of the capital city of Managua. *Las Asambleas de Dios* was among the original founding members of CEPAD. This alliance took responsibility for the distribution of food, clothing, medical supplies and other emergency materials to the earthquake victims. CEPAD soon became a permanent evangelical organization, known as the Evangelical Committee for Development Aid, which involved itself not only in development but in politics as well. CEPAD was ardently opposed to the Somoza regime and later, in the opinion of certain groups such as *las Asambleas de Dios*, became aligned with the Sandinistas. There has been a controversial and sometimes bitter debate between CEPAD and *las Asambleas de Dios* over political issues. In 1990 *las Asambleas de Dios* withdrew its membership from CEPAD. It should be clearly understood that the decision of *las Asambleas de Dios* to sever relationships with CEPAD was not based on a difference of philosophy regarding the involvement of evangelical/Pentecostal churches in social projects. The division took place over political disagreements. The leadership of *las Asambleas de Dios* in Nicaragua, particularly in the early years of the Sandinista government, felt that CEPAD had politically aligned itself with the Sandinista government and, therefore, could not objectively represent *las Asambleas de Dios* before the government. A series of salvos were fired from both sides. In the July–August 1989 official *CEPAD REPORT*, CEPAD stated that the first Pentecostal missionaries to Nicaragua in 1912 (who two years later, according to the report, formed the Assemblies of God) arrived in the same year as the invasion of the U. S. marines, inferring that the formation of the Assemblies of God was integrally linked to the arrival of U.S. military forces. The report declared that as 'any school child here can tell you . . . their appearance [the Pentecostal missionaries] in such close proximity to the arrival of the U.S. occupation forces is more than a coincidence'.(1) Further, CEPAD claimed that *las Asambleas de Dios* had 'never gained autonomy, members received subtle but persistent reinforcement that all good things around them are sent from "above," where the denominations are headquartered in U.S. states like Missouri ... A collusion of ideologies and world view served the needs of the empire better than any conspiracy concocted by national intelligence agencies'(2). Additionally, CEPAD accused *las Asambleas de Dios* of practising a dispensational theology that 'can do nothing to solve earthly problems... such a theology of indifference does not motivate people to immerse themselves in the revolution, and, in fact, often encourages them to distrust the revolution as a Satanic project' (10). The report included an additional series of charges against Pentecostals in general. In light of the accusations levelled by CEPAD, the *presbiterio general* of *las Asambleas de Dios* felt they had little choice but to withdraw from CEPAD. In a written response to the official board of CEPAD and in particular to its president Dr. Adolfo Parajon Dominquez on May 8, 1990 they listed each of the accusations from the CEPAD REPORT, which they (*las Asambleas de Dios*) undoubtedly took personally, and asked the following rhetorical question: 'We ask ourselves, for what purpose would the editor of CEPAD in their article publish such damaging and malicious accusations? Just the title of the report 'The Other Invasion' seems to be a call of alert to the Sandinistas to restrain, censure and imprison evangelicals that they [CEPAD] call the "Christian Right." It seems that the purpose of CEPAD is to end all their religious opposition and at the same time constitute a Super-church that will be recognized and guaranteed by the Sandinista state.' *Las Asambleas de Dios* felt strongly that further alliance with CEPAD, given the above reasons, was untenable and consequently on May 8, 1990 'the *PRESBITERIO GENERAL* of the Evangelical Pentecostal Conference of *las Asambleas de Dios* de Nicaragua resolved to: disaffiliate from CEPAD'. *Carta de Desafiliación al CEPAD* May 8, 1990 (Managua, Nicaragua). (The copy of the letter is in the possession of the author and is used with the permission of the *presbíterio ejecutivo de las Asambleas de Dios de Nicaragua.*) For a historical review of CEPAD from a sympathetic perspective see Adolpho Miranda Sáenz. 'The Political Metamorphosis of Evangelicals in Nicaragua'. in *TRANSFORMATION: An International Evangelical Dialogue on Mission and Ethics* 9 (July/September 1992): 20–25.

Bibliography

Allen, Roland. *Missionary Methods: St. Paul or Ours?* (Grand Rapids, MI: Wm. B. Eerdmans Publishing Co., 1962).

Amerding, Carl E. *Evangelicals and Liberation.* (Phillipsburg, NJ: Presbyterian and Reformed Publishing Co., 1979).

Anderson, Dole A. *Management Education in Developing Countries: The Brazilian Experience.* Latin American Monograph Series. (Michigan State University, Boulder, CO: Westview Press, 1987).

Anderson, Robert Mapes. *Vision of the Disinherited: The Making of American Pentecostalism.* (New York, NY: Oxford University Press, 1979).

Andrews, Stuart. *Methodism and Society.* (London: Longmens, 1970).

Annis, Sheldon. *God and Production in a Guatemalan Town.* (Austin, TX: University of Texas Press, 1987).

Assman, Hugo. *La Iglesia Electronica y su impacto en America Latina.* (San José, Costa Rica: Editorial Departamento Ecuménico de Investigaciónes [DEI], 1987).

Barratt, Thomas Ball. *The Truth about the Pentecostal Revival.* (Larik, Norway: Alfons Hansen and Soner, 1927).

Barrett, David B. *World Christian Encyclopedia.* (New York, NY: Oxford University Press, 1982).

Bartleman, Frank. *How Revival Came to Los Angeles: As It was in the Beginning.* (Los Angeles: n. p., 1924).

Bastian, Jean-Pierre. *Protestantismo y Sociedad en México.* (Mexico City: Casa de Publicaciones Unidas, 1983).

Bastide, Roger. *The African Religions of Brazil.* (Baltimore, MD: John Hopkins University Press, 1970).

Bedell, George C., Leo Sanden, Jr., and Charles T. Wellborn, eds. *Religion in America.* (New York, NY: Macmillan Publishing Company, 1975).

Belo, Fernando. A. *A Materialist Reading of the Gospel of Mark.* Translated by Matthew J. O'Connell. (Maryknoll, NY: Orbis Books, 1981).

Berger, Peter, and Thomas Luckman. *The Social Construction of Reality.* (New York, NY: Doubleday, 1967).

Birch, Bruce C. *Let Justice Roll Down: The Old Testament, Ethics, and Christian Life.* (Louisville, KY: John Knox Press, 1991).

Bloch-Hoell, Nils. *The Pentecostal Movement; Its Origin, Development, and Distinctive Character.* (Oslo: Universitetsflorlaget, 1964).

Blumhoffer, Edith L. *The Assemblies of God: A Chapter in the Story of American Pentecostalism.* 2 Vols. (Springfield, MO: Gospel Publishing House, 1989).

Boff, Leonardo. *Jesus Christ liberator: a critical Christology for our time.* Translated by Patrick Hughes. (Maryknoll, NY: Orbis Books, 1978).

———. *La Trinidad, la Sociedad y la Liberación.* (Buenos Aires: Ediciones Paulinas, 1988).

Bonhoeffer, Dietrich. *Letters and Papers from Prison.* Revised ed. (NY: SCM Press, 1971).

Boudewijnse, Barbara, Andre Droogers, and Frans Kamsteeg, eds. *Algo más que opio: Una lectura antropológica del pentecostalismo latinoamericano y caribeño.* (San José, Costa Rica: Departamento Ecuménico de Investigaciones [DEI], 1991).

Bright, John. *The Kingdom of God.* Nashville, (TN: Abingdon-Cokesbury Press, 1963).

Brown, Diana D. *Umbanda: Religion and Politics in Urban Brazil.* Ann Arbor, (MI: University Microfilms International Press, 1986).

Brown, Robert McAfee. *Gustavo Gutiérrez: An Introduction to Liberation Theology.* (Maryknoll, NY: Orbis Books, 1990).

———. *Theology in a New Key.* (Philadelphia, PA: Westminster Press, 1978).

Burke, Emory S., ed. *The History of American Methodism.* 3 Vols. (New York, NY: Abingdon Press, 1961).

Burrell, Gibson, and Morgan Gareth. *Sociological Paradigms and Organizational Analysis.* (Portsmouth, NH: Heinemann, 1979).

Cameron, Richard. *Methodism and Society in Historical Perspective.* (New York, NY: Abingdon Press, 1961).

Cerillo, Augustus Jr., and Murray W. Dempster, eds. *Salt and Light: Evangelical Political Thought in Modern America.* (Grand Rapids, MI: Baker Book House, 1989).

Chafer, L. S. *Systematic Theology.* 5 Vol. (Dallas, TX: Dallas Theological Seminary, 1944).

Comblin, José. *Holy Spirit and Liberation.* (Maryknoll, NY: Orbis Books, 1989).

Conn, Charles W. *Where the Saints Have Trod: A History of the Church of God Missions.* (Cleveland, TN: Pathway Press, 1959).

Cook, David. *Living in the Kingdom: the Ethics of Jesus.* (London: Hodder & Stoughton, 1992).

———. *The Moral Maze: A way of exploring Christian Ethics.* (London: SPCK, 1983).

Cook, Guillermo. *The Expectation of the Poor: Latin American Base Ecclesial Communities in Protestant Perspective.* (Maryknoll, NY: Orbis Books, 1982).

Cullman, Oscar. *Christ and Time.* Translated by Floyd Filson. (Philadelphia, PA: The Westminster Press, 1950).

Cummings, William K. *Low-Cost Primary Education: Implementing an Innovation in Six Nations.* (Ottawa, ONT: International Development Research Centre, 1986).

Damboriena, Prudencia. *El Protestantismo en America Latina.* 2 Vols. (Freiburg,

Madrid: Oficina Internacional de Investigaciones Sociales de FERES, 1963).

Dayton, Donald. *Theological Roots Of Pentecostalism*. (Grand Rapids, MI: Zondervan Publishing House, 1987).

De los Reyes, Alfonso. *La Responsibilidad Social de la Iglesia*. (Mexico City, Mexico: Editorial Cristiana Continental de Las Asambleas de Dios, 1992).

Diamond, Sara. *Spiritual Warfare: The Politics of the Christian Right*. (London: Pluto Press, 1989).

Dodd, C. H. *The Founder of Christianity*. (New York, NY: Macmillan Press, 1970).

——. *The Parables of Jesus*. (London: Nisbett, 1935).

Dominguez, Roberto. *Pioneros de Pentecostes*. Vol 2. (San Salvador: Literature Evangelica, 1975).

Durkeim, Emile. *Suicide: a study in sociology*. Edited by George Simpson. Translated by John A. Spaulding and George Simpson. (London: Routledge & Kegan Paul, 1952).

Dussel, Enrique. *A History of the Church in Latin America: Colonialism to Liberation*. Translated and revised by Alan Neeley. (Grand Rapids, MI: Wm. B. Eerdmans Publishing Co., 1981).

Eckstein, Susan, ed. *Power and Popular Protest: Latin American Social Movements*. (Berkely, CA: University of California Press, 1989).

Ellis, Marc H., and Otto Maduro, eds. *Expanding the View: Gustavo Gutiérrez and the Future of Liberation Theology*. (Maryknoll, NY: Orbis Books, 1990).

Escobar, Arturo and Sonia E. Alvarez, eds. *The Making of Social Movements in Latin America: Identity, Strategy, and Democracy*. (Boulder, CO: Westview Press, 1992).

Fals Borda, Orlando, ed. *The Challenge of Social Change*. (Beverly Hills, CA.: Sage Publications Inc., 1985).

Fee, Gordon. *Gospel and Spirit, Issues in New Testament Hermeneutics*. (Peabody, MA: Hendrickson Publishers, 1991).

Frankena, William K. *Ethics*. 2d ed. (Englewood Cliffs, NJ: Prentice Hall, 1973).

Freire, Paulo. *The Pedagogy of the Oppressed*. (New York, NY: Herder and Herder, 1970).

Ganunza, José María. *Los sectas nos invaden*. (Caracas, Venezuela: Ediciones Paulinas, 1978).

Gaxiola-Gaxiola, Manuel Jesús. *La Serpiente y la Paloma, Analisis del Crecimiento de la Iglesia Apostólica de la Fe en Cristo Jesus de México*. (Pasadena, CA: William Carey Press, 1975).

General Council of the Assemblies of God. *Ministers and Missionaries of the General Council of the Assemblies of God*. Rev. to September 25, 1992. (Springfield, MO: Gospel Publishing House, 1992).

Goff, James R. Jr. *Fields White Unto Harvest: Charles F. Parham and The Missionary Origins of Pentecostalism*. (Fayetteville, AK: The University of Arkansas Press, 1988).

Gustafason, James M. *Christian Ethics and the Community*. (Philadelphia, PA: Pilgrim Press, 1971).

Gutiérrez, Gustavo. *A Theology of Liberation: History, Politics and Salvation*. Revised ed. Translated by Caridad Inda and John Eagleson. (Maryknoll, NY: Orbis Books, 1988).

———. *The truth shall make you free: confrontations*. Translated by Matthew J. O'Connell. (Maryknoll, NY: Orbis Books, 1990).

———. *We Drink From Our Own Wells*. Translated by Matthew J. O'Connell. (Maryknoll, NY: Orbis, 1984).

Harrell, David Edwin, Jr. *All Things are Possible: The Healing and Charismatic Revivals in Modern America*. (Bloomington, IN: Indiana University Press, 1975).

Henry, Carl F. H. *The Uneasy Conscience of Modern Fundamentalism*. (Grand Rapids, MI: Wm. B. Eerdmans Publishing Co., 1947).

Hodges, Melvin A. *The Indigenous Church*. (Springfield, MO: Gospel Publishing House, 1953).

———. *The Indigenous Church and the Missionary*. (Pasadena, CA: William Carey Library, 1978).

———. *A Theology of the Church and Its Mission*. (Springfield, MO: Gospel Publishing House, 1977).

Holland, Joe and Peter Henriot. *Social Analysis: Linking Faith and Justice*. (Maryknoll, NY: Orbis Books, 1984).

Hollenweger, Walter J. *The Pentecostals*. (Minneapolis, MN: Augsberg Publishing House, 1972).

Hoover, Willis C. *Historia del Avivamiento Pentecostal en Chile*. (Valparaiso, n. p., 1948).

Horsley, Richard. *Sociology of the Jesus Movement*. (New York, NY; Crossroad, 1989).

Instituto Interamericano de Cooperación para la Agricultura (IICA). *Centroamérica en cifras*. (San José, Costa Rica: Facultad Latinoamericana de Ciencias Sociales (FLASCO), 1991).

Ireland, Rowan. *Kingdoms Come: Religion and Politics in Brazil*. Pittsburgh, PA: University Press, 1991.

Jeremias, Joachim. *New Testament Theology: Part I. The Proclamation of Jesus*. Translated by John Bowden. (London: SCM, 1971).

Johns, Cheryl Bridges. *Pentecostal Formation: A Pedagogy Among the Oppressed*. (Sheffield: Sheffield Academic Press, 1993).

Jones, Charles Edwin. *Perfectionist Persuasion: A Social Profile of the National Holiness Movement*. (Metuchen, NJ: Scarecrow Press Inc., 1974).

Kaiser, Walter J. Jr. *Toward Old Testament Ethics*. (Grand Rapids, MI: Academie Books, 1983).

Kendrick, Klaude. *The Promise Fulfilled: A History of the Modern Pentecostal Movement*. (Springfield, MO: Gospel Publishing House, 1961).

Kessler, John B. A. *A Study of the Older Protestant Missions and Churches in Peru and Chile.* (Goes, Netherlands: Oosterbaan and Le Cointre, 1967).

Kirk, J. Andrew. *Liberation theology: an evangelical view from the Third World.* (London: Marshall, Morgan & Scott, 1979).

Knowles, James Purdie. *Samuel A. Purdie: his life and letters.* (Plainfield, IN: Publishing Association of Friends, 1908).

Koebel, W. H. *Central America: Guatemala, Nicaragua, Costa Rica, Honduras, Panama and Salvador.* (London: T. F. Unwin Ltd., 1927).

LaBerge, Agnes N. O. *What God Hath Wrought.* (Chicago: IL: Herald Publishing Co., 1921).

Ladd, George Eldon. *Presence of the Future: The Eschatology of Biblical Realism.* (Grand Rapids, MI: Wm. B. Eerdmans Publishing Co., 1974).

——. *A Theology of the New Testament.* (Grand Rapids, MI: Wm. B. Eerdmans Publishing Co., 1974).

LaFeber, Walter. *Inevitable Revolutions: The United States in Central America.* (New York, NY: W. W. Norton and Company, 1983).

Lalive d'Epinay, Christian. *Haven of the Masses: A Study of the Pentecostal Movement in Chile.* (London: Lutterworth, 1969).

Lehmann, Paul L. *Ethics in a Christian Context.* (London: SCM Press LTD., 1963).

Los Niños de las Américas: *Supervivencia, Protección y Desarrollo Integral de la Niñez en el Decenio de 1990.* (Santa Fe de Bogotá: UNICEF, 1992).

Lourié, Sylvain. *Education and Development: Strategies and Decisions in Central America.* (Paris: United Nations Educational, Scientific, and Cultural Organization, 1989).

Luna, David Alejandro. *Manual de historia económica de El Salvador.* (El Salvador: Editorial Universitaria, 1971).

Lyon, David. *Karl Marx: an assessment of his life and thought.* 2d. ed. (Australia: Lion, 1980).

Mackay, John A. *The Other Spanish Christ: a study in the spiritual history of Spain and South America.* (New York, NY: The Macmillan company, 1933).

Mahan, Asa. *Baptism of the Holy Ghost.* New York, NY: W. C. Palmer, Jr., 1970.

Malherbe, Abraham. *Social Aspects of Early Christianity.* (Philadelphia, PA: Fortress Press, 1983).

Malina, Bruce. *The New Testament World: Insights from Cultural Anthropology.* (Louisville, KY: John Know Press, 1981).

Mannheim, Karl. *Ideology and Utopia: An introduction to the Sociology of Knowledge.* Translated by Louis Wirth and Edward Shils. (London: Routledge & Kegan Paul, 1936).

Maríz, Cecelia Loreto. *Coping With Poverty: Pentecostals and Christian Base Communities in Brazil.* (Philadelphia, PA: Temple University Press, 1994).

Martin, David. *Tongues of Fire: The Explosion of Protestantism in Latin America.* (Cambridge, MA: Basil Blackwell, Inc., 1990).

Marx, Karl, and James Engel. *The German Ideology.* Translated by S. Ryazanskaya. (Mascon: Lawrence and Wishart Ltd., 1964).

Masferrer, Alberto. *El Rosal Deshojado.* 2d ed. (El Salvador: Ministerio de Educación, Dirección General de Publicaciones, 1965).

——. G̲ *Que Debemos Hacer?: cartas a un obrero.* 5 ed. (San Salvador: Dirección General de Cultura, Direccion de Publicaciones, 1968).

McLellan, David. *Essential Writings.* Oxford: (Oxford University Press, 1988).

——. *Marxism and religion: a description and assessment of the Marxist Critique of Christianity.* (London: Macmillan, 1987).

Meeks, Wayne. *The first urban Christians: the social world of the Apostle Paul.* (New Haven, CT: Yale University Press, 1983).

Menzies, William. *Anointed to Serve: The Story of the Assemblies of God.* (Springfield, MO: Gospel Publishing House, 1971).

Merton, R. K. *Social Theory and Social Structure.* (Glencove, IL: Free Press, 1957).

Míguez Bonino, José. *Christians and Marxists: The Mutual Challenge to Revolution.* (London: Hodder and Stoughton, 1976).

——. *Doing Theology in a Revolutionary Situation.* (Philadelphia, PA: Fortress Press, 1975).

——. *Protestantismo y Liberación.* (Nueva Creación: Buenos Aires, Argentina, forthcoming).

——. *Toward a Christian Political Ethics.* (Philadelphia, PA: Fortress Press, 1983).

——. ed. *Faces of Jesus: Latin American Christologies.* Translated by Robert A. Barr. (Maryknoll, NY: Orbis Books, 1984).

Minus, Paul M. *Walter Rauschenbusch: American Reformer.* (New York, NY: Macmillan Publishing Company, 1988).

Miranda, José. *Marx and the Bible.* (Maryknoll, NY: Orbis Books, 1974).

Moltmann, Jürgen. *The Crucified God: The cross of Christ as the Foundation and Criticism of Christian Theology.* Translated by R. A. Wilson and John Bowden. (New York, NY: Harper & Row, 1974).

——. *The Trinity and the Kingdom of God: The Doctrine of God.* (London: SCM Press Ltd., 1981).

Mott, Stephen. *Biblical Ethics and Social Change.* (New York, NY: Oxford University Press. 1982).

Munro, Dana G. *The Five Republics of Central America.* (New York, NY: Oxford University Press, 1918).

Nelson, Jack. *Hunger for Justice: The Politics of Food and Faith.* (Maryknoll, NY: Orbis Books, 1980).

Nelson, Wilton. *Protestantism in Latin America.* (Grand Rapids, MI: Wm. B. Eerdmans Publishing Co., 1984).

Nida, Eugene. *Understanding Latin Americans.* (Pasadena, CA: William Carey Library, 1974).

Núñez C., Emilio A., and William D. Taylor. *Crisis in Latin America: An Evangelical Perspective.* (Chicago, IL: Moody Press, 1989).

Parham, Charles. *Apostolic Faith.* (Baxter Springs, Kansas: n. p., 1919–1920).

Parham, Sarah E. *The Life of Charles S. Parham.* Joplin, MO: Tri-State Printing Co., 1930; reprint, (Birmingham, AL: Commercial Printing Co., 1977).

Parker, Joseph I., ed. *Interpretative Statistical Survey of the World Mission of the Christian Church.* (New York, NY: International Missionary Council, 1938).

Polmerville, Paul. *The Third Force in Missions.* (Peabody, MA: Hendrickson Publishers, 1985).

Putman, George Palmer. *The Southland of North America.* (New York, NY: G. P. Putman's Son, 1913).

Quartanciono, Antonio. *Sectas en América Latina.* (Guatemala City, Guatemala: Consejo Episcopal Latinoamericano, 1981).

Rasmussen, Larry, and Bruce Birch. *Bible and Ethics in the Christian Life.* (Minneapolis, MN: Augsberg, 1976).

Read, William R., Victor M. Monterroso, and Harmon A. Johnson. *Latin American Church Growth.* (Grand Rapids, MI: Wm. B. Eerdmans Publishing Co., 1969).

Reglamento Local: Manual de Doctrinas y Prácticas de las Asambleas de Dios. (San José, Costa Rica: Asociación Cristiana de las Asambleas de Dios, 1992).

Roberts, Bryan. *Organizing Strangers.* (Austin, TX: University of Texas Press, 1973).

Rolim, Francisco Cartaxo. *Religiao e Classes Populares.* (Petropolis, Brazil: Editorial Vozes, 1980).

Rothery, Agnes. *Central America and the Spanish Main.* (Boston, MA: Houghton Mifflin Company, 1929).

Rowland, Christopher, and Mark Corner. *Liberating Exesesis: The Challenge of Liberation Theology to Biblical Studies.* (London: SPCK, 1990).

Ruhl, Arthur. *The Central Americans: adventures and impressions between Mexico and Panama.* (New York, NY: C. Scribner's Sons, 1929).

Ruiz, Bartolomé Matamoros. *Historia de las Asambleas de Dios en Nicaragua.* (Managua, Nicaragua: Editorial Vida, 1984).

Ryrie, C. C. *Dispensationalism Today.* (Chicago, IL: Moody Press, 1965).

Samandú, Luis E. *Protestantismos y Procesos Sociales en CentroAmérica.* (San José, Costa Rica: Editorial Universitaria Centroamericana, 1991).

Schäfer, Heinrich. *Protestantismo y crisis social en América Central.* (San José, Costa Rica; Investigaciones Departamento Ecuménico de Investigación [DEI], 1992).

Schweitzer, Albert. *The Quest of the Historical Jesus.* Translated by W. Montgomery. (London: Black, 1913).

Segundo, Juan Luis. *The Hidden Motives of Pastoral Action: Latin American Reflections.* Translated by John Drury. (Maryknoll. NY: Orbis Books, 1978).

——. *Jesus Of Nazareth Yesterday and Today: Faith and Ideology.* Vol. 1. (Maryknoll, NY: Orbis Books, 1984).

——. *The Liberation of Theology.* (Maryknoll, NY: Orbis Books, 1976).

Shaw, S. B., ed. *Echoes of the General Holiness Assembly.* (Chicago, IL: S. B. Shaw, 1901).

Sobrino, Jon. *Christology at the Crossroads.* Translated by John Drury. (Maryknoll, NY: Orbis Books, 1978).

Spain, Mildred. *And in Samaria: A Story of Fifty Years Missionary Witness in Central America, 1890–1940.* (Dallas, TX: Central American Mission, 1940).

Spittler, Russell, ed. *Perspectives in the New Pentecostalism.* (Grand Rapids, MI: Baker Book House, 1976).

Stoll, David. *Is Latin America Turning Protestant? The Politics of Evangelical Growth.* (Berkeley, CA: University of California Press, 1990).

Stronstad, Roger. *The Charismatic Theology of St. Luke.* (Peabody, MA: Hendrickson Publishers, 1984).

Sullivan, Lawrence Eugene. *Ichanchu's drum: an orientation to meaning in South American religions.* (New York, NY: Macmillan Publishing Co., 1988).

Synan, Vinson. *The Holiness-Pentecostal Movement in the United States.* (Grand Rapids, MI: Wm. B. Eerdmans Publishing Company, 1971).

——, ed. *Aspects of the Pentecostal-Charismatic Origins.* (Plainfield, NJ: Logos International, 1975).

Thompson, Wallace. *Rainbow Republics of Central America.* (New York, NY: E. P. Dutton and Company, 1926).

United Nations, Population Division. *Human Development Report, 1992.* (New York, NY: Oxford University Press, 1992).

Verhey, Allan. *The Great Reversal: Ethics and the New Testament.* (Grand Rapids, MI: Wm. B. Eerdmans Publishing Co., 1984).

Vigil, James Diego. *From Indians to Chicanos: A Sociocultural History.* (London: C. V. Mosby Co., 1980).

Villapando, Waldo Luis, ed. *Las Iglesia del Transplante: Protestantismo de Migración en la Argentina.* (Buenos Aires: Centro de Estudios Cristianos, 1970).

Von Harnack, Adolf. *What is Christianity?* Translated by W. Montgomery. (New York, NY: G. P. Putman, 1901).

Waggoner, George R., and Barbara Asbton Waggoner. *Education in Central America.* (Lawrence, KS: The University Press of Kansas, 1971).

Wagner, C. Peter. *Look Out! The Pentecostals Are Coming.* (Carol Stream, IL: Creation House, 1973).

Walker, Louise Jeter. *Siembra y Cosecha.* 2 Vols. (Springfield, MO: Gospel Publishing House, 1992).

Weber, Max. *The Protestant Work Ethic and the Spirit of Capitalism.* (New York, NY: Charles Scribner's Sons, 1958).

Weiss, Johannes. *Jesus' Proclamation of the Kingdom of God.* Translated by R. H. Hiers and D. L. Holland. (Philadelphia, PA: Fortress Press, 1971).

Wesley, John. *Plain Account of Christian Perfection.* (New York, NY: Track Department, n.d).

White, Alistair. *El Salvador.* (New York, NY: Praeger Publications, 1973).

White, R. E. O. *Biblical Ethics.* (Atlanta, GA: John Knox Press, 1979).

Wilder, A. N. *Eschatology and Ethics in the Teachings of Jesus.* (New York, NY: Harper and Row, 1950).

Wilkerson, David. *The Cross and the Switchblade.* (New York, NY: Dell Publishing Co., 1958).

Willems, Emilio. *Follower's of the New Faith: Culture Change and the Rise of Protestantism in Brazil and Chile.* (Nashville, TN: Vanderbilt University Press, 1967).

Williams, J. Rodman. *Renewal Theology.* 3 Vols. (Grand Rapids, MI: Zondervan Publishing House, 1990).

Wrede, William. *The messianic secret.* Translated by J. C. G. Greig. (Cambridge: Clark, 1971).

Yoder, John Howard. *The Politics of Jesus.* (Grand Rapids, MI: Wm. B. Eerdmans Publishing Co., 1972).

BOOK CHAPTERS

Aker, B. C. 'Initial Evidence, A Biblical Perspective'. In *Dictionary of Pentecostal and Charismatic Movements*, eds., Stanley M. Burgess and Gary B. McGee, 455–459. (Grand Rapids, MI: Zondervan Publishing House, 1988).

Bammel, E. 'Poor'. In *Theological Dictionary of the New Testament.* (Grand Rapids, MI: Wm. B. Eerdmans Publishing Co., 1983. 6:885–915).

Barrett David B. 'Statistics, Global'. In *Dictionary of Pentecostal and Charismatic Movements*, eds., Stanley M. Burgess and Gary B. McGee, 810–830. (Grand Rapids, MI: Zondervan Publishing House, 1988).

Bernales, Andrés Opazo. 'El Movimiento Protestante en Centroamérica: Una Aproximación Cuantitativa'. In *Protestantismo y Procesos Sociales en Centroamérica*, ed. Luis Samandú. (San José, Costa Rica: Editorial Universitaria Centroaméricana, 1991).

Blumhofer, E. L. 'Assemblies of God'. In *Dictionary of Pentecostal and Charismatic Movements*, eds., Stanley M. Burgess and Gary B. McGee, 23–28. (Grand Rapids, MI: Zondervan Publishing House, 1988).

——. 'John Alexander Dowie'. In *Dictionary of Pentecostal and Charismatic Movements*, eds., Stanley M. Burgess and Gary B. McGee, 248–249. (Grand Rapids, MI: Zondervan Publishing House, 1988).

Bundy, David. 'Keswick Higher Life Movement'. In *Dictionary of Pentecostal and Charismatic Movements*, eds., Stanley M. Burgess and Gary B. McGee, 518–519. (Grand Rapids, MI: Zondervan Publishing House, 1988).

Burdick, John. 'Rethinking the Study of Social Movements: The Case of Christian Base Communities in Urban Brazil'. In *The Making of Social*

Movements in Latin America: Identity, Strategy and Democracy, eds., Arturo Escobar and Sonia E. Alvarez, 171–184. (Oxford: Westview Press, 1992).

——. 'Struggling Against the Devil: Pentecostalism and Social Movements in Urban Brazil'. In *Rethinking Protestantism in Latin America*, eds. Virginia Garrard Burnett and David Stoll. (Philadelphia, PA: Temple University Press, 1993).

Conn, Charles W. 'Christian Perfection (A Pentecostal Perspective)'. In *Dictionary of Pentecostal and Charismatic Movements*, eds., Stanley M. Burgess and Gary B. McGee, 169–180. (Grand Rapids, MI: Zondervan Publishing House, 1988).

Dayton, Donald. 'From "Christian Perfection" to the "Baptism of the Holy Ghost"'. In *Aspects of Pentecostal-Charismatic Origins*, ed. Vinson Synan. (Plainfield, NJ: Logos International, 1975).

Dempster, Murray W. 'Evangelism, Social Concern, and the Kingdom of God'. In *Called and Empowered: Global Mission in Pentecostal Perspective*, eds. Murray W. Dempster, Byron D. Klaus and Douglas Petersen. (Peabody, MA: Hendrickson Publishers, 1991).

Fee Gordon D. 'The Kingdom of God and the Church's Global Mission'. In *Called and Empowered: Global Mission in Pentecostal Perspective*, eds. Murray W. Dempster, Byron D. Klaus and Douglas Petersen. (Peabody, MA: Hendrickson Publishers, 1991).

Gerlach, Luther P. 'Pentecostalism: Revolution or Counter-Revolution?' In *Religious Movements in Contemporary America*, eds. Iwing I. Zaretsky & Mark P. Leone. (Princeton, NJ: Princeton University Press, 1974).

Greenway, Roger S. 'Protestant Missionary Activity in Latin America'. In *Coming of Age*. (Lanham, MD: University Press of America, 1994).

Hocken, Peter D., and Desmond W. Cartwright. 'European Pentecostalism'. In *Dictionary of Pentecostal and Charismatic Movements*, eds., Stanley M. Burgess and Gary B. McGee, 268–278. (Grand Rapids, MI: Zondervan Publishing House, 1988).

Hoffnagel, Judith Chambliss. 'Pentecostalism: A Revolutionary or Conservative Movement'. In *Perspectives on Pentecostalism; Case Studies from the Caribbean and Latin America*, ed. Stephen D. Glazier. (Lanham, MD: University Press of America, 1980).

Horne, J. W. 'Sermon'. In *Peniel; or Face to Face with God*, ed. A. McLean and J. W. Eaton. (New York, NY: W. C. Palmer, Jr., 1869).

Jones, C. E. 'Holiness Movement'. In *Dictionary of Pentecostal and Charismatic Movements*, eds., Stanley M. Burgess and Gary B. McGee, 406–409. (Grand Rapids, MI: Zondervan Publishing House, 1988).

Kuzmič, Peter. 'History and Eschatology: Evangelical Views.' In *Word and Deed: Evangelism and Social Responsibility*, ed. Bruce Nicholls. (Grand Rapids, MI: Wm. Eerdmans Publishing Co., 1985).

Ladd, George Eldon. 'Eschatology and Ethics'. In *Baker's Dictionary of Christian Ethics*, ed. C. F. H. Henry. (Grand Rapids, MI: Baker Book House, 1973).

Maldonado, I. E. 'Building Fundamentalism from the Family in Latin America'. In *Fundamentalism and Society*, eds. Martin E. Marty and R. Scott Appleby. (Chicago, IL: University of Chicago Press, 1993).

Margolies, Luise. 'The Paradoxical Growth of Pentecostalism'. In *Perspectives on Pentecostalism; Case Studies from the Caribbean and Latin America*, ed. Stephen D. Glazier. (Lanham, MD: University Press of America, 1980).

McGee, Gary. B. 'Alice Eveline Luce'. In *Dictionary of Pentecostal and Charismatic Movements*, eds., Stanley M. Burgess and Gary B. McGee, 543–544. (Grand Rapids, MI: Zondervan Publishing House, 1988).

——. 'Henry Cleophas Ball'. In *Dictionary of Pentecostal and Charismatic Movements*, eds., Stanley M. Burgess and Gary B. McGee, 40. (Grand Rapids, MI: Zondervan Publishing House, 1988).

——. 'Missions, Overseas by 1910 (North American)'. In *Dictionary of Pentecostal and Charismatic Movements*, eds., Stanley M. Burgess and Gary B. McGee, 612. (Grand Rapids, MI: Zondervan Publishing House, 1988).

Míguez Bonino, José. 'Confrontation as a Means of Communication in Theology, Church and Society'. In *The Right to Dissent*, eds. H. Kung and J. Möltmann. (New York, NY: Seabury Press, 1982).

——. 'For Life and Against Death: A Theology That Takes Sides'. In *Theologians in Transitions: The Christian Century "How my mind has changed" series*, ed. James M. Wall. (New York, NY: Crossroads, 1991).

——. 'A God Who Acts and Renews His Church'. In *Social Justice and the Latin Churches*, ed. Church and Society in Latin America. Translated by Jorge Lara Braud. (Richmond, VA: John Knox Press, 1969).

——. 'Historia y misión'. In *Protestantismo y liberalismo en America Latina*, eds. Carmelo Alvarez, José Míguez Bonino and Roberto Craig. (San José, Costa Rica: Departamento Ecuménico de Investigaciones [DEI], 1993).

——. 'Historical Praxis and Christian Identity'. In *Frontiers of theology in Latin America*, ed. Rosino Gibellini. (Maryknoll, NY: Orbis Books, 1979).

——. 'Statement by José Míguez Bonino'. In *Theology in the Americas* (Detroit II Conference Papers), eds. Sergio Torres and John Eagleson. (Maryknoll, NY: Orbis Books, 1976).

Padilla, C. René. 'Hermeneutics and Culture'. In *Down to Earth: Studies in Christianity and Culture*, eds. J. R. W. Scott and R. Coote. (Grand Rapids, MI: Eerdmans Publishing Co., 1980).

——. 'Liberation Theology: An Appraisal'. In *Freedom and Discipleship: liberation theology in an Anabaptist perspective*, ed. Daniel Schipani. (Maryknoll, NY: Orbis Books, 1989).

Petersen, Douglas. 'The Kingdom of God and the Hermenuetical Circle: Pentecostal Praxis in the Third World'. In *Called and Empowered: Global Mission in Pentecostal Perspective*, eds. Murray W. Dempster, Byron D. Klaus and Douglas Petersen. (Peabody, MA: Hendrickson Publishers, 1991).

Rauschenbusch, Walter. 'The New Evangelism'. In *American Protestant Thought:*

The Liberal Era, ed. William R. Hutchinson. (New York, NY: Harper and Row, 1968).

Reed, D. A. 'Oneness Pentecostalism'. In *Dictionary of Pentecostal and Charismatic Movements*, eds., Stanley M. Burgess and Gary B. McGee, 644–651. (Grand Rapids, MI: Zondervan Publishing House, 1988).

Riss, R. M. 'Finished Work Controversy'. In *Dictionary of Pentecostal and Charismatic Movements*, eds., Stanley M. Burgess and Gary B. McGee, 306–309. (Grand Rapids, MI: Zondervan Publishing House, 1988).

——. 'William H. Durham'. In *Dictionary of Pentecostal and Charismatic Movements*, eds., Stanley M. Burgess and Gary B. McGee, 255–256. (Grand Rapids, MI: Zondervan Publishing House, 1988).

Robeck, Cecil M. Jr. 'Frank Bartleman'. In *Dictionary of Pentecostal and Charismatic Movements*, eds., Stanley M. Burgess and Gary B. McGee, 50–51. (Grand Rapids, MI: Zondervan Publishing House, 1988).

——. 'National Association of Evangelicals (NAE)'. In *Dictionary of Pentecostal and Charismatic Movements*, eds., Stanley M. Burgess and Gary B. McGee, 634–636. (Grand Rapids, MI: Zondervan Publishing House, 1988).

Rocha, Abelino Martínez. 'Comportamientos Sociales en el Protestantismo y en el Pentecostalism Popular Nicaragüense'. In *Protestantismos y Procesos Sociales en Centroamérica*, ed. Luis Samandú. (San José, Costa Rica: Editorial Universitaria Centroamericana, 1991).

——. 'Los Protestantismos en la Crisis Salvadoreña'. In *Protestantismo y Procesos Sociales en Centroamérica*, ed. Luis Samandú. (San José, Costa Rica: Editorial Universitaria Centroamericana, 1991).

Sepúlveda, Juan. 'Pentecostal Theology in the Context of the Struggle for Life'. In *Faith born in the struggle for life: a rereading of Protestant faith in Latin America today*, ed. Dow Kirkpatrick. Translated by L. McCoy. (Grand Rapids, MI: Wm. B. Eerdmans Publishing Co., 1988).

Stendahl, Krister 'Biblical Theology, Contemporary'. *Interpreter's Bible Dictionary*, Vol. 1. (New York, NY: Abingdon Press).

Sugden, Christopher. 'A Presentation of the Concern for Kingdom Ethics'. In *Kingdom and Creation in Social Ethics*. Grove Ethical Series, no. 79. (Nottingham: Grove Books Ltd., 1990).

Synan, H. Vinson. 'Classical Pentecostalism'. In *Dictionary of Pentecostal and Charismatic Movements*, eds., Stanley M. Burgess and Gary B. McGee, 219–222. (Grand Rapids, MI: Zondervan Publishing House, 1988).

——. 'Fundamentalism'. In *Dictionary of Pentecostal and Charismatic Movements*, eds., Stanley M. Burgess and Gary B. McGee, 326. (Grand Rapids, MI: Zondervan Publishing House, 1988).

——. 'William Joseph Seymour'. In *Dictionary of Pentecostal and Charismatic Movements*, eds., Stanley M. Burgess and Gary B. McGee, 778–781. (Grand Rapids, MI: Zondervan Publishing House, 1988).

Thiselton, A. C. 'The New Hermeneutic'. In *New Testament Interpretation: Essays on Principles and Methods*, ed. I. Howard Marshall. (Grand Rapids, MI: Wm. B. Eerdmans Publishing Co., 1977).

Wagner, Peter. 'Church Growth'. In *Dictionary of Pentecostal and Charismatic Movements*, eds., Stanley M. Burgess and Gary B. McGee, 185. (Grand Rapids, MI: Zondervan Publishing House, 1988).

Warner, Wayne E. 'Publications'. In *Dictionary of Pentecostal and Charismatic Movements*, eds., Stanley M. Burgess and Gary B. McGee, 744. (Grand Rapids, MI: Zondervan Publishing House, 1988).

Wilson, Everett A. 'Dynamics of Latin American Pentecostalism'. In *Coming of Age: Protestantism in Contemporary Latin America*, ed. Daniel R. Miller. (Lanham. MD: University Press of America, 1994).

——. 'Francisco Olazábal'. In *Dictionary of Pentecostal and Charismatic Movements*, eds., Stanley M. Burgess and Gary B. McGee, 643–644. (Grand Rapids, MI: Zondervan Publishing House, 1988).

——. 'Hispanic Pentecostalism'. In *Dictionary of Pentecostal and Charismatic Movements*, eds., Stanley M. Burgess and Gary B. McGee, 390–400. (Grand Rapids, MI: Zondervan Publishing House, 1988).

——. 'Identity, Community, and Status'. In *Earthen Vessels: American Evangelicals and Foreign Missions, 1880–1980*, eds. Joel A. Carpenter and Wilbert R. Shenk. (Grand Rapids, MI: Wm. B. Eerdmans Publishing Co., 1990).

——. 'Juan L. Lugo'. In *Dictionary of Pentecostal and Charismatic Movements*, eds., Stanley M. Burgess and Gary B. McGee, 544. (Grand Rapids, MI: Zondervan Publishing House, 1988).

——. 'La Crisis de integración nacional en El Salvador'. In *El Salvador de 1840–1935; Estudiado y Analizado por los Extranjeros*, eds. Rafael Menjivar y Rafael Guidos Vejar. (San Salvador: Universidad Centroaméricana José Simeon Canas, 1978).

——. 'Passion and Power: A Profile of Emergent Latin American Pentecostalism'. In *Called and Empowered: Global Mission in Pentecostal Perspective*, eds. Murray W. Dempster, Byron D. Klaus and Douglas Petersen. (Peabody, MA: Hendrickson Publishers, 1991).

Yrigoyen, Charles Y., Jr. 'United Methodism'. In *Encyclopedia of the American Religious Experience*, eds. Charles H. Lippy and Peter W. Williams, 3 vols, I: 525–537. (New York, NY: Charles Scribner's Sons, 1988).

JOURNAL, MAGAZINE AND REFERENCE ARTICLES

Aguilar, Edwin Eloy, and others. 'Protestantism in El Salvador: Conventional Wisdom versus Survey Evidence'. *Latin American Research Review* 28 (1993): 119–140.

'Al margen de la implantación en El Salvador del impuesto sobre el capital y la renta y del proyecto de contribución territorial'. *Revista Económica*, (12 November 1924): 19.

Alvarez, Carmelo E. 'Latin American Pentecostals: Ecumenical and Evangelicals'. *Catholic Ecumenical Review* 23 (October 1986): 91–95.

Alvarez, Eduardo. 'Vialidad, moralidad'. *Actualidades* VII (February 1926): 457.

Anderson, Gordon. 'Pentecostal Hermeneutics'. *Paraclete: A Journal of Pentecostal Studies* 28 (Spring 1994): 13–22.

Apostolic Faith (Los Angeles), I (Sept. 1906).

'Base Ecclesial Communities'. *Transformation* 3 (July–September 1986): 1–29.

Bastian, Jean-Pierre. 'The Metamorphosis of Latin American Protestant Groups: A Sociohistorical Perspective'. *Latin American Research Review* 28 (1993): 33–61.

Behrman, Jere R. 'Schooling in Latin America: What Are the Patterns And What Is The Impact?' *Journal Of Interamerican Studies* 27 (Winter 1985–86): 21–35.

Bueno, John. *Reflexiones sobre el Origen y Filosofía del Programa Integral de Educación de las Asambleas de Dios, PIEDAD.* (San Salvador: Documents of PIEDAD, 1984).

Cavaness, Barbara. 'God Calling: Women in Assemblies of God Missions'. *PNEUMA: The Journal of the Society for Pentecostal Studies* 16 (Spring 1994): 49–62.

Cleary, Edward L. 'John Paul Cries 'Wolf': Misreading the Pentecostals'. *Commonweal* 7 (November 20 1992): 7–8.

Cook, Guillermo. 'The Evangelical Groundswell in Latin America'. *Christian Century*, (12 December 1990): 1175.

Dempster, Murray W. 'The Church's Moral Witness: A Study of Glossolalia in Luke's Theology of Acts'. *Paraclete: A Journal of Pentecostal Studies* 23 (Winter 1989): 1–7.

———. 'Christian Social Concern in Pentecostal Perspective: Reformulating Pentecostal Eschatology'. *Journal for Pentecostal Theology* 2 (1993): 51–64.

———. 'Pentecostal Social Concern and the Biblical Mandate of Social Justice'. *PNUEMA: The Journal of the Society for Pentecostal Studies* 9 (Fall 1987): 129–153.

Diament, Mario. 'Corrupt to the Core'. *Hemisphere* 3 (Summer 1991): 21.

Ellis, T. 'Pentecostal Revival Touches India'. *Heritage* (Winter 1982–1983).

Escobar, Samuel. 'A New Reformation'. *Christianity Today*, 6 April 1992, 30–31.

Fee, Gordon. 'Response to Roger's Stronstad's 'The Biblical Precedent for Historical Precedent'.' *Paraclete: A Journal of Pentecostal Studies* 27 (Summer 1993): 1–14.

Flora, Cornelia B. 'Pentecostal Women in Colombia: Religious Change and the Status of Working-Class Women'. *Journal of Interamerican Studies and World Affairs* 17 (November 1975): 411–425.

———. 'Pentecostalism and Development: The Colombian Case'. in *Perspectives on Pentecostalism: Case Studies from the Caribbean and Latin America*, 81–93.

Gaxiola, Adoniram. 'Poverty as a Meeting and Parting Place: Similarities and

Contrasts in the Experiences of Latin American Pentecostalisms and Ecclesial Base Communities'. *PNUEMA: The Journal of the Society for Pentecostal Studies* 13 (Fall 1991): 167–174.

Gaxiola-Gaxiola, Manuel J. 'Latin American Pentecostalism: A Mosaic within a Mosaic'. *Pnuema: The Journal of the Society for Pentecostal Studies* 13 (Fall 1991): 107–129.

——. 'The Pentecostal Ministry'. *International Review of Mission* 66 (January 1977): 57–63.

Gros, Jeffrey. 'Confessing the Apostolic Faith from the Perspective of the Pentecostal Churches'. *PNUEMA, The Journal of the Society for Pentecostal Studies* 9 (Spring 1987): 5–16.

Herrera, J. Alberto. 'La Emigración salvadoreña'. *Isidro Menéndez* 2 (May–June 1925): 11–14.

Hollenweger, Walter J. 'The Religion of the Poor is not a Poor Religion'. *The Expository Times* 87 (May 1976): 228–232.

Huntington, Deborah. 'The Prophet Motive'. *NACLA Report on the Americas.* 18 (January/February 1984): 2–11.

'Impresiones de un sabio alemán sobre El Salvador; notas de viaje del doctor Sapper'. *Pareceres* 1 (December 1926): 3.

'Joseph es sanado de sus huesos'. *Noti-PIEDAD: Un Noticiero de las Escuelas de las Asambleas de Dios,* San José, Costa Rica: setiembre 1993.

Kirk, J. Andrew. 'Christian Understanding of Liberation'. *Evangelical Review of Mission* 10 (April 1986): 129–136.

'La crisis del maiz'. *Patria* (San Salvador, El Salvador), 18 January, 1929.

Ladd, George Eldon. 'The Search for Perspective'. *Interpretation* 25 (1971): 41–62.

Long, Jan Harris. 'No Longer a Silent Majority'. *Christianity Today* 5 (April 1993): 72.

Mackay, John A. 'Latin America and Revolution—II: 'The new mood in the Churches'. ' *Christian Century,* 24 November 1965, 1439.

McGavran, Donald. 'What Makes Pentecostal Churches Grow'. *International Bulletin of Church Growth* 13 (January 1977): 97–99.

'Medio millón de niños: Generación sin futuro'. *Barricada* (Managua, Nicaragua), (28 Noviembre 1993), 12.

Meyers, Brant L. 'State of the World's Children: Critical Challenge to Christian Mission'. *International Bulletin of Missionary Research* 18 (July 1994): 98–102.

Míguez Bonino, José. 'The Biblical Roots of Justice'. *Word and World: Theology for Christian Ministry* 7 (Winter 1987): 12–21.

——. 'Conversion, New Creature and Commitment'. *International Review of Mission* 72 (July 1983): 324–332.

——. 'How Does United States Presence Help, Hinder or Compromise Christian Mission in Latin America'. *Review and Expositor* 74 (Spring 1977): 174–177.

——. 'The Pentecostal Movement'. *International Review of Mission* 66 (January 1977): 77–78.

Moltmann, Jürgen. 'On Latin American Theology: An Open Letter to José Míguez Bonino'. *Christianity and Crisis*, 29 March 1976, 62.

Navarro C., Garma. 'Liderazgo Protestante en una lucha campesina en México'. *América Indígena* 44 (1984): 127–141.

Nida, Eugene. 'The Indigenous Churches in Latin America'. *Practical Anthropology* 8 (May-June 1961): 97–105.

Open Letter. 'Pedagogismo y mediocre educación'. *La Nación* (San José, Costa Rica) 6 de febrero 1994, 14A.

Padilla, C. René. 'Liberation Theology, Part I'. *The Reformed Journal* 33 (June 1983): 21–23.

Palma, Marta. 'A Pentecostal Church in the Ecumenical Movement'. *The Ecumenical Review* 37 (April 1985): 223–229.

Parker, Garry. 'Evangelicals Blossom Brightly amid El Salvador's Wasteland of Violence'. *Christianity Today*, 8 (May 1981): 34.

Paulston, Rolland G. 'Ways of Seeing Education and Social Change in Latin America: A Phenomenographic Perspective'. *Latin American Research Review* 27 (1992): 177–202.

Plüss, Jean-Daniel. 'Azusa and Other Myths: The Long and Winding Road from Experience to Stated Belief and Back Again'. *PNEUMA: The Journal of the Society for Pentecostal Studies* 15 (Fall 1993): 189–201.

Ricoeuer, Paul. 'The Critique of Religion'. *Union Seminary Quarterly Review* 28 (1973): 203–212.

Roberts, Bryan. 'Protestant groups and coping with urban life in Guatemala City'. *American Journal of Sociology* 73 (1968): 753–767.

Samandú, Luis E. 'El pentecostalismo en Nicaragua y sus raíces religiosas populares'. *Pasos* 17 (May-June, 1988): 1–10.

Saracco, J. Norberto. 'Type of Ministry Adopted by Latin American Pentecostal Churches'. *International Review of Mission* 66 (January 1977): 64–70.

Schultze, Quentin J. 'TV Religion as Pagan-American Missions'. *Transformation: An International Evangelical Dialogue on Mission and Ethics* 9 (October/ December 1992): 2–5.

Segundo, Juan Luis. 'La opción por los pobres como clave hermeneútica para entender el Evangelio'. *Sal Terrae* (June 1986): 473–82.

Self, Charles E. 'Conscientization, Conversion, and Convergence: Reflections on Base Communities and Emerging Pentecostalism in Latin America'. *PNEUMA: The Journal of the Society for Pentecostal Studies* 14 (Spring 1992): 59–72.

Sepúlveda, Juan. 'Pentecostalism as Popular Religiosity'. *International Review of Mission* 72 (July 1983): 324–332.

——. 'Reflections on the Pentecostal Contribution to the Mission of the Church in Latin America'. *Journal of Pentecostal Theology* 1 (October 1992): 93–108.

Sheppard, Gerald. 'Pentecostals and the Hermeneutics of Dispensationalism: The

Anatomy of an Uneasy Relationship'. *PNEUMA: The Journal of the Society for Pentecostal Studies* 6 (Fall 1984): 5–33.

Stockwell, Eugene. 'Editorial: Responses to the Spirit; pt. 2: Charismatics'. *International Review of Mission* 75 (April 1986): 113–157.

Stoll, David. 'A Protestant Reformation in Latin America?' *Christian Century* 17 January 1990, 44–48.

Stronstad, Roger. 'The Biblical Precedent for Historical Precedent'. *Paraclete: A Journal of Pentecostal Studies* 27 (Summer 1993): 1–14.

—— 'Pentecostal Experience and Hermeneutics'. *Paraclete: A Journal of Pentecostal Studies* 15 (Winter 1992): 14–30.

Volf, Miraslov. 'On Loving with Hope: Eschatology and Social Responsibility'. *TRANSFORMATION: An International Dialogue on Evangelical Social Ethics* 7 (July/September 1990): 28–31.

Wacker, Grant. 'Planning for the End, the Enduring Appeal of Prophecy Belief'. *Christian Century*, 19 January 1994, 48–52.

Wallace, Anthony F. C. 'Revitalization Movements'. *American Anthropology* 58 (April 1956): 264–281.

Wilson, Everett A. 'The Central American Evangelicals: From Protest to Pragmatism'. *International Review of Mission* 77 (January 1988): 94–106.

——. 'Latin American Pentecostalism: Challenging the Stereotypes of Pentecostal Passivity'. *TRANSFORMATION: An International Evangelical Dialogue on Mission and Ethics* 11 (January/March 1994): 19–24.

——. 'Latin American Pentecostals: Their Potential for Ecumenical Dialogue'. *PNEUMA: The Journal of the Society for Pentecostal Studies* 8 (Fall 1986): 85–90.

——. 'Sanguine Saints: Pentecostalism in El Salvador'. *Church History* 52 (June 1983): 186–98.

UNPUBLISHED MATERIALS

Annual Report, Las Escuelas Cristianas de las Asambleas de Dios de Costa Rica. San José, Costa Rica: Asociación Evangélica de las Asambleas de Dios de Costa Rica, March 1994.

Annual Report, Asambleas de Dios de Guatemala. Guatemala: Las Asambleas de Dios de Guatemala, 1992.

Canaca Jiménez, Mario Antonio. 'En Busca de la Excelencia Academica'. San Pedro Sula, Honduras: SIEELA, 15 March 1987.

——. 'Filosofia del programa PIEDAD frente a la educación publica'. San Pedro Sula, Honduras: SIEELA, 15 March 1987.

——. 'La actividad académica y los servicios estudiantiles en los centros educativos cristianos 'Asambleas de Dios' en Honduras'. Tegucigalpa, Honduras: SIEELA, 20–25 May 1985.

Chugg, Norman, and Kenneth Larson. 'Chugg-Larson Report to TEAM's [The Evangelical Alliance Mission] 1970 Conference on Their Church Planting

Study Trip to Central America'. Wheaton, Il: Evangelical Alliance Mission, 1970.

'Constitution and statutes,' Asociación Social de Bienestar Social del Centro Evangelístico, San José, Costa Rica.

Country reports of CELAD. Panama City, Panama: Consejo de Ejecutivos Latin Americans de las Asambleas de Dios, 25–29 November 1992.

Dempster, Murray W. 'Old Testament Foundations of Christian Social Concern'. San Salvador, El Salvador: SIEELA, 20–26 May 1985.

——. 'Soundings in the Moral Significance of Glossolalia'. A paper presented at the 1983 Annual meeting of the Society for Pentecostal Studies, Cleveland, Tennessee, 4 November 1983.

'Estatutos,' Instituto de Desarrollo Social de las Asambleas de Dios (IDSAD). Managua, Nicaragua, 1990.

Evans, Timothy E. 'Percentage of Non-Catholics in a Representative Sample of the Guatemalan Population,' a paper presented to the panel, Protestantism in Latin America: The Social and Political Implications. Washington, D.C.: Latin American Studies Association, 4 April 1991.

García, Joaquín. 'La Mística de PIEDAD'. San Pedro Sula, Honduras: SIEELA, 30 March 1987.

García, Miguel. 'Un Reto Para Servir'. Sermon presented at the Consejo de Ejecutivos Latinoamericanos de las Asambleas de Dios, Panama City, Panama, 12 November 1993.

Guerrero, José Alfredo. 'Origin, Desarrollo Y Filosofia de los Liceos Cristianos'. San Salvador, El Salvador: SIEELA, 18 May 1984.

'Hogar Cuna: ¿Por qué existimos?' Asociación Social de Bienestar Social del Centor Evangelístico, San José, Costa Rica.

Jones, Charles Edwin. 'The Beulah Land and the Upper Room: Reclaiming the Text in Turn-of-the-Century Holiness and Pentecostal Spirituality'. A paper presented at the 22nd Annual Meeting of the Society for Pentecostal Studies, Springfield, MO: 12–14 November 1992.

'Manual de Ministerios Femeniles,' Asociación Evangélica de las Asambleas de Dios de Costa Rica. San José, Costa Rica, 1993.

Miscellaneous archival materials of the Conferencia Nacional de las Asambleas de Dios de Nicaragua. Managua, Nicaragua.

Mission Statement of Latin America ChildCare. Tegucigalpa, Honduras: SIEELA, 15 February 1993.

Muñoz, Lucas. *The Church Goes On* (video). Springfield, MO: Department of Foreign Missions of the Assemblies of God, 1991.

Nelson, Douglas. 'For Such a Time as This: The Story of Bishop William J. Seymour and the Azusa Street Revival'. Unpublished Ph. D. diss., Birmingham: University of Birmingham, 1981.

'Nueva Evangelización, Promoción Humana, Cultura Cristiana,' final document of the IV General Conference of the Latin American Bishops held in Santo

Domingo, Dominican Republic, 12–28 October 1992. (México: Ediciones DABAR S.A., 1992): 107–108.

Origen y desarrollo de las Asambleas de Dios en Guatemala. Guatemala: Concilio Nacional de las Asambleas de Dios de Guatemala, 1987.

Petersen, Douglas. 'New Testament Foundations for Social Concern'. San Salvador, El Salvador: SIEELA, 20–25 May 1985.

——. 'Análisis, Reflexión y Acción Pastoral'. San Pedro Sula, Honduras: SIEELA, 15 March 1987.

Sibaja, María. Memorandum describing the LACC Los Guido project, San José, Costa Rica. San José, Costa Rica: Escuelas Cristianas, n.d.

Wacker, Grant. 'Character and the Modernization of North American Pentecostalism'. A paper presented at the 21st Annual Meeting of the Society for Pentecostal Studies, Lakeland, Florida, 7–9 November 1991.

INTERVIEWS

García, Joaquín. Interview by author, 19 April 1992 and 25 February 1994.

Míguez Bonino, José. Interview by author, 17 January 1993 and 28 November 1993, Buenos Aires, Argentina.

Rodriguez, Carmela, and Rev. Carlos Bermudez [respectively mother and pastor of LACC student—Sara Rodriguez]. Interview by author, 25 September 1990, San José, Costa Rica.

Rodriguez, Cecilia. Conversations with author, San Salvador, El Salvador, 26 February 1993.

Archila, Adrian Fernando. Interview by author, 28 February 1994, San Salvador, El Salvador.

Index